Governing the EU in an Age of Division

NEW THINKING IN POLITICAL ECONOMY

Series Editor: Peter J. Boettke, *George Mason University, USA*

New Thinking in Political Economy aims to encourage scholarship in the intersection of the disciplines of politics, philosophy and economics. It has the ambitious purpose of reinvigorating political economy as a progressive force for understanding social and economic change.

The series is an important forum for the publication of new work analysing the social world from a multidisciplinary perspective. With increased specialization (and professionalization) within universities, interdisciplinary work has become increasingly uncommon. Indeed, during the 20th century, the process of disciplinary specialization reduced the intersection between economics, philosophy and politics and impoverished our understanding of society. Modern economics in particular has become increasingly mathematical and largely ignores the role of institutions and the contribution of moral philosophy and politics.

New Thinking in Political Economy will stimulate new work that combines technical knowledge provided by the 'dismal science' and the wisdom gleaned from the serious study of the 'worldly philosophy'. The series will reinvigorate our understanding of the social world by encouraging a multidisciplinary approach to the challenges confronting society in the new century.

Titles in the series include:

Debt Default and Democracy
Edited by Giuseppe Eusepi and Richard E. Wagner

The Political Economy of Non-Territorial Exit
Cryptosecession
Trent J. MacDonald

Tax Tyranny
Pascal Salin

The Rule of Law, Economic Development, and Corporate Governance
Nadia E. Nedzel

Neoliberal Social Justice
Rawls Unveiled
Nick Cowen

Toward a Political Economy of the Commons
Simple Rules for Sustainability
Meina Cai, Ilia Murtazashvili, Jennifer Brick Murtazashvili and Raufhon Salahodjaev

Governing the EU in an Age of Division
Dalibor Rohac

Governing the EU in an Age of Division

Dalibor Rohac

Senior Fellow, Foreign and Defense Policy, American Enterprise Institute, USA

NEW THINKING IN POLITICAL ECONOMY

Cheltenham, UK • Northampton, MA, USA

Published by
Edward Elgar Publishing Limited
The Lypiatts
15 Lansdown Road
Cheltenham
Glos GL50 2JA
UK

Edward Elgar Publishing, Inc.
William Pratt House
9 Dewey Court
Northampton
Massachusetts 01060
USA

A catalogue record for this book
is available from the British Library

Library of Congress Control Number: 2022944604

This book is available electronically in the **Elgar**online
Political Science and Public Policy subject collection
http://dx.doi.org/10.4337/9781802208733

ISBN 978 1 80220 872 6 (cased)
ISBN 978 1 80220 873 3 (eBook)

Printed and bound in Great Britain by TJ Books Limited, Padstow, Cornwall

Contents

v

Preface

In the morning of June 24, 2016, the world woke to an astonishing piece of news. By a sizeable margin, the British voted to leave the European Union, proving most pundits and pollsters wrong. Within hours, the U.K.'s prime minister David Cameron, who had campaigned for the country to remain in the EU, stepped down. For many, the result, which has since upended British political life, was a victory of retrograde nationalism, anti-immigration sentiments, and nostalgia for a simpler past over the material benefits and peace brought about by decades of European integration. Euroskeptics, Guy Verhofstadt, a vocal liberal Member of European Parliament and the former prime minister of Belgium, quipped, "[wanted] to go back to the past, to put up all the old borders, and the so-called sovereignty of the nation states."[1] The Brexit monomania appeared not only dangerous for British democracy, but it risked being the beginning of the end of the European project, with more countries following the British to the exit.

A little over two years earlier, in the early morning of February 27, 2014, men in unmarked uniforms took over the Verkhovna Rada of the Autonomous Republic of Crimea in its capital of Simferopol. Within hours, Crimea's legally elected leadership was dismissed and replaced with the Kremlin's stooges. Before the Western world could mount a response, a new political reality – a landgrab – had been asserted on the ground, literally at gunpoint. To elites on both sides of the Atlantic, the brazen move was dumbfounding, as if harking from a different, less civilized era – and thus bound to fail. "Let's let Putin play that game if he chooses," a *Los Angeles Times* writer opined. "If Obama and European leaders employ their economic weapons smartly, Putin can be taught a harsh lesson about real power in the modern world."[2]

Today, the United Kingdom is no longer a member of the EU. Many side-products of Brexit, from disputes over fishing rights to vexing questions about the Irish border continue to act as irritants. Yet, by any far account, the U.K. is a normal, prosperous country that remains deeply involved in commerce with the European continent and engaged in its security. The EU, too, seems to have survived the loss of one of its key members just fine. And, contrary to expectations, Vladimir Putin has not been chastened by the "smart" response from the EU and from successive U.S. administrations. Emboldened by the West's continuing fecklessness, he decided to launch a full-scale invasion of Ukraine in February 2022. Both of these examples exposed blind spots of a meta-ideological perspective that sees the European project, as well as the rules-based 'liberal international order,' as manifestations of an inexorable march of history toward progress. From that vantage point, it was obvious that the nativism behind Brexit and other populist movements, or Putin's retrograde warmongering and imperial nostalgia had "no place in the 21st century." Alas they do. The arc of moral universe, to paraphrase the turn of phrase of Martin Luther King Jr. frequently invoked by former U.S. president Barack Obama, does not bend toward justice on its own – it does so only under the right cultural, institutional, and political conditions, which are never guaranteed once and for all.

Few other policy initiatives or international organizations reflect the faith in ineluctability of progress as strongly as the EU. For decades, the organization drew its strength from the shared understanding of Europe's political elites that the horrors of the first half of the 20th century could never be repeated. In its institutional DNA, the Europe project carries the ambition not only to manage the messy, pluralistic, and querulous Europe as it exists, but also to reshape it into a new political form in pursuit of an 'ever-closer union.' Unlike earlier efforts at European unification, which were often just thinly veiled efforts at imposing hegemony on the continent, the European project is infused with a sincere belief that seeks to place conflict and power politics in the rear view mirror. Those who internalized Francis Fukuyama's thesis about 'end of history'[3] incorrectly as implying that all important political, economic, and institutional questions had been settled – rather than as the more pedestrian and defensible observation that after the collapse of communist regimes, democratic capitalism faced no coherent and appealing alternatives – might have reasons to see the turbulences of the 2010s as temporary abominations on humankind's upward trajectory. The failure of progress to materialize makes many despondent. Brexit, Trump's presidency, resurgent Russia and China, democratic backsliding in Eastern Europe, and the West's failure to address the challenge of climate more effectively pierce through the illusion of progress as an inevitable historic force, gyrating public debate between a complacent faith in progress and moral panics, each appearing as an existential threat. In the EU's case, important questions arise about the bloc's effectiveness as a policymaking body and about its own relevance in a world that may not conform to the optimistic tenets that underpinned its founding meta-ideology.

This book focuses on the key shortcoming of treating European Union as a mechanism of progress and political unity: the disregard of such an approach for the actually existing diversity of the European continent. Diverse groups of Europeans and different European nations have conflicting interests. They have varied understandings of what 'progress' and common good look like – and sometimes they disagree over deeply held political and moral values. To operate under the assumption that such sources of disagreement are bound to disappear over time sidesteps the central question that the EU should seek to address: how can continental divisions, disagreements, and conflicts be adequately managed, and how they can be used as a basis for learning, cooperation, and a positive-sum competition between member states and other actors?

The EU's internal heterogeneity has increased dramatically through its successive enlargements: first to the south, in the 1980s, and later to the east, in the 2000s. These have put the meta-ideology underpinning the EU to test and found it wanting. For one, events have provided a clear answer to the question of whether a trade-off exists between the EU's width and the depth of its integration. As the patchwork of the EU's ad hoc, intergovernmental responses to crises of the 2010s reveals, the trade-off is very real indeed. Vastly different sets of policies can be reasonably pursued by groups of likeminded countries – say, the six original founding members of the European Economic Community – than by the EU at its 27 member states. That is not necessarily a bad thing. Cooperation across more countries also carries substantial gains, as does the existence of a single European market, encompassing over 500 million customers. As a result, it is not the contention of this book that the EU's enlargements should be seen as failures – quite the contrary. On most metrics that matter, enlargements have been resounding successes. Rather, the point is that the EU's leadership have not fully grappled with the implications of the bloc's increased diversity.

The book integrates two intellectual interests which are usually pursued on separate tracks – and which I long treated as separable in my own work. On the one hand, the book studies the implications of Europe's heterogeneity, disagreement, and pluralism for the EU's governance. On the other hand, it does so through a very specific, Eastern European set of lenses, by revisiting some of the debates about legacies of post-communist transitions, 'neoliberalism,' and the role played by international economic and political integration in Eastern Europe. The connections between the two are obvious. For one, Eastern enlargements have led to a dramatic increase in the EU's internal diversity, imposing limits on the form of integration that has been feasible within the EU. Second, the EU's own institutional set-up and ambitions have not been always geared toward managing the continent's growing diversity. Frequently, the quest for one-size-fits-all solutions has pitted different groups of member states, including Eastern European, post-communist ones, against each other. To accommodate its underlying diversity and channel it to productive uses, this book argues, the EU has to move away from the increasingly stale dogma of 'ever-closer union.' Doing so must avoid the equally empty promises of populist Euroskepticism. As Brexit has demonstrated, leaving the EU raises at least as many issues as it purports to solve – about market access, regulatory alignment, or about political and security cooperation. Even a country that has extricated itself formally from the EU will arguably find it in its interest to preserve the existing economic links to the EU and to work with its European partners in addressing shared policy challenges – in other words, to replicate, with higher transaction costs, a lot of the arrangements existing under the EU's aegis. An alternative to these two extremes is to help turn the EU into a flexible, rules-governed platform which allows national governments to solve policy problems through their own initiative. Sometimes, solutions can (and must) be devised at the level of all 27 members, but frequently, smaller coalitions of like-minded countries can work more effectively. Pursuing that path would involve functionally disaggregating the EU and not treating it as a monolithic organization but rather as a plethora of separate 'integration projects' running in parallel, under the umbrella of common institutions and a thin layer of rules. Doing so would dull the sharpness of the distinction between the EU's members and non-members. Different countries, both members and non-members, can participate in different combinations of European policy initiatives. That would not be a dramatic departure from the status quo. There are non-members participating in the single market and the Schengen zone of free travel (Iceland, Norway), using the common currency (Kosovo), and playing a significant security role on the continent (United Kingdom). Making such a flexible form of integration the default, and making the layer of non-negotiable common European rules and requirements thinner would go a long way toward alleviating the problems of paralysis and lowest-common-denominator solutions that plague European policymaking. It would also neutralize the common concern, often amplified by nationalist and populist leaders, that the European project is primarily a vehicle for a narrow ideological agenda of progressivism, cosmopolitanism, and liberal moralism, seeking to 'impose' from the outside a set of norms, which could not withstand domestic democratic scrutiny. Furthermore, the EU's disaggregation offers practical avenues for extending, in real time, many of the membership's benefits to a country such as Ukraine, which does not have the luxury of allowing the traditional accession process to run its course.

The EU is not a state and it should not aspire to become one. It follows that it should not aspire to be a 'superpower' either. Its belated awakening to Russia's aggression against Ukraine, ongoing since 2014, its effort to compartmentalize different aspects of its relationship with China, and sheer powerlessness in the face of adverse developments in its immediate neighborhood (say, the Western Balkans or North Africa) reveal that the quest for unity and a single European voice at 27 members is more often than not a fool's errand. That does not mean that Europeans should not do more for their security and in asserting their foreign policy interests. They should – but they have to proceed in a way that amounts to more than just chest-puffing rhetoric and watered-down statements that characterize the current approach. Once again, ad hoc coalitions of members and non-members, accountable to their own publics and embedded in a thin layer of common rules, can do much more than the EU-27 ever could.

The vision of Europe presented in this book is not an inherently exciting one. It accepts the EU's flaws, ambiguities, and divides at their face value, instead of seeking to overcome them through forces of historic change or some clever tweaks to its institutional architecture. I am all the more thankful to the countless individuals for their advice and their support of this small-c conservative project, geared toward preserving and marginally improving European modus vivendi instead of providing an impetus for grand European reform. Most importantly, my colleagues and the leadership at the American Enterprise Institute have provided me with an unparalleled intellectual home for this endeavor. Leon Aron, Stefan Auer, Hal Brands, Angelos-Stylianos Chryssogelos, Andrew Goodhart, Bill Kristol, Julian Mueller, Vít Novotný, Federico Reho, Dan Rothschild, Kori Schake, Gary Schmitt, and Stan Veuger generously took the time to read and critique early versions of the manuscript, although they bear no responsibility for any errors that remain. I also presented an early version of ideas that led to this book at a Zoom event "Coexisting in a Pluralist Society," convened by Jennifer Brick Murtazashvili and Paul Dragos Aligica at the Center for Governance and Markets at the University of Pittsburgh and the Institute for Humane Studies at George Mason University. Some of the arguments germinated or were cultivated through columns and articles in *American Purpose*, *Foreign Policy*, *Cosmos and Taxis*, *Law & Liberty*, and *European Politics and Society*. I am grateful to the editors and referees for giving me the space and much needed feedback. Lance Kokonos and Benjamin Noon provided excellent research assistance. As always, I'm indebted to my wife Petra for bearing the brunt of the burden associated with writing this book. Finally, this book is dedicated to my son Egon, a bearer of both a European (Slovak) and American identity. May his generation inherit a Europe that is spared of the mistakes of the past, including by avoiding the common error of turning empty promises of a utopia into the enemy of an imperfect yet serviceable status quo.

Arlington, Virginia
March 16, 2022

NOTES

1.   Cited in Adams (2019).
2.   Horsey (2014).
3.   Fukuyama (1992).

1.   A glass half full or half empty?

Even before Russia's invasion of Ukraine in 2022, one could detect a tone of apprehension among European officials and elites. At the height of the EU's refugee crisis in 2015, and shortly after the terror attacks in Paris, Germany's finance minister Wolfgang Schäuble ominously called uncontrolled mass migration into the EU a "rendezvous of our society with globalization" and compared the events of 2015 to an "avalanche."[1] In a speech in October 2016, the president of the European Commission Jean-Claude Juncker admitted that "[w]e should stop talking about the United States of Europe [...] because the peoples of Europe do not want them,"[2] breaking with a decades-long embrace of political union as the explicit goal of European integration. Since the European election in 2019, the new European Commission has featured a post of vice president for "Promoting our European Way of Life," implying that even Europe's *savoir vivre* may be under threat. In 2021, the EU's High Representative of the Union for Foreign Affairs and Security Policy, Josep Borrell, warned that if the bloc continues on its current path, "from the point of view of the practical implications on the game of power politics, we will become irrelevant."[3] It is not just immigration and the outside world; even new technologies are a problem. According to another of the Commission's vice presidents, Margrethe Vestager, big tech "threatens our freedoms, our opportunities, even our democracy."[4]

The growing concern about Europe's future, its place in the world, and its ability to cope with change is a departure from what the Italian political scientist Giandomenico Majone called "a political culture of total optimism," which characterized the European project since its inception. The contrast is particularly vivid when the new tone is compared with the complacent hubris of the early 2000s. At that time, Europe's steady progress, peace, and prosperity seemed like a given. "I remember vividly the celebrations of our accession on 1 May [2004] in Dublin," Slovakia's former prime minister Mikuláš Dzurinda, who led his country to join the EU, reminisces. "We were like little kids – Kwaśniewski, Chirac, Blair – we were all laughing like crazy, thinking that everything important had been sorted out, once and for all."[5] The veteran journalist T. R. Reid suggested that the EU was on the path to become a global superpower, rivaling the role of the United States.[6] The British writer Mark Leonard concurred, predicting in his book that "Europe will run the 21st century."[7] As late as 2013, at the height of the Eurozone crisis, the president of the European Commission José Manuel Barroso called for "a fresh impetus in a new rapprochement" and the looming "coming together between the people of Europe and the European Union."[8]

It is not a puzzle why the bombast has given way to more somber tones. For more than a decade, the EU has been in a firefighting mode, mired in a concatenation of crises, which have resulted both from external events and from the inadequacy of the EU's underlying institutions. First, the Eurozone was hit with a sovereign debt and banking crisis, which had devastating effects on its Mediterranean periphery. Greece, which came the closest to defaulting on its debt and crashing out of the common currency, lost over a quarter of nominal output during the protracted economic downturn. While Greece's situation was extreme, sluggish growth has long been the new normal in Europe, propelling the continent's economic decline both in relative and, in the case of some countries, absolute terms. The size of the EU's market remains formidable and the bloc is still home to some of the world's most iconic corporations – think Volkswagen, Airbus, Siemens, IKEA, or Inditex. Conspicuously, however, 'unicorns' – private companies worth $1 billion or more – are almost completely missing from the continent. Unicorns matter because they are unmistakable signs of economic dynamism, entrepreneurial churn, and innovation. In 2021, the EU was home to merely 40 unicorns, valued jointly at $78 billion. For comparison, the joint valuation of the 19 unicorns hailing only from South Korea, Singapore, and Indonesia was $76 billion. And whereas six unicorns grew in Indonesia, none of them did in Italy, the EU's third largest economy.[9]

In the past decade, the EU also saw a refugee crisis, with almost two million asylum seekers arriving on Europe's shores in just one year (2015), a wave of terror attacks, a hot war in its immediate neighborhood prompting an even larger refugee wave in 2022, a referendum leading to the acrimonious exit of an influential member state, recurrent confrontations with a revanchist Russia, chronic disagreements with its American ally, as well as a global pandemic. Normalized by population, several EU countries – most notably Bulgaria, Hungary, the Czech Republic, and Croatia – have suffered some of the heaviest death tolls from Covid-19, ahead not only of the United States and the U.K., but also of much poorer countries such as Jordan or Georgia.

Ironically, one of the things that Europeans did do right in the early days of the pandemic was to shut down national borders to all international travel. That, together with lockdowns and a quick and widespread adoption of masking, enabled particularly the post-communist countries of Central and Eastern Europe to essentially avoid the first wave of the pandemic and its death toll altogether. Those measures, however, violated both the spirit and the letter of the core rules underpinning the EU as an entity *defined* by freedom of movement. National governments closed their borders unilaterally and without much consideration for their neighbors, much less for any European rules. A similar move would have been unthinkable in the United States. Even if travel restrictions between U.S. states would have slowed down the spread of the virus in the spring months of 2020, state-level border closures would not have survived their first contact with federal law and courts. In the EU, in contrast, that remains a moot point – even if the European Commission or the Court of Justice of the European Union had weighed in, it is unlikely that the behavior of national governments would have changed on an issue where the protection of public health and lives was at stake.

Adding insult to injury, when European countries emerged from their first lockdowns in the late spring and early summer of 2020, they did not restore the status quo ante of the Schengen Agreement. Instead, countries created ad hoc travel corridors on a bilateral basis, building a confusing cobweb of restrictions, quarantines, and conflicting test requirements – a far cry from a unified European system. As late as in the summer of 2021, by when the EU had rolled out its 'vaccine passports,' most EU countries continued to uphold the local restrictions, including on travelers from other EU countries.

Concerned that the rollout of vaccines would follow a similarly chaotic route, with national governments engaged in a zero-sum bidding war, European leaders delegated the task of vaccine procurement to the European Commission. Initial results were underwhelming – largely because of the risk-averse and bureaucratic nature of the organization. In July of 2020, shortly after promising results of early trials started coming in, the U.S. government ordered 500 million vaccine doses from Moderna and 600 million from Pfizer/ BioNTech. The EU's aim, by contrast, was to "build a diversified portfolio of vaccines based on different technologies."[10] As a result, in August and October of 2020, the bloc concluded contracts with Sanofi, Johnson & Johnson, and AstraZeneca – even though it was already clear that Pfizer/BioNTech and Moderna were firmly in the lead in the vaccine race. Only in November did the European Commission place a firm order for 200 million Pfizer/BioNTech doses, with an option for 100 million more. Similarly, it ordered 80 million doses from Moderna, with an option for another 80 million to be delivered later. According to *Der Spiegel*'s report, both Pfizer/BioNTech and Moderna had ample spare capacity.[11] Respectively, the two companies offered to provide the EU with 500 million and 300 million initial doses but were turned down – notwithstanding pleading from Germany's health minister Jens Spahn. The main reason? Reportedly, the French government intervened in favor of Sanofi, which would not produce a working vaccine until 2022. Vaccinations in the EU have also been held back by a longer approval process. The European Medicines Agency (EMA) gave a green light to the Pfizer/BioNTech vaccine only on December 21, 2020 – three weeks after the U.K., which has been criticized by Europeans as "hasty."[12] The EMA waited until early January 2021 to approve the Moderna vaccine, notwithstanding its earlier rollout in the United

States. Although the EU did catch up eventually with the United States and the United Kingdom, for much of 2021 the EU's vaccination rates lagged behind the more agile early movers. The consequences of the EU's slow response were also geopolitical. Some EU governments turned to the less effective Russian and Chinese vaccines, whose sales likely carried a variety of strings attached. Across Central Europe, the vaccine issue destabilized governments and deepened divisions in way that can only benefit the EU's adversaries.[13]

GEOPOLITICAL NON-ENTITY

Efforts to turn the EU into a global superpower, or at least into a coherent player on the world stage, have been faltering. The creation of the position of a High Representative for Foreign and Security Policy in 2008 was portrayed as a breakthrough, alongside the setting up of the EU's dedicated diplomatic service, the European External Action Service (EEAS) and a permanent presidency of the European Council. The job of the EU's top diplomat ended up being reserved for a succession of mostly inoffensive lower-tier figures – from Catherine Ashton, through Federica Mogherini, to Josep Borrell – leaving truly consequential foreign and security policy firmly in the hands of national leaders and foreign ministers. The arguable successes of the EU's foreign policy of the past decade, from Yanukovich's departure from power in Ukraine in February 2014, facilitated by Polish, French, and German foreign ministers; the Minsk Accords and the deal with Turkey's Recep Tayyip Erdoğan, brokered by Angela Merkel; or the Paris Climate Accord and the Iran Deal – insofar as those can be seen as successes – were overwhelmingly products of initiatives by national governments or their coalitions instead of being spearheaded by European institutions.

On many issues, persistent disagreements between member states are a source of ambiguity about where the EU stands. What is its view of China, for example? Official documents maintain that China is simultaneously the EU's "negotiating partner," a "competitor," and a "systemic rival."[14] Some European governments have taken principled positions both on subjects such as Taiwan and on protecting their technological infrastructure, such as 5G networks, against Chinese interference. Simultaneously, pushed by Germany and France, the European Commission finalized a Comprehensive Agreement on Investment (CAI) – concluded in the last days of 2020 – only for it to be blocked by the European Parliament several months later. Hungary, too, has developed a tight relationship with China, joining the Belt and Road Initiative and effectively derailing the EU's efforts to hold China accountable for the 2020 crackdown in Hong Kong, for example.[15]

Following Russia's aggression against Ukraine in 2014, the EU implemented a comprehensive regime of sanctions, which has since remained in place. Yet, that has not prevented the German government from pursuing a natural gas pipeline project (Nord Stream 2), which placed Ukraine and other Eastern European countries in a vulnerable position relative to Russia and which was only abandoned following Russia's wholesale invasion of Ukraine. Following a clearly rigged presidential election and the government's heavy-handed crackdown of mass protests in Belarus in August 2020, the EU refused to recognize the results, stated that Lukashenko's new presidential mandate lacked "any democratic legitimacy," and called for "an inclusive national dialogue and responding positively to the demands of the Belarusian people for new democratic elections."[16] Forceful actions were not forthcoming, however. Only after almost two months since the fraudulent election did the EU impose sanctions against the Belarusian regime, largely because Cyprus had been blocking the action as a bargaining chip in its own unrelated dispute with Turkey – effectively holding the entire EU hostage to its own demands. As the Kremlin threatened to invade Ukraine in the early weeks of 2022, some European governments were concerned more about the economic fallout from a possible escalation of U.S. and EU sanctions than about Russian belligerence.[17] Of course, the invasion itself prompted an unprecedented response from the EU, alongside the United States and other allies. However, it would be a mistake to celebrate this seismic shift as a success. If anything, it was a sign of the EU and the West's prior failure to deter Russian aggression – perhaps because the Kremlin's plans were firm regardless of any prospective damage inflicted by Western sanctions or because Western and European governments did not communicate clearly (and were likely genuinely unsure) about how far they were willing to go in the case of a Russian invasion.

The extraordinary nature of the Russian invasion in 2022 provided a moment of unity to a bloc that oftentimes disagrees over questions of foreign policy. Moreover, the EU is held back by a lack of capacity at both the EU and national level, which will likely be remedied only gradually following Russia's invasion of Ukraine in 2022. To intervene in the civil war in Libya, for example, the Franco-British coalition had to rely on U.S. capabilities, provided reluctantly by the Obama administration.[18] On the EU and NATO's Eastern flank, effective deterrence continues to be impossible without a sizeable U.S. presence. Successive U.S. administrations have stressed the need for European allies to step up, yet Europe was not fully awoken from its slumber even by the abuse directed at it during Donald Trump's presidency. Rhetorically, and formally, the issue of 'strategic autonomy' has taken center stage, leading to the creation of Permanent Structured Cooperation (PESCO) on security and defense and the European Defence Fund (EDF). Without a commitment by member states to invest more resources into their militaries, either jointly or independently, such formal structures remain empty shells – not to mention the inevitable backlash if European governments had indeed tried to build up a

'European army' under the control of European institutions instead of national governments.

HAS THE EU FAILED?

A lot has been written about the EU's shortcomings and about the trade-offs of political and economic integration. One influential set of lenses through which the European project and economic integration have been viewed was provided by Harvard economist Dani Rodrik in the form of the so-called 'Rodrik's Trilemma.' In his widely cited article, he explains the tension that exists between democracy, the nation state, and deep economic integration.[19] Because deep economic integration – of the kind pursued by the EU – affects many aspects of domestic policy and regulation, it clashes with democratic governance existing at the national level. The pursuit of deep economic integration thus means either a deepening democratic deficit, in which national politics becomes increasingly constrained by rules and regulations coming from the outside, or the emergence of democratic decision-making at the supranational level. As of today, the EU involves an uneasy combination of rules and bureaucratic oversight that tie the hands of national, democratically elected politicians and institutions (most notably the European Parliament) that seek to imbue the EU's decisions with a sense of popular legitimacy. Whether those arrangements are satisfactory has been a subject of debates among academics. Princeton's Andrew Moravcsik famously argued that the EU possessed democratic legitimacy – particularly when compared against *real-world* examples of democracy existing within nation states and not some idealized version thereof. If there appears to be a disconnect from voters across Europe, as documented by chronically low turnout in European elections, he argues, it is mainly because it deals with questions that are technical in character – say, trade, competition policy, central banking, or technical administration.[20] That argument, however, falls flat in an era in which European institutions have placed themselves at the frontlines of many intimately political battles, some of them removed far from the EU's original purview – over immigration, fiscal policy, LGBTQ rights, or vaccine mandates. Even quintessentially technical subjects, such as regulatory convergence through trade agreements, have become subjects of heated political contestation as the EU was seeking to conclude a trade agreement with the United States in the 2010s, the Transatlantic Trade and Investment Partnership (TTIP).[21]

There is another source of friction in the European project, identified by the Dutch historian and political philosopher Luuk van Middelaar. An important distinction exists between the politics of rules, at which the EU is quite adept, and the politics driven by events – which requires improvisation, risk-taking, and alertness to opportunities.[22] Much of the European project can be seen as an effort to supersede the chaotic and violent politics of events of yesteryear with a more orderly form of political organization and decision-making based squarely on rules. In order to make power competition between France and Germany impossible, the European project merged their steel and coal industries, preventing their rearmament. To prevent beggar-thy-neighbor protectionism and economic nationalism, the EU has created a massive marketplace governed by common rules. To curb the political temptations of irresponsible deficit spending within a shared monetary union, it instituted strict fiscal rules under the Stability and Growth Pact. On many fronts, that approach has delivered. Unlike in the past, an armed conflict between EU member states is indeed unthinkable. Notwithstanding the many structural problems plaguing European economies, the single market has made Europeans wealthier and more globally competitive than they would otherwise be.

However, no set of rules can engineer away the fundamentally unpredictable and oftentimes conflictual character of social and political life. It was precisely in those unforeseen circumstances, which involved conflicts between different values or interests – when the monetary union was at risk of unraveling, when the Schengen Area was overrun with asylum seekers, or when the pandemic hit – that the EU found itself at its weakest. The problem is not just the bureaucratic and risk-averse nature of the EU's executive, the European Commission. A deep-seated aversion to political conflict from the EU's most important country, Germany, amplifies the problem. Instead of facing challenges head on, the can is often kicked down the road under the rubric of 'strategic patience.' When action does become unavoidable, solutions are rarely subject to open, democratic deliberations. Rather, they are presented, often by the Commission, in technocratic terms and as 'having no alternative' – effectively assuming away the clashes of ideas, values, and interests that characterize political decision-making.[23]

The answer to the question of whether these constraints and shortcomings necessarily set the EU up for failure or not depends on what one thinks the ultimate purpose of European integration is. There are two alternative ways to understand the EU's end goal, which have been in tension since the project's inception.

Under the first, dominant dispensation, the purpose of European integration is to usher in a qualitatively new form of governance in Europe, to overcome Europe's atavistic divides and to serve as a vehicle of progress. The mindset, which is found in abundance across European institutions and among the continent's liberal elites, is reminiscent of Woody Allen's quip in *Annie Hall*: "A relationship, I think, is like a shark, you know? It has to constantly move forward or it dies." As such, the New York University legal scholar Joseph Weiler notes that European integration has rarely been justified through traditional means of input/output, or process/result legitimacy. The EU's deficiencies as a democratic polity have long been apparent, as has the bloc's failure to deliver some essential Europe-wide public goods. Instead, "the justi-fication for action and its mobilizing force derive [...] from the ideal pursued, the destiny to be achieved, the promised land waiting at the end of the road."[24] In that sense, the EU has closely mirrored developments in Western political thought at large. The philosophical underpinnings of Western liberal democ-racies, too, have moved away from more modest, classical forms of liberalism which sought to establish a tolerable if unsatisfying modus vivendi for free, self-governing societies toward far more ambitious conceptions of freedom and equality.

The progressive, forward-looking conception of European integration is itself ridden with contradictions. On the one hand, its ultimate purpose is to transcend the destructiveness of nationalism of the past and yield a form of governance from which the entire world can learn, which would be substan-tively different from the nation state. In practice, however, this approach has often consisted of efforts to slavishly scale up the nation state to the European level. Already, the bloc has acquired many state-like features: a currency, a directly elected parliament, a flag, and an apex court. Frequently, political leaders such as France's president Emmanuel Macron make allusions to 'European sovereignty.' The term is particularly arresting, as sovereignty has traditionally referred to forms of political power that are "indivisible, supreme and absolute" – and not to federal arrangements that involve an association of self-governing political units.[25] Particularly in recent years, as the tenor of the integration project has grown more pessimistic, fearful, and inward-looking, the state-like view of the EU promises to essentially replicate the behaviors of nation states on a larger scale instead of persisting with the ambitious, outward-looking mindset that once fueled the EU's Eastern enlargements.[26] Building border barriers, erecting obstacles to trade and investment including from friendly countries such as the United States, Switzerland or the United Kingdom, and fretting about the 'European way of life' blurs the distinction between the proponents of the integration project and petty nationalists who are seeking to do the same thing, only on a smaller, national scale.[27]

There has also been a considerable lack of imagination in the thinking sur-rounding the EU's immediate future. True, the EU must heed the lessons of history. According to some proponents of Europe's 'federalization,' "historical record shows that successful unions have resulted not from gradual processes of convergence in relatively benign circumstances, but through sharp ruptures in periods of extreme crisis."[28] The right model thus seems to be England's union with Scotland, struck in 1707 in the aftermath of the War of the Spanish Succession and, most prominently, America's Constitutional Convention of 1787, conducted in the midst of a debt crisis after the War of Independence. However, the EU has tried – and failed – in its own attempt at a constitutional convention (2001–03). Like the early United States, it was also exposed to an unprecedented combination of shocks and crises over the course of the past decade. Yet, the political leadership needed for a big-bang 'federalization' of the EU (in reality, the creation of a European state) has been absent.

There might be good reasons for that failure. An obvious one is that successful political unions of the past, unlike the EU, had a robust sense of shared political identity prior to their founding. The conventional wisdom that, in the United States, strong state-based ties trumped citizens' allegiance to the common political project is an artifact of the polarized politics leading to the Civil War, rather than an accurate description of America at the time of its founding. In fact, a sense of shared American identity and common purpose was presumed already in the 1754 Albany Plan. In *Federalist 2*, predating the U.S. Constitution, John Jay talks of "one connected country" given by Providence to

> one united people – a people descended from the same ancestors, speaking the same language, professing the same religion, attached to the same principles of government, very similar in their manners and customs, and who, by their joint counsels, arms, and efforts, fighting side by side throughout a long and bloody war, have nobly established general liberty and independence.[29]

If the purpose of European integration is the creation of a European super-state or some other form of utopia, then the European project has failed and is bound to fail again. Fortunately, the EU does not *have* to be understood in those hyper-ambitious, teleological terms. In the second, alternative understanding, the EU can be seen simply as a platform, necessarily flawed, for managing relationships between European countries and for exploiting gains from cooperation and trade, a nexus of institutions, rules, and relationships linking together and constraining national governments, creating a space for economic competition and political cooperation. This far more restrained view of European integration conceptualizes the EU as an order instead of a teleological, forward-looking project. It carries with itself a dose of agnosticism about the EU's ultimate purpose, about the meaning of Europeanness, and about the relevant scope of joint European action. Instead of articulating a bold European policy agenda, it contents itself with providing tools to relevant actors, most notably European governments, to resolve conflicts and reap gains from cooperation, competition, and trade.

ROOTS OF THE EUROPEAN IDEA

The idea of a united Europe goes back centuries. Some Catholics, such as Dante Alighieri who called for a new universal Roman Empire "governed temporally by an emperor and spiritually by the pope," were dissatisfied with Europe's political fragmentation – at odds with the universal character of Christendom. Similarly, Frenchman Pierre Du Bois argued in favor of empowering the pope to resolve disputes between princes, who would be constituted as a Christian Council.[30] With the Reformation, such discussions shifted toward accommodating Europe's religious diversity. William Penn, a 17th-century Quaker, sought to set up an "Imperial Parliament" with a rotating presidency that would settle disputes while preserving the internal sovereignty of every participating nation.[31] The tension between more and less ambitious visions of a European polity continued throughout the Enlightenment era. In Immanuel Kant's understanding, the purpose of an international federation was to secure peace by creating a rules-based international order.[32] While secular in his outlook, utopian thinker Henri de Saint-Simon saw the European project in almost messianic, religious terms, as the continent's chance of redemption from the sins of the past.[33]

Consolidation of Europe's nation states and aggressive nationalism that led to World War I gave a new impetus to efforts to unify the continent. Perhaps the most prominent among those was the Paneuropean Movement led by Count Richard von Coudehove-Kalergi. "A fragmented Europe," writes von Coudenhove-Kalergi,

> leads to war, oppression, misery; a united Europe to peace, freedom, prosperity! Once this either-or in its full meaning is clear to Europeans – then everyone will choose which of these two paths they want to go down: the path of European anarchy – or the way towards European organization; the path of death – or the way of life.[34]

While it was a distinctly elite phenomenon with little traction in European politics, the movement pursued detailed plans of prospects for Europe's political and economic unification.

As the situation on the continent continued to deteriorate, the idea of a European federation was making headway with intellectuals of very different ideological stripes. Months before the outbreak of World War II, the Austrian economist and later Nobel Laureate Friedrich August von Hayek argued that "one of the main deficiencies of nineteenth-century liberalism [was] that its advocates did not sufficiently realize that the achievement of the recognized harmony of interests between the inhabitants of the different states was only possible within the framework of international security."[35] To rectify this omission, Hayek believed an international authority ought to be set up to constrain the nation state, particularly from pursuing nationalist and protectionist economic policies. Governments would delegate the power to this authority, the idea went, to "[prevent] individual states from interfering with economic activity in certain ways" without necessarily giving it also the "positive power of acting in their stead."[36] This classical liberal vision of European federalism was as much about devolving power as it was about setting up a supranational political authority. Hayek, for instance, saw Nazism not as a one-off aberration. Rather, it was an extension of the much earlier project of Germany's political consolidation and militarization. Accordingly, he argued in 1944,

> the victors should not regard Bismarck's creation of a highly centralized Germany as an irreversible fact, and that, if Germany is ever to fit as a peaceful member into the European family of nations, it will be necessary partly to undo Bismarck's work and to reconstruct Germany with a decentralized and truly federal structure.[37]

Such a policy of domestic decentralization had to "be supplement[ed] by the enforcement of complete free trade, external and internal, for all these German states."[38] Likewise, the German 'ordoliberal' economist Wilhelm Röpke rejected the suggestions that Europe ought to be organized politically by moving sovereign power from the nation states to a European federation. Instead, Röpke, who was among the most prominent representatives of the pro-market ordoliberal tradition associated with the University of Freiburg, argued, "the excess of sovereignty should be abolished instead of being transferred to a higher political and geographical unit."[39]

The restrained view of European integration stood in sharp contrast with a more ambitious vision pursued by thinkers on the political left. For Altiero Spinelli, a communist politician who later became a prominent member of the European Commission, integration represented a radical break with everything Europe had seen in the past. As the *Ventotene Manifesto*, co-authored by Spinelli, put it, "[w]e must know how to discard old burdens, how to be ready for the new world that is coming, that will be so different from what we have imagined. Among the old, the inept must be put aside; and among the young, new energies are to be stimulated."[40] Spinelli and his disciples stressed the need to immediately create "a secure and strong European power based on a democratic consensus among Europeans" as a vital institutional prerequisite to establishing an "effective economic, military and diplomatic unit" in Europe.[41] In fact, the argument went, common European political institutions ought to be built *before* the postwar reconstruction of Europe's nation states takes place.[42] The progressive approach to European federalism relied on a unitary view of sovereignty, and stressed the hierarchical nature of the relationship between federal power and states. Notwithstanding the rhetoric of historical progress, a centralized European government was meant to proceed in much the same way as unifications of Europe's nation states took place in the 19th century – presumably to be accompanied by a similar degree of top-down cultural and social homogenization.

For some, such as France's maverick philosopher Alexandre Kojève, Europe's integration was a corollary of unstoppable historic forces transcending the nation state and creating empires. A Marxist and Hegelian thinker, he not only trained a generation of influential French postwar philosophers but also worked in high-level positions at France's Ministry of the Economy, participating directly in negotiations leading to the formation of the European Coal and Steel Community (ECSC). "[I]t [i]s impossible to jump from the Nation to Humanity without going through Empire,"[43] Kojève argued, describing the nascent European project as a "Latin Empire," encompassing the culturally, linguistically, and politically like-minded nations of France, Spain, Italy, and Portugal, which would join an economic union in order to "create and inspire" a new "specifically political ideology," which would be geared toward securing not so much power or 'greatness' but rather autonomy. "A will to autonomy" is not necessarily imperialist or militarist, as "'militarism' and 'imperialism' are outgrowths of a fundamentally underdeveloped will to autonomy and do not use truly powerful means of execution."[44]

Occupying the space between the minimalist classical liberal views of European integration and the unbounded progressive ones was a spectrum of Christian Democratic thinkers, whose ideas came to dominate Europe's political life after World War II, including among some of the early architecture of the European project. The resurgence of Christian Democracy followed decades of an uneasy adaptation of Catholic intellectuals and leaders to political life in pluralistic, liberal democracies, which characterized later decades of the 19th century. Leo XIII's encyclical, *Rerum Novarum*,[45] outlined a novel political and a policy agenda that sought to charter a middle course between laissez-faire liberalism and temptations of the left, emphasizing an organic, covenantal nature of society, from the family, through local community and market relationships, to national and international politics. Philosophically, these ideas were developed most fully through the works of 'personalist' authors such as Emmanuel Mounier, Dennis de Rougemont, and Jacques Maritain. Personalism was grounded in the personal nature of God in Christianity and the resulting centrality of the individual as the *Imago Dei*, placing humans and their dignity at the center of political life – again, to provide an alternative to both collectivist ideologies of the time and to the oft-caricatured individualism of free-market liberals. Making "democracy safe for Catholics,"[46] personalism saw society as based on the "cooperation between independent decision-making centres and restructuring of the whole of society, both based on freely entered into contracts."[47] This vision was difficult to reconcile with the reality of centralized nation states, especially as those grew increasingly oppressive at home, and aggressive in their international outlook.

Catholic politics were heterogeneous and evolving. They involved distinctly illiberal and anti-pluralist currents, exemplified by France's *Action Française*.

Some personalist thinkers, such as Maritain, were initially distrustful of liberal democracy, but gradually came to embrace it.[48] By and large, however, the emerging personalist outlook increasingly emphasized decentralization and federalism[49] as natural responses to the pluralistic nature of society and of the organic nature of bonds tying human societies together. Also a Catholic, though more culturally than politically and spiritually, Jean Monnet ended up pioneering a very different, technocratic functionalist view of European integration, which naturally complemented the ambitious progressive vision rather than the organic personalist view of international federalism. Monnet's toolbox differed from Spinelli's, who was transparent about the imperative to "organize power at the European level" through discrete political moves.[50] Monnet's method eschewed direct challenges to national sovereignty in favor of a gradual pooling of competencies, which was supposed to open the way to gradual political unification – "the [European] Community is only a step towards organizational forms of tomorrow."[51] Growing economic ties will feed an ongoing cycle of political integration, "establishing de facto solidarity, from which a federation would gradually emerge."[52] The common state would thus emerge out of necessity, not out of a discrete political choice. While his toolkit was different, Monnet concurred with the progressives on the obvious desirability and indeed inevitability of the ultimate goal – of 'ever-closer union.' In other words, "Europe is late on a path on which it has already embarked deeply."[53] Furthermore, "[t]he realities will themselves allow to create a political union," Monnet wrote in his memoirs. "The idea is clear: Europe will be built by men, at the right moment, from the reality that is available to them."[54]

In varying proportions, Europe's postwar history carries the footprint of all these competing ideas. Röpke, for example, shared his intellectual pedigree with the ordoliberal Chancellor of Germany Ludwig Erhard. Distinctly federalist in the classical liberal sense, Germany's constitution includes to this day a number of 'super-rigid' provisions that make it difficult, if not impossible, to fundamentally alter the democratic character of its regime. Similarly to German ordoliberals, the second president of Italy, Luigi Einaudi, maintained a classical liberal view of European integration as "the opposite of subjugating the various states and the various regions to a single centre."[55] Instead, it simply meant "assigning to the federal authority certain economic tasks strictly defined in the constitutional document of the federation [...] it is necessary to reduce to a minimum absolutely necessary the number of tasks assigned to the federation from the beginning."[56] An ordoliberal view of Europe, as a thin rules-based order enabling social market economy to thrive, was reflected in the emergence of the European Commission as a guardian of a level playing field. Its oversight role, which dates back to the 1950s, grew stronger through cases such as *Dassonville*, which curbed the ability of governments to impose arbitrary trading restrictions. "All trading rules," the European Court of Justice decided, "enacted by Member States, which are capable of hindering, directly or indirectly, actually or potentially, intra-Community trade are to be considered as measures having an effect equivalent to quantitative restrictions."[57] Later, the Single European Act, a highly complex piece of legislation going far beyond just issues of economic integration (e.g., covering questions of voting procedures, the European Commission's powers in areas of environmental, social, and regional policy), entrenched the principle of free movement of goods, people, services, and capital.[58] Since then, the Commission has successfully curbed state aid to national champions, broken up numerous publicly owned monopolies in network industries, deregulated the airline industry, and dismantled barriers to the integration of financial markets. The relative rigidity in the enforcement of state aid rules in the past few decades has been a primary ingredient in the creation of the single market, reflecting a distinctly ordoliberal view of the world. With a few exceptions, they ban any discretionary intervention from member states that may result in a distortion of the commerce between or within the member states themselves. As a result of the EU's commitment to the single market, a number of product and service markets in Europe, most prominently airlines and telecoms, are more competitive than in the United States.[59] Furthermore, Christian Democrats among the founding fathers of the integration project, such as Italy's prime minister Alcide De Gasperi or Germany's Konrad Adenauer, were well-versed in personalist philosophy.[60]

Yet, the ideological outlook that most shaped the EU and its precursors from the 1950s onward bore relatively little resemblance to either ordoliberalism or personalism. Rather, it amalgamated Monnet's technocratic functionalism and Spinelli's ambitious progressivism. To the extent to which Catholic thinking played a role, it provided a quasi-religious zeal to the effort rather than a sense of restraint and deference to bottom-up forms of social organization. Consider the messianic tone apparent in the 1950 Schuman Declaration, drafted largely by Jean Monnet and his team, which included a commitment to integrate the coal and steel industries of the six European nations, France, Germany, Italy, Belgium, Luxembourg, and the Netherlands:[61]

> [T]he pooling of coal and steel production should immediately provide for the setting up of common foundations for economic development as a first step in the federation of Europe, and will change the destinies of those regions which have long been devoted to the manufacture of munitions of war, of which they have been the most constant victims.
> The solidarity in production thus established will make it plain that any war between France and Germany becomes not merely unthinkable, but materially impossible. The setting up of this powerful productive unit, open to all countries willing to take part and bound ultimately to provide all the member countries with the basic

elements of industrial production on the same terms, will lay a true foundation for their economic unification.

This production will be offered to the world as a whole without distinction or exception, with the aim of contributing to raising living standards and to promoting peaceful achievements. With increased resources Europe will be able to pursue the achievement of one of its essential tasks, namely, the development of the African continent. In this way, there will be realized simply and speedily that fusion of interest which is indispensable to the establishment of a common economic system; it may be the leaven from which may grow a wider and deeper community between countries long opposed to one another by sanguinary divisions.[62]

France's foreign minister Robert Schuman, who read out the declaration at Quai d'Orsay on the anniversary of the end of World War II, was himself a pious Catholic who saw the integration project as a fundamentally spiritual quest: "Europe is searching for an identity; it is aware that it has its own future in hand. It has never been so close to the goal. May God not let Europe miss the hour of its destiny, its final chance of salvation," he wrote in his memoir.[63] Similarly, De Gasperi saw the integration project as a version of "universal res publica Christiania," echoing the medieval and early modern dreams of a universal polity based on Christian principles.[64]

THE CHALLENGE OF PLURALISM

Europe's diversity is key to an understanding of why this ambitious version of the integration project has reached a dead end – and why a reconceptualization of the EU as an order geared to manage pluralism is in order. The European project, mind you, started with merely six countries. Belgium, France, Italy, Luxembourg, the Netherlands, and West Germany had sizeable (in most cases dominant) Catholic populations and they all had just emerged from the horrors of World War II. With successive enlargements, the EU has grown dramatically more heterogeneous. The United Kingdom, which joined in 1973, maintained throughout the period of its membership an uneasy attitude toward many aspects of the integration project, culminating in the 2016 Brexit referendum. The Southern enlargements of the 1980s, bringing Greece, Spain, and Portugal into the club, widened the EU's internal economic differences and planted the seeds of the asymmetric economic crisis that almost tore the Eurozone apart in the early 2010s. Finally, the Eastern enlargements of the 2000s and the 2010s brought post-communist countries, counting almost 100 million people, into the fold.

The impact of the Eastern enlargements on the EU's functioning remains the main focus of discussion throughout this book. That does not imply essential-izing the difference between 'old' and 'new' member states, neither of which makes for a homogeneous group. Real incomes and numerous other metrics of well-being in, say, the Czech Republic or Estonia, exceed today those in many of the 'old' members. Moreover, the first batch of Central and Eastern European countries have now been a part of the EU for almost two decades, yet those countries are still being referred to as 'new' member states. No one referred to Austria, Finland, or Sweden as 'new' member states after their accession in 1995 – not even in 2000, when a right-wing populist party joined a government coalition in Austria, portending the much-discussed democratic 'backsliding' that has been taking place prominently in some post-communist countries a decade or so later.

The casual orientalism that often infuses conversations about the place of post-communist countries in the EU is unwarranted. A similar reasoning could be applied to the EU's earlier enlargements, including to the Mediterranean periphery, or to the rush of 'Southern' members to join the Eurozone. What matters in both cases is that enlargements have made the EU more economically, politically, and socially heterogeneous. And it is simply a fact that the footprint left by the big-bang enlargement of 2004, which brought the first batch of eight post-communist countries into the Union together with Cyprus and Malta, followed by Romania and Bulgaria and then Croatia some years later, exceeds that of earlier instances of the EU's expansion. At the time of Austria, Finland, and Sweden's accession in 1995, average income in the EU's poorest member state, Greece, was at almost 40 percent of the income in the EU's wealthiest state, Luxembourg. When Bulgaria joined the EU in 2007 as its poorest member state, that ratio dropped to 15 percent. Since then, the gap between the wealthiest and poorest member state has narrowed only slightly, to 20 percent in 2020.[65] Since 2019, the EU also includes a country that is categorized by Freedom House only as "partly free" (Hungary).[66] European populations have widely different attitudes toward questions of social tolerance and minorities. While 88 percent of Swedes, for example, support the institution of same-sex marriage, only 27 percent of Hungarians and 32 percent of Poles do so.[67]

That the EU's successive enlargements, particularly to the East, have dramatically increased the EU's heterogeneity is by no means a bad thing – quite the contrary. Diversity has always been one of Europe's strengths. Historian David Landes, for example, famously argued that Europe's historical divisions were fundamental to the continent's technological and economic rise in the early modern period.[68] At the same time, diversity and disagreement place new demands on governing institutions. In particular, deep disagreements over values require mechanisms that defuse possible society-wide conflicts, for example by devolving relevant political decisions to lower levels of government, closer to the individuals and local communities. Moreover, having the right set of institutions helps adjudicate also the more 'shallow,' empirically driven disagreements – say over effects of particular policies, institutions, or informal practices. A correctly structured polity would allow not only for a much greater variation of policies informed by such competing claims but also for learning and selection on the basis of resulting "natural experiments."[69] Ideally, an enlarged EU ought to be a space for Europe-wide competition of perspectives, ideas, and policies that fuel learning, innovation, and progress. When managed by a set of institutions unfit for that purpose, in contrast, diversity becomes a source of friction and paralysis. Unfortunately, too often, that is the story of European integration under the dominant paradigm, which seeks to turn a rambling, heterogeneous, and quarrelling continent featuring dozens of ethnic and national identities, hundreds of languages, and vastly different histories into a neat, homogenous polity.

Many are in denial about the fundamental incompatibility of the ambitious, teleological form of European integration and Europe's pluralistic nature. Some studies show, for example, that enlargements did not noticeably slow down production of new European legislation, denying thus the existence of a trade-off between the EU's 'widening' and 'deepening.' Major policy and legislative initiatives, the data show, proceeded in Parliament and the Council even as the membership base expanded.[70] That misleadingly places emphasis on the inputs, not outputs, of European policymaking. Not all EU legislation, after all, is born equal. The proliferation of narrow, technical norms tells one little about the ability of the EU to adapt and respond to new challenges. It is undeniable that both the EU's policies and the bloc's overall ethos have been deeply affected by the presence of new member states. Even the most ambitious, if not utopian, in the founding generation understood the inevitability of that trade-off. Kojève, driven by his vision of a culturally connected European project built as an alternative both to the Soviet empire and to an equally alien 'Anglo-Saxon' world, played a central role in derailing the U.K.'s accession to the European Economic Community.[71]

Without a recalibration of the EU's governance and institutions toward managing diversity and maintaining a European modus vivendi, away from the ambitious teleological agenda of unification, the EU will continue to suffer from a mismatch between its unrealistically high-minded ends and the dearth of tools needed to pursue them. The danger is not, as it seemed a few years ago, an unraveling of the EU at the hands of reckless populists. The British example, which made clear the difficult trade-offs involved in disentangling an economy from decades of deep economic and political integration with the EU, has inspired few followers on the continent – even in hard-line populist and nationalist circles. The more likely risk to the EU is one of its gradual hollowing out and irrelevance. Myriad international organizations linger on despite outliving their original mandates. The International Monetary Fund (IMF) was set up originally to manage the Bretton Woods system of fixed rates, defunct since the early 1970s. The IMF has since reinvented its mission in creative ways, including by taking on issues as remote as women's economic empowerment.[72] Other institutions persist through inertia while being largely inconsequential for policy outcomes. Not many people have even heard, much less follow the work, of the UN's Economic Commission for Europe in Geneva or the Council of Europe Development Bank in Paris or any number of international organizations that once played an important role on the world stage. Similarly, a hollowed-out version of the EU, with much of its bureaucratic apparatus, could live on for decades, animating the Brussels bubble with new initiatives and white papers, while European governments and publics largely get on with their lives.

The argument unfolding in the following chapters is not an 'anti-European' or a 'Euroskeptic' one – quite the contrary. It is unabashedly *pro-European*, both in the sense that it wishes prosperity and peace for the European continent and in the sense that it sees the EU and much of its institutional architecture as important components of its success. If anything, it is the self-styled prophets of 'ever-closer union' whose support for Europe is made conditional on the continent's embrace of their institutional and policy agenda. This book, in contrast, embraces Europe as it exists, not as an abstraction or as a hypothetical end state, accepting it in its unwieldy, pluralistic complexity and taking limitations of top-down approaches to policymaking as given.

In practical terms, the much needed recalibration starts from recognition that the EU is not a single, monolithic entity but rather a number of functionally separate integration projects running in parallel. There is no inherent reason why membership in the EU's single market has to overlap with membership in the Schengen Area, with participation in the Common Agricultural Policy, or in the monetary union. And, indeed, those integration projects do not always overlap. Numerous EU members show no intention of joining the Euro. EU non-members, such as Norway or Switzerland, are in the single market, while Ireland is not in the Schengen Area of passport-less travel.

'Unbundling' the EU does not necessitate dramatic changes to European treaties, though some would help. More importantly, it requires a change in the habits of mind of European leaders and Brussels institutions themselves. Instead of seeing new policy initiatives as being, by default, one-size-fits-all solutions, European policies can emerge from horizontally organized coalitions of members (and non-members), with European institutions playing primarily a supportive, rather than a leading role. Such an approach, which would involve voluntary associations of self-governing, democratic political units, would provide a more organic response to the challenge represented by the Rodrik Trilemma than the essentially utopian effort to create a European democracy from the top down. As a result, it would neutralize much of the opposition to the European project, which is grounded in the not-unjustified concern that EU membership provides a one-way street toward ever-more delegation of decision-making to Brussels, at the expense of national governments.

NOTES

1. Cited in Deutsche Welle (2015).
2. Juncker (2016).
3. Borrell (2021).
4. Vestager (2020).
5. Dzurinda (2021).
6. Reid (2004).
7. Leonard (2005b).
8. Barroso (2013).
9. CBInsights (2021).
10. European Commission (2021e).
11. Becker et al. (2020).
12. Guarascio (2020).
13. Rohac (2021d).
14. European Commission (2019b).
15. Rohac (2021c).
16. Council of the EU (2020a).
17. See Nardelli et al. (2022).
18. Clinton (2016, 295–312).
19. Rodrik (2000).
20. Moravcsik (2002).
21. Bauer (2016).
22. Middelaar (2019).
23. Auer (2019).
24. Weiler (2011, 683).
25. Reho (2018).
26. See, e.g., Kundnani (2020, 2021).
27. Even sophisticated scholarly proponents of an expansive understanding of the EU embrace integration as an essentially state-building exercise. See, e.g., Kelemen and McNamara (2022).
28. Simms (2012, 50).
29. Jay (1787).
30. Nelsen and Guth (2015, 126).
31. Nelsen and Guth (2015, 126–7).
32. Kant (1983).
33. Swedberg (1994).
34. Coudenhove-Kalergi (1923).
35. Hayek (1948, 270).
36. Hayek (1948, 267).
37. Hayek (1945, 12).
38. Hayek (1945, 13).
39. Quoted in Majone (2014, 267).
40. Spinelli and Rossi (1941).
41. Spinelli (1985, 151–62).
42. Majone (2014, 296).

43.   Quoted in Kletzer (2006, 146).
44.   Cited in Kletzer (2006, 147).
45.   Leo XIII (1891).
46.   Nelsen and Guth (2015, 124).
47.   Burgess (2000, 152).
48.   Nelsen and Guth (2015, 124).
49.   For a discussion of the relationship between personalism and federalism, see Kinsky (1979).
50.   Burgess (1996, 4).
51.   Monnet (1985, 617).
52.   Quoted in Burgess (2000, 35).
53.   Monnet (1985, 617).
54.   Monnet (1985, 506).
55.   Einaudi (1945).
56.   Einaudi (1945).
57.   European Court of Justice (1974).
58.   Gillingham (2003, 228–58).
59.   Gutiérrez and Philippon (2019).
60.   See, e.g., Kaiser (2007).
61.   The prominence of Catholicism rose in the Netherlands during the interwar period, making the Catholic People's Party (KVP) the dominant political force of the postwar era.
62   Schuman (1950)
63.   Quoted in Nelsen and Guth (2015, 198).
64.   Quoted in Nelsen and Guth (2015, 195).
65.   World Bank (2021).
66.   See Freedom House (2021).
67.   Lipka and Masci (2019).
68.   Landes (1998).
69.   Müller (2019).
70.   Toshkov (2017) is the most notable of these. Best et al. (2010) is a survey of earlier literature.
71.   Kletzer (2006, 140).
72.   International Monetary Fund (2021a).

2.   The light that did not fail

Any debate about the EU's supposed failures must retain a sense of perspective. The advent of the integration project was preceded by the unimaginable horrors of World War II. The EU's enlargements, meanwhile, came after the collapse of a monstrous totalitarian regime that held captive a large portion of Europe. Anyone who crossed the Iron Curtain before 1990 can attest that the trip was tantamount to moving from a color movie to a black and white one, or vice versa, depending on the direction of travel. All the common stereotypes about communism were true: long lines and near-empty shelves in stores in the East, taciturn faces, the monotony of gray urban and rural landscapes, and the oppressive apparatus of secret police – a far cry from the vibrancy and material prosperity of free societies, oftentimes just a few miles away.

Pandemic-era disruptions aside, crossing the border today could not be a more forgettable experience, if only because of the absence of formal border controls. True, the roads might still be in worse shape in the East, though that has been changing too thanks to the inflow of EU-funded investments in the infrastructure of new, poorer member states. If anything, it is the East that now looks more colorful with its chaotic excess of visual ads contrasting with the orderly looking German and Austrian countryside. Unlike in the 1980s, there are no shortages of *any* goods or services on the Eastern side of the border. Urban centers of post-communist countries have been painstakingly restored to their former glory after decades of neglect, the restaurant scene is improving, and affluent-looking locals can be seen driving the latest models of foreign-made cars. Notwithstanding scandals surrounding the government's use of spyware against political opponents in countries such as Hungary,[1] unchecked state surveillance is overwhelmingly a thing of the past, too.

In short, there is a lot to celebrate about the past 30 years in Eastern Europe. The EU, moreover, is an important reason why. In material terms, a large chunk of the post-communist world – specifically, the four Visegrád countries, the Baltic States, Slovenia, Croatia, Romania, and Bulgaria – have made it. If a time traveler from 1989 were offered a glimpse of Prague, Ljubljana, Bratislava, or Budapest today and saw the overwhelming sense of abundance and prosperity, they would surely declare post-communist transitions a resounding success. Data only corroborate that impression. While in some countries the early years of communist rule went hand in hand with productivity-enhancing industrialization and urbanization, the growth potential of planned economies had been largely exhausted by the 1960s. The stagnation of subsequent decades continued to widen the gap between Western European economies and the ossified communist bloc. In real terms, Czechoslovakia's per capita GDP exceeded that of Austria at the time of communism's onset in 1948. By 1990, Czechoslovak incomes fell in relative terms to barely half of those in the neighboring Austria.[2] Devastated by war, Poland's real per capita income was a little over half that of Finland in 1948, a relatively low-income European economy. By 1990, Finland was almost three and a half times wealthier than Poland. The border regions in countries such as Austria or Germany, once the periphery of the Western world, have also benefitted from new trade and market opportunities, resulting in rising employment and incomes.[3]

In all of this, European integration has played an important, albeit subtle, role. It was *not* the inflow of EU funds that made Eastern Europe prosperous, nor was it the adoption of the EU's body of rules and regulations – the 'acquis communautaire'. Rather, it was the competition of economic policies and reforms between Eastern European governments joining the EU's single market, which aimed at attracting foreign direct investment. That competition has also left an imprint on Western European economies, the governments of which made some efforts at making them more flexible and dynamic. Some Eastern Europeans, furthermore, brought a breath of fresh air into stale debates about Europe's geopolitical role, its responsibilities, and the transatlantic alliance.

RAGS TO RICHES

Given the initial disruption caused by the collapse of communist economic planning, things were bound to get worse before they would start improving – hence the famous 'J-curve' followed by essentially all post-communist economies. The adjustment of the early 1990s was particularly dramatic in Russia, which lost one third of its GDP and half of its industrial production. In Poland, the early years of the transition shaved off more than 20 percent of GDP.[4] There were dramatic short-term costs to income, production, and employment in the newly independent Baltic States, which were tightly integrated with the Soviet economy. Other post-communist countries suffered smaller shocks, especially if they had been partly exposed to markets and international competition during the communist era. Yet, survey data on incomes suggest significant short-term hardship even in countries that seemed to have gotten off lightly, such as Hungary.[5]

Planned economies were characterized by wasteful and inefficient production. Industrial production activity in the Soviet Union, for example, was several times more steel-intensive, for example, than production in the West.

Absent incentives to economize on inputs, such as labor, communist-era enterprises had little reason to innovate, automate, or improve their efficiency. In fact, factories that exceeded the centrally set plan would risk seeing their output targets increased or their inputs cut by central planners in the future. Instead of rewarding factory managers for efficiency gains, the logic of central planning meant that success in the pursuit of the collective goals placed one in a more difficult situation later. Without the profit motive, managers were thus incentivized to maximize the amount of available slack. For any prescribed amount of output, a rational factory manager would request the maximum possible allocation of resources. And conversely, for a given quantity of inputs, the manager sought to ensure that production targets were set as low as possible. Given the information asymmetries – central planners had limited means to independently verify the information that was provided to them by managers of state-owned enterprises or to compare it to market data – factory managers were able to get away with behavior that led to wastefulness, inefficiency, and ultimately endemic shortages of goods.[6]

Whatever temporary disruption brought about by the transition in the 1990s, it has since been outweighed by the economic gains made over the longer horizon. Real per capita incomes have almost tripled in Poland and Slovakia since the fall of communism. Even among the poorer EU latecomers, Bulgaria and Romania, the average citizen today is more than twice as well as off as in 1989. And while the catching up has not been complete, the Czech Republic's real per capita GDP today is approaching three quarters of that of Austria. Finland's real per capita GDP, meanwhile, is only 40 percent higher than that of Poland – a dramatic degree of economic convergence over just a generation and a half. In real terms, a big part of post-communist Central and Eastern Europe already outperforms economies on the EU's Mediterranean periphery – Portugal, Greece, and, in some cases, Spain.

If anything, aggregate statistics may underestimate the magnitude of economic progress. Planned economies were plagued by constant shortages of consumer goods. GDP figures do not capture waiting times in lines to buy necessities such as fruit or meat. For durable goods, such as cars or apartments, the waiting times were counted in years. In 1990, there were only 138 cars per 1,000 inhabitants in Poland.[7] Today, the figure exceeds 700.[8] In real terms, a Škoda car in the 1980s would cost its owner twice as much as a new entry-level Škoda today – a far more comfortable, reliable, powerful, safer, and less polluting car.[9] Instead of the shortage-induced wait times and high prices for subpar automobiles, the sudden explosion in car ownership has created a new category of public policy problems, especially at the local level – unruly parking and congestion, especially in cities. While not trivial, problems of abundance are generally far more pleasant to deal with than those of poverty.

Quality improvements and an explosion in diversity of consumer products are also imperfectly captured by income statistics. Those happened across the board, virtually overnight. During the communist era, many services and commodities were next to non-existent – think exotic holidays or video recorders – or were available only in a limited selection at low quality. Food safety standards in communist countries, for instance, were far weaker than in the West and their enforcement was typically kept away from public scrutiny since socialist-era agriculture relied far more heavily on the use of chemicals. Compared to the present, the use of fertilizer per acre was roughly double and, in the 1970s, it was estimated that Czechoslovak farmers used five times as many pesticides per acre as French farmers.[10] Embarrassingly, a large shipment of Czechoslovak ham was turned away by U.S. authorities in 1984 for its high content of polychlorinated biphenyls, industrial chemicals which tend to accumulate in the fat tissues of animals and humans, and are associated with developmental problems in children. An investigation by Czechoslovak authorities, not disclosed to the public, later revealed ubiquity of the substance across the food supply chain.[11] In 1989 – at the high water mark of 'glasnost' – a study reported elevated levels of cadmium, zinc, and lead in cheese and dairy products across 80 percent of samples from 10 different manufacturers in Czechoslovakia.[12]

The progress seen since 1990 has not been limited to the economy. Since the fall of communism, Central and Eastern Europe has also become much healthier as a result of reduced pollution, better diets, rising incomes and other factors. Catching up with the West, life expectancy has gone up by 12 years (from 68 to 81 years) in Slovenia – and by 10 years in Poland. Infant mortality in, say, Hungary has been reduced fivefold, from 15.7 per 1,000 live births in 1990 to 3 in 2019, placing much of post-communist Central and Eastern Europe below the EU average. Even in Romania, the reduction has been dramatic – from 25.8 in 1990 to 5.7 in 2019.[13] For adults between the ages of 30 and 70, mortality from cardiovascular diseases, diabetes, and chronic respiratory disease is down by around a quarter.[14] In Poland, plagued with chronic pollution, asthma deaths have declined more than fourfold between 1990 and the present.[15] There are important caveats, of course. The catastrophic decline in life expectancy in Russia during the 1990s is the most important exception, from which the country has since recovered only in part. Life expectancy fell by five years over just four years, driven by economic and social turmoil, depression, and tobacco and alcohol consumption – and a deterioration of the health care system.[16]

Russia's story is an exception. Together with other, less fortunate post-Soviet republics it stands in contrast to the countries that joined the EU and NATO and saw remarkable health gains. Many of those have been related to an improved quality of the environment. While air pollution remains a problem, exposure to small particle pollutants (PM 2.5) – associated with chronic respiratory diseases – is down by roughly a third across the Visegrád states relative to 1990 levels. Aggregate greenhouse gas pollution in post-communist countries is down too – including by over 50 percent in the Baltic States.[17] The legacies of communist-era heavy industry and agriculture, relying on unrestrained use of polluting inputs, have not disappeared overnight. Even today, Central and Eastern European countries remain among the most polluted in the EU. For instance, Poland's reliance on coal persists – in part because coal miners are a well-organized interest group, but also because of the national security implications of using Russian natural gas, an obvious alternative to coal. Still, EU accession meant adopting much stricter standards concerning air pollution, water management, waste management, and the protection of ecosystems. Even earlier, the 1990s brought about the end to many of the economically unsustainable heavy industrial practices of the communist era, with heavy environmental tolls. Surface extraction of lignite in the north of Bohemia, which transformed the region into a moon-like landscape, has been brought to a halt. Chronic water pollution has been curbed – and in many parts of Central and Eastern Europe crayfish, long considered extinct, returned to rivers.[18]

The list of good news continues. Contrary to the common perception of the post-communist world as a land of unfettered gangster capitalism, the successful economies of the region managed to complete their transition to markets while remaining relatively egalitarian. Of course, in its early stages the transition meant a sudden increase in inequality, largely over by the late 1990s. For one, the administratively set wage structure of the communist era was gone and there was no upper limit to how much employees could earn on the market. The opening of the economy and privatization, furthermore, provided ample opportunities to some to get wealthy quickly. Price liberalization, the need to balance public finances in the face of the sudden economic contraction, and unemployment – basically non-existent in planned economies – meant that vulnerable groups saw their real incomes squeezed. In some countries, the shock was significant. Headcount poverty rate in Poland, for example, went up from 6 percent to 20 percent – before falling again throughout the 2000s and the 2010s.

Economists Branko Milanovic and Lire Ersado find that 'large' privatization amplified inequality by quickly moving sizeable assets into private hands. In contrast, 'small' privatization, which involved selling shops, newspaper stands, and restaurants – most of them owned collectively under the previous regime – into private hands reduced inequality. Keeping inflation under control, too, helped to keep inequality at bay, as did effective and early democratization – arguably by making policy responsive to the citizens' needs.[19] Since the end of the 1990s, inequality has plateaued across most post-communist countries. It has reached higher levels in the Baltic States,

Bulgaria, and Romania. In Visegrád economies and Slovenia, however, Gini coefficients today are between 0.25 and 0.3 – a range comparable to Germany and Sweden.

MARKETS, INVESTORS, AND 'NEOLIBERAL' REFORMS

The credit for addressing economic legacies of communist rule, particularly for eliminating the distortions created by planning, goes to early post-communist governments. Operating in completely uncharted territory, policymakers took on difficult decisions, often at steep political costs. Once exposed to market competition, the existing state-run companies were not competitive and could not be sustained on their own. In some countries, the issue was addressed through mass privatization and eventual restructuring by private owners. In others, government policies sought to protect employment, even at the cost of perpetuating the existence of companies that were not commercially viable. There are individual cases of particularly large companies, such as Polish shipyards, which were managed successfully by governments for considerable periods of time.[20] Alas, such efforts generally resulted in asset stripping by managers who started selling salvageable assets to companies connected to them, below market prices. Yet, in practically all instances and regardless of the privatization and restructuring strategy, a host of unintended consequences materialized. While the Czech Republic moved ahead with mass privatization through the so-called voucher scheme, it left its banking sector in government hands. Banks, furthermore, set up 'investment funds' which were buying vouchers from the public and exchanging them for shares in companies that were being privatized. What resulted was a situation dubbed 'banking socialism,' in which state-owned banks not only exercised a degree of control over the corporate sector but were also its main source of financing – leading straight to a financial crash in the final years of the 1990s.[21]

Whatever their short-term costs, the initial wave of economic reforms – involving price liberalization, privatization, and accompanying measures aimed at macroeconomic stabilization – was over quickly. Later in the 1990s and in the 2000s, post-communist reformers decided to go much further than to put in place measures allowing a market economy to exist. In fact, during the period 1990–2006, the region was home to the strongest wave of economic liberalization in the world.[22] At the turn of the century, a swathe of post-communist countries adopted simple flat tax regimes and cut corporate tax rates dramatically, sometimes acting against the advice of international authorities. They proceeded with partial privatizations of pension systems to make their old-age pensions fiscally sustainable over the longer term and also to encourage investment and a wider culture of shareholder capitalism. Some countries, such as Estonia, drastically improved their business environments to make themselves attractive to high-tech industries, start-ups and innovators.

Some of the subsequent reforms were products of sheer necessity. The governments of Slovakia or the Czech Republic did not have the resources to simply bail out their state-owned and state-connected banks overflowing with non-performing loans from the 1990s. A cleaning of balance sheets – costly to the taxpayer – and a privatization of 'revitalized' banks by sales to reputable foreign investors was quite literally the only feasible option. In other instances, post-communist reform zeal went hand in hand with equally energetic efforts at political and economic integration with the West. The interaction of the two is often misunderstood, as joining NATO and particularly the EU meant meeting a long list of political, legal, and economic requirements, including (in the EU's case) adopting the vast body of European legislation. In their influential book, *The Light that Failed*, Ivan Krastev and Stephen Holmes talk about the "copycat mind" and "politics of imitation," which sought to reshape post-communist Central and Eastern Europe to resemble the West, in part through the process of modeling local formal institutions after those prevailing in Western European countries.[23]

Yet, the fashionable image of post-communist countries as pursuing merely superficial formal changes to tick boxes on EU-prescribed laundry lists of reforms is a caricature that denies post-communist reformers and voters their agency. In fact, evidence suggests that 'conditionality' was redundant in the case of genuine reform frontrunners while being ineffective in the case of entrenched post-Soviet regimes that never saw real efforts at reform.[24] "Estonia did its pension reform because we realized that the pay-as-you-go system was not sustainable," the country's former president Toomas Hendrik Ilves (2006–16) says. "There was no EU requirement on pension reform." Similarly, Estonia "had a more liberal trade policy before joining the European Union."[25] At most, conditionality played a significant role in coalescing pro-Western political forces in countries that found themselves at a cross-roads – as Slovakia did ahead of its 1998 parliamentary election, having been excluded from the first wave of the EU's enlargement, or Bulgaria and Romania. In Slovakia, the EU's initial decision not to pursue accession negotiations accession negotiations in the first wave of enlargements was "a highly mobilizing civilizational menace," according to Ivan Mikloš who became the deputy prime minister and later minister of finance in the two reformist governments in Slovakia (1998–2006), spearheading bold economic reforms.[26] At a granular level, however, "the fact that we were meeting the criteria for membership and progressing with the accession negotiations had zero practical effect on domestic reforms as such," adds Mikloš' former boss, the former prime minister Mikuláš Dzurinda (1998–2006).[27]

If it was not European technocrats and Western 'best practices' that unleashed the wave of economic reforms in Eastern Europe, who or what did it? It was, it turns out, the EU's single market and the ethos of economic openness that the EU had fostered. With EU accession negotiations completed or underway, post-communist economies were both opening to the world and eliminating regulatory, non-tariff barriers standing between them and the economic powerhouses of Western Europe, most notably Germany. Moreover, they were doing so *simultaneously*, all chasing a pool of mobile capital in order to kick-start their growth. The resulting process of institutional and tax competition amounted to the most significant instance of economic liberalization in the world in the period 1990–2006.[28] There is no question that it worked. "FDI [foreign direct investment] did not just start trickling in," Dzurinda reminisces, "we were flooded by it."[29] In fact, around the time of their EU accession, countries of the region saw larger inflows of FDI than any other region in the world.

'NEOLIBERAL' REVOLUTION GOES WEST

Western European economies benefitted from the EU's enlargements and the 'neoliberal' moment in Eastern Europe as well. First, Eastern Europe was a new export market. Second, the private sector seized the opportunity to adjust production networks and set up new plants across the EU. Unsurprisingly, between 2003 and 2006 the proportion of respondents in the EU-15 countries who feared that future enlargements would increase domestic unemployment rose from 43 percent to 63 percent – and reached 80 percent in Germany.[30] Such fears of 'delocalization' materialized only in a small number of sectors, such as food, clothing, and car manufacturing. In many others, the investment and growing employment in 'new' member states was connected with employment creation in 'old' member states as the expanding companies grew more efficient and more competitive internationally.[31] Furthermore, the real alternative to the explosion of FDI in the Eastern region was not a preservation of the status quo. Given that barriers to trade and investment had been falling globally, Western businesses could have easily moved elsewhere, including to China and other Asian economies.

Contrary to Western fears, exemplified by the famous 'Polish plumber' scare in France, there is no evidence of Eastern European workers 'stealing' jobs in large numbers in the West. The U.K. was one of the few 'old' members to open its labor market to the newcomers without any transitional periods and as a result experienced elevated inflows of Eastern European workers, which would have been likely attenuated if other countries had opened theirs. Yet, even under those circumstances, the inflow of cheaper Eastern European labor exercised a strongly positive effect on British public finances, while having only a small impact on the labor market, where it led to wage increases at higher echelons of the wage distribution and a very modest downward pressure on low-wage professions. Needless to say, the latter effect was noticeable enough to feed into the anti-EU backlash that was building up in the U.K. in the run-up to the 2016 Brexit referendum.[32] Paradoxically, *emigration* had a similar effect on wage distribution that can be observed in Poland, the most populous 'new' member state, which accounted for a plurality of immigrant flows to the U.K. Wages of medium- and high-paying professions increased, arguably as a result of the brain drain – while wages in low-paying jobs declined.[33]

The rising FDI flows to the East and a churn on Europe's labor markets did not leave many 'old', typically highly taxed and highly regulated member countries, enthusiastic. A lot of handwringing about supposedly harmful tax competition ensued, driven by fear that post-communist reformist zeal would lead to a zero- or negative-sum game in which European governments compete for a mobile tax base (capital) by cutting their tax rates to the point of endangering the health of public finances. While the case against tax competition as a collectively harmful race to the bottom made sense in theory, it is hard to see in practice how the competitive pressure was harmful. For one, it made Eastern Europe's tax system more streamlined, less prone to tax fraud, and more economically efficient, without necessarily affecting the revenue side of the budget adversely. "Slovakia's flat tax reform was designed to be revenue-neutral – which it was, in its first year," according to its author Ivan Mikloš. "A year later, revenue started to grow dramatically."[34]

Furthermore, "the notion that this would come at the expense of the EU's 'old' members was nonsense," Mikloš argues. "Insofar as the new tax system helped newcomers grow more rapidly, it shortened the time during which we were net recipients of EU funds."[35] The reforms, however, did put competitive pressure on other governments, including Western European ones. Slovakia's immediate neighbor, Austria, cut its corporate income tax to 25 percent in response to the Slovak reform. After she became the leader of the Christian Democratic Union (CDU), Angela Merkel visited Bratislava to learn about the country's reform experience and the flat tax was *almost* featured in the party's election manifesto in 2005.[36] In fact, during the 2000s, Italy, Spain, the Netherlands, the U.K., and Germany, made substantial cuts to their corporate income taxes – arguably to keep up with the more dynamic newcomers.[37] Already during Gerhard Schröder's chancellorship, Germany undertook an ambitious and effective program of economic reforms. Known as the 'Hartz Reforms,' they involved a consolidation of welfare and unemployment assistance into a single system, a limit to the duration of full unemployment benefits, and liberalization of part-time and temporary work, alongside measures facilitating new business formation.[38] Even in France, President Nicolas Sarkozy arrived in office in 2007 with substantial reformist ambitions. A Commission for the Liberation of French Growth, presided over by economist Jacques

Attali, made far-reaching recommendations to modernize France's stale social model.[39] The Commission's report called for a streamlining of France's byzantine system of public administration, tax cuts – particularly of social security contributions made by employees – pension reform, and an overall shift of policy focus toward encouraging entrepreneurship. The efforts at reform, however, were off to an awkward start when Sarkozy rejected out of hand, at the official launch of the Commission's final report in January 2008, a number of the Commission's recommendations, including regional administration reform and ending the use of the precautionary principle.[40] Even those changes that Sarkozy's government did pursue in the area of pensions and labor market regulation were met with fierce resistance from labor unions and were largely abandoned. Yet, 'new Europe' is not to blame for the difficulties of reforming France – a challenge that proved insurmountable not only for Sarkozy but also for his predecessors and successors at Elysée. Quite the contrary, the problem was not *too much* competitive pressure from post-communist countries that had joined the single market, but rather that there was *not enough* of it to break through the stasis of French politics.

MIND THE GAP

To acknowledge that the West had and still has lessons to learn from post-communist economies does not entail harboring any illusions about them. While post-communist countries mostly avoided large spikes in income inequality, skeptics have noted that economic growth is concentrated in big cities, at the expense of increasingly stagnant and depopulated rural areas. Real per capita incomes in Slovakia or the Czech Republic lag behind the EU average, yet their leading metropolitan areas, Prague and Bratislava, count among the continent's wealthiest, with almost double the EU's per capita GDP.[41] The gap between urban and rural economies is not closing either, notwithstanding growing productivity rates in agriculture.[42] The resulting clustering of economic activity in urban areas and the associated sociological and political polarization is not unique to post-communist countries. However, what does set the region apart, the skeptics note, is the fact that the economic growth in metropolitan areas has been driven by foreign direct investment. Understandably, much of the profit earned by foreign corporations ends up being repatriated. Some years ago, economist Thomas Piketty circulated a chart, in which outflows of profits and property incomes were compared against the inflows of EU transfers.[43] Somewhat unsurprisingly, in Visegrád countries the outflows were distinctly larger than the EU's largesse, supposedly explaining the Eastern Europeans' aggrieved sense of being only second-class European citizens. Of course, Piketty's was an apples-to-oranges comparison. The EU's structural funds, aimed at leveling differences in economic development within the

EU and building new infrastructure, are transfers. They result from political decisions and are paid for by European taxpayers, who are not necessarily getting anything tangible in return. Profits of Western European companies result from earlier investments that those companies made – which also led to dramatic gains in incomes, employment, and productivity. Without those investment projects, and without the subsequent 'outflows' of profits, ordinary Central and Eastern Europeans would be far worse off. Across the region, lists of the largest private-sector employers prominently feature Western European (Volkswagen Group), American (General Electric), or East Asian (Foxconn) companies which either took over some of the more promising state-owned enterprises or built manufacturing plants from scratch. They did so because of the profit motive, yet by doing so they boosted dramatically the economic prospects of countries on the receiving end of that investment.

Yet, Piketty's cheap attempt at grievance politics touches on a genuine conundrum. Is the FDI-driven growth model sustainable indefinitely? If not, how will post-communist countries close the remaining income and productivity gaps with the West? Or will they? The combination of factors that have made the region attractive to foreign investors – lower wages, geographic proximity to Western Europe, an abundance of trained labor in areas with previously existing industrial production, and favorable tax and business environments – might dissipate over time. Even if membership in the single market is an important advantage relative to economies further to the East, Eastern European governments will have to make up for the rising costs by improving their business environments even further, investing in better infrastructure and human capital. Alas, the momentum behind structural reforms appears a thing of the past, in part because the imperative of catching up with the West has grown weaker, but also because the low-hanging fruit of big-bang reforms opening the economy to competition and slashing red tape has been largely picked. The policy and institutional changes that can help post-communist economies transition to economic activity with higher value added are more intricate than the conceptually simple changes made in previous decades. Investment into human capital, or research and development, also takes longer to come to fruition in the form of increased productivity and incomes.

Measures of economic competitiveness and quality of business environment do not point to dramatic improvements in recent years. With some exceptions, post-communist countries rank about as highly on the World Economic Forum's Global Competitiveness Index, or the World Bank's Doing Business survey, as they did a decade and a half ago.[44] Improvements in education, critical for the accumulation of human capital and rising productivity, have been uneven across the region. Few countries have succeeded in pushing through and sustaining deeper reforms of the education system. Poland's case, where the curriculum was modernized in 1999 alongside the introduction of independent testing and a restructuring of schools, remains an exception – in most other post-communist countries reforms were piecemeal, haphazard, and easily reversible.[45] Since 1989, for example, Slovakia has seen 20 different education ministers – most of whom attempted (and typically failed) in over-hauling the underlying education machinery. As a result, on PISA evaluation, monitoring student performance in reading, mathematics, and science, some post-communist countries (Poland, Estonia) tend to perform better than the global average, and show signs of improvement – many, however, lag far behind (Romania) and in some cases student test scores have steadily declined (Slovakia, Hungary). Higher education does not offer a more cheerful picture. Only a handful of Central and Eastern European universities make it to the Shanghai Ranking, dominated by institutions in the United States and the Anglosphere, China, and Western Europe. Charles University in Prague comes 201st–300th, followed by the University of Warsaw (301st–400th), Jagellonian University in Cracow (401st–500th) and the University of Tartu in Estonia (401st–500th).

As a result, many post-communist countries might be set for a long con-vergence. True, in purchasing power parity, average incomes in the Czech Republic and Estonia already exceed those in Greece and Portugal, the poorest among the 'old' member states. Yet, extrapolating its growth rates from 2010 to 2019, Bulgaria would take until 2076 to get to the EU's average income levels. For the EU, that means extended periods of regional economic dispar-ities – in other words, of diversity and by extension also of disagreement and conflicting interests – which will continue to constrain the EU's operation and policymaking. Consider, for example, how realistic it is to envisage a common minimum wage among countries at such widely different levels of economic development. Why would Eastern Europeans seek to drive up their wage costs, one of the main selling points to international investors? How appealing is the political pitch for more European redistribution toward poorer regions, if prospective net payers and net recipients are easy to identify in advance – or indeed for a common fiscal stabilization policy that would likely entail the same distributional effects? Not very, particularly in wealthier countries whose taxpayers can reasonably expect to be in the former category, notwithstanding rhetorical flourishes about European solidarity. The logic cuts in the opposite way, too – an EU-wide unemployment insurance scheme, tied to existing wage levels in different countries, would arguably lead to net redistribution to higher-wage economies in the West, at the expense of taxpayers in poorer Eastern European countries.

And it is not just about the economy. A 2015 study by economists Simeon Djankov, Elena Nikolova, and Jan Žilinský revealed a substantial difference in life satisfaction between post-communist Central and Eastern and Western Europe – a gap that cannot be fully explained by lingering differences in standards of living, life expectancy or cultural legacies such as that of Orthodox Christianity. The difference, the authors argue based on rich survey evidence, boils down to a much lower sense of satisfaction with how their governments function.[46] It is no surprise, then, that support for populist and anti-establishment parties across the region is at record highs. In Brussels, meanwhile, 'new Europe' has not become a synonym for the reinvigoration of the decades-old integration project. Rather, it is a synonym of frequent headaches.

The persistence and, in some cases, a widening of some gaps between Central and Eastern Europe and the West is sometimes subsumed in the catchphrase of 'backsliding.' The term is unfortunate as it suggests a reversal to a previously existing form of political and social organization – in this case, one-party rule and a planned economy. In that sense, post-communist countries are neither 'backsliding' nor are they at any risk of it. For all the nostalgia for the old days, overwhelming majorities approve of multi-party democracy and market economy, do not want to return to pre-1989 socialism, and recognize the material progress made over the past three decades.[47] As the following chapters show, the evolution of post-communist countries and their political dynamics once in the EU have not always matched the more naïve expectations of the 1990s in several important respects. For one, the foundations of future economic growth that would help the region close the income gap with the West remain fragile. Social and cultural attitudes in post-communist nations remain different in important ways from those prevailing in the West. And, perhaps most significantly, some post-communist democracies continue to look markedly different from their Western liberal versions.

To note that a counterfactual in which Central and Eastern Europe becomes indistinguishable from the West was never on the menu is not to reify the East–West divide or the 'otherness' of post-communist countries.[48] In the past, some parts of post-communist Central Europe (Bohemia, Silesia, Gdańsk) were more economically advanced than many regions of 'old' Europe. The West's history, furthermore, is replete with growth miracles – most recently the rise of Ireland, once an economic backwater –as well as growth disasters. In real terms, after all, per capita income in Italy was lower in 2020 than it was in 1996 – in sharp contrast to the vigorous catch-up growth of post-communist countries.[49] Yet, both 'old' and 'new' European countries live with a great variety different political, cultural, and economic legacies, which have not been fully bridged by the European project: Europe's North and South rarely see eye to eye on matters of fiscal policy and questions of political patronage.[50] Like Central and Eastern Europe, Greece, Spain, and Portugal live with relatively recent legacies of autocratic rule, which continue to shape, albeit differently, their politics today.

The fact that catch-up growth of Eastern Europe may be difficult, and that the region will continue to be different from other parts of the EU, is neither a negation of the enormous progress achieved in the past three decades nor is it an indictment of the role played by the EU. If anything, the post-1989 history of the region provides a powerful illustration of what the EU does best: leveraging diversity, through a shared institutional framework, to encourage economic dynamism and learning. What follows, in contrast, is a tale of what the EU has done less well: repeatedly seeking and failing to turn the enlarged and more diverse EU into a state-building project.

NOTES

1.　Walker (2021).
2.　Bolt and van Zanden (2020).
3.　Crozet et al. (2004).
4.　Milanovic (1998).
5.　Milanovic (1998, 34).
6.　Kornai (1979).
7.　Pucher (1999).
8.　European Automobile Manufacturers Association (2021).
9.　Imlauf (2016).
10.　Potočár (2020).
11.　Šťovíček and Šuta (2017).
12.　Pápajová and Hermanová (1989).
13.　World Bank (2021).
14.　World Bank (2021).
15.　Human Progress (2021).
16.　Notzon et al. (1998).
17.　European Environment Agency (2021).
18.　Štambergová et al. (2009).
19.　Milanovic and Ersado (2010).
20.　Johnson et al. (1995).
21.　Kreuzbergová (2006).
22.　Appel and Orenstein (2018).
23.　Krastev and Holmes (2020).
24.　Schimmelfennig (2007).
25.　Ilves (2021b).
26.　Mikloš (2021).
27.　Dzurinda (2021).
28.　Appel and Orenstein (2018, 92).
29.　Dzurinda (2021).
30.　Barysch (2006, 79).
31.　Buti et al. (2009).
32.　Dustmann and Frattini (2014); Ruhs and Vargas-Silva (2012).
33.　Dustmann et al. (2015).
34.　Mikloš (2021).
35.　Mikloš (2021).
36.　Mikloš (2021); Dzurinda (2021).
37.　Appel and Orenstein (2018, 113).
38.　Grässler (2014).

39.   Attali (2008).
40.   Bouin (2008).
41.   Eurostat (2019).
42.   Macours and Swinnen (2006).
43.   Piketty (2018).
44.   Schwab (2019).
45.   Wiśniewski and Zahorska (2020).
46.   Djankov et al. (2016).
47.   Wike et al. (2019a).
48.   Epstein and Jacoby (2014).
49.   Federal Reserve Bank of St. Louis (2021).
50.   Trantidis (2018).

3.   The enlargement hangovers

Celebrations of the 30th anniversary of the fall of the Berlin Wall and, more broadly, of the collapse of communism in Eastern Europe, hit an oddly somber note in 2019. "Liberal democracy is being challenged and questioned," the German president Frank-Walter Steinmayer said in a speech to mark the occasion, while the Chancellor Angela Merkel urged Europeans to revitalize "the values on which Europe is founded – freedom, democracy, equality, rule of law, human rights."[1] The perceived malaise runs deeper than just the EU's policy failures. It reflects the sense that liberal democracy is under siege, particularly in countries that have embraced it after the fall of communism. Whatever triumphalism was present at the supposed 'end of history' in the early 1990s – a term coined by Kojève, long before Fukuyama – it has since given way to lamentations about "the bitter repudiation of liberalism itself, not only [in Eastern Europe] but also back in the heartland of the West," as the cover of Krastev and Holmes' acclaimed book puts it. Striking a similarly pensive note, the journalist and historian Anne Applebaum recently described a New Year's Eve party hosted by her and her husband, who would go on to become Poland's next foreign minister, at their country house in Chobielin, Poland in 1999. The guests, who hailed from both sides of the Atlantic, included budding political figures, journalists, and intellectuals. "At that moment," Applebaum writes, "when Poland was on the cusp of joining the West, it felt as if we were all on the same team. We agreed about democracy, about the road to prosperity, about the way things were going." Yet, in the years that followed, the attendees moved in different and sometimes surprising political directions:

> Some of my New Year's Eve guests continued, as my husband and I did, to support the pro-European, pro-rule-of-law, pro-market centre-right – remaining in political parties that aligned, more or less, with European Christian Democrats, with the liberal parties of Germany and the Netherlands, and with the Republican Party of John McCain. Some now consider themselves centre-left. But others wound up in a different place, supporting a nativist party called Law and Justice … [which] has embraced a new set of ideas, not just xenophobic and deeply suspicious of the rest of Europe but also openly authoritarian.[2]

Why the apprehensive tone, particularly given the unquestionable progress seen in Applebaum's adopted homeland of Poland? This chapter focuses on two causes of the angst that permeates a lot of today's discussions about the region and of its role in the EU. The first one is a mismatch between the tools that were assumed to bring about such convergence – adoption of formal rules, scrutiny of national institutions by European authorities, and financial assistance from the EU – and the nature of the problem at hand. The second one is the fact that some of the expectations about the future of Eastern Europe and its convergence, not just economic but also political and cultural, with the West were unfounded. The two sources of today's disappointment are connected. Both are based in a view of the integration project as one of political and cultural homogenization, even state-building, instead of an effort to manage Europe's diversity. Today, the EU and the West at large need to find an alternative approach to the problem of 'democratic backsliding': one that recognizes that conflicts between EU countries are inherently political and require political, not legal, solutions and one that is able to distinguish between different dimensions of the problem – most notably between those that can be addressed constructively at the European or international level and those where such engagement is unlikely to play a constructive role.

EUROPEAN PROJECT GONE AWRY

The most important gap between the EU's Eastern European member states and the West is the quality of their institutions. There is no question that countries that joined the European Union had made significant strides to improve the quality of their democratic governance. The 'Copenhagen Criteria'[3] required candidate countries to have a functioning market economy, a sufficient state capacity to implement and apply European legislation and to meet political criteria of democracy, rule of law, human rights, and protection of minorities. In practice, candidate countries had no choice but to deal with the most egregious forms of corruption, run free and fair elections, and guarantee the independence of the judiciary and other apolitical public bodies. Overwhelmingly, these reforms have been successful and 'sticky.' Neither are bad institutions an inescapable trap, as the example of Estonia's extraordinarily clean legal system and public administration illustrates. An effective digitalization of public services and e-government proved to be an extraordinarily effective antidote to institutional legacies of Soviet communism. "What in Greece is called fakelaki, or 'little envelope', which you offer in order to get any kind of service doesn't exist in Estonia," Ilves explains. "You don't have that in this country because you don't do anything face-to-face, you do it all digitally."[4]

Yet, young democracies operate differently from more established ones. For one, they often lack channels through which politicians could make credible promises about public policy. Instead of political parties and candidates offering competing policy agendas, electoral competition involves competition between different forms of redistribution and patronage – something that is much more easily observable than policy outcomes.[5] Patronage-based politics can persist for decades, as it has in Greece following its democratization in the 1970s. Second, the international pressure for effective institutional reforms, improving the rule of law, and curbing corruption largely disappeared with EU accession. Once post-communist countries were in the exclusive club, they faced no further pressure to change. While, in principle, new EU members are bound to abide by the acquis and by the rules that they sign up to, monitoring and enforcement mechanisms are qualitatively different from those imposed on prospective members.[6] The difference boils down to credibility: because of the unanimity rule, any current member holds veto power over the accession of new members. There is no legal mechanism through which a member state could be expelled. Sanctioning an existing member state under Article 7 of the Lisbon Treaty requires unanimity of remaining members[7] – an essentially impossible task if there are several 'rogue' states. After joining the EU, Bulgaria and Romania were subjected to a Cooperation and Verification Mechanism (CVM) to monitor the effort to fight corruption – yet the strength of such monitoring was far less effective than in the period before accession.[8] According to the World Bank's Worldwide Governance Indicators, corruption in Bulgaria *worsened* after accession. Today, corruption in both Bulgaria and Romania remains roughly the same as at the time when the two countries joined the EU in 2007.[9] Elsewhere in the region, improvements on common measures of institutional quality have also been limited and uneven. Not only have they belied the idea that EU membership guarantees a straightforward 'path to Denmark,' as development economists would put it, but defective institutions endemic in the region also play an important role in perpetuating the economic divide that continues to exist between Eastern Europe and the more affluent, 'old' member states.

The EU's canonical response to the economic gap between richer and poorer member states has been a form of development assistance: EU funds. Yet, not unlike development aid in other contexts, the inflow of European money facilitated the entrenchment of patronage-based politics, corruption, and erosion of domestic institutions instead of kick-starting economic growth and investment. Within the 2014–20 Multiannual Financial Framework (MFF), the EU spent over €360 billion to narrow disparities between member states. It does so through several structural and investment 'funds' (European Regional Development Fund, European Social Fund, Cohesion Fund, Youth Employment Initiative). The European Regional Development Fund is the largest of them and supports the building of infrastructure and job creation. Out of those resources, over €200 billion went to post-communist 'new' member states, most prominently to Poland (€77 billion). Under the current MFF (2021–27) the amount of structural and investment funds under the rubric of 'Cohesion, Resilience, and Values' exceeds €426 billion. In addition, the post-pandemic recovery package, Next Generation EU (NGEU), involves €750 billion divided between loans and grants, a significant part of which are flowing again to the East.

EU funds have never been a completely free lunch. For one, national governments are co-financing the projects, sometimes matching EU funding one-to-one, and providing the bulk of administrative support to the program. Neither are the economic benefits of the spending completely obvious since, as an IMF working paper put it, "it is unclear whether the EU funds are crowding out or augmenting domestic spending."[10] Assessing the effect of EU funds on growth is complicated since aid tends to flow to underdeveloped (i.e., low-growth) regions of the EU. Studies that address the problem of 'endogeneity' and yet find a positive association between EU funds and growth also recognize that the spending can play a more significant, positive role in more developed environments (i.e., places that have arguably less need for such funding).[11] In Italy, significant amounts of EU funds did little to narrow the productivity divide existing between the country's industrialized North and its persistently poor South.[12] In the EU's two poorest countries, Bulgaria and Romania, the spending has had "an ambivalent effect on the national economies of the two countries."[13]

Development economists studying poor economies with large natural resource endowments have noted that the inflow of revenue that is detached from the domestic tax base, together with weak institutions, can have pernicious effects as it changes the incentives of local elites – away from cultivating the domestic tax base through pro-growth reforms toward policies that entrench the current elites and siphon away rents.[14] A similar mechanism to the 'resource curse' appears to be at play in the case of EU funds and Eastern Europe. A 2013 study found that EU funds have "provided additional public resources available for corrupt rent extraction" of more than 1 percent of GDP (a substantial figure given that the total value of EU funds in Central and Eastern Europe (CEE) countries is of the order of several percentage points of GDP), leading to a measurable adverse effect on corruption.[15] Together with Romania and Bulgaria, Hungary is the EU member state most plagued by corruption, according to common measures.[16] Since its accession in 2004, it also happens to be the largest per capita recipient of EU funds. The decision-making authority over disbursement of funds lies directly in the office of the prime minister. Hungary is the only EU country that has continued to rely on unannounced "negotiated procedures" instead of tenders open to multiple bidders competing on criteria announced in advance.[17] As a result, the government can strike a procurement deal with essentially any company without having to go through an open competition. In 2019, more than half of all public contracts were awarded in tenders featuring single bidders.[18]

Irregularities were found in all 35 projects that the EU's anti-fraud office, OLAF, reviewed in Hungary between 2011 and 2015.[19] Line 4 of Budapest's metro was completed in 2014 thanks to funding from the EU. An investigation by OLAF alleged "serious irregularities – fraud and possible corruption" in relation to the line, and recommended that the European Commission should recover €280 million of funds that were misused.[20] Elios, a company co-owned by Orbán's son-in-law István Tiborcz won EU-funded contracts worth €65m to install LED street lights across Hungary – although prices of LED bulbs were falling during the time under consideration, lamps installed by Elios were 56 percent more expensive than usual.[21] Lőrinc Mészáros, the mayor of Felcsút, Orbán's home village, owns hundreds of companies and last year topped Forbes's Hungarian rich list. Hungarian investigative journalism outlet *Atlatszo* showed that companies held by Mészáros or his family won tenders to the tune of 486 billion forints (€1.5 billion) between 2010 and 2017, with 83 percent of the contracts on EU-funded projects.[22] In 2018, Brussels provided 93 percent of the 265 billion forints (€760 million) worth of public contracts he received. When asked once what he owed his success to, he responded: "God, luck and Viktor Orbán."[23]

In practically every post-communist country, similar stories are being told, featuring most prominently EU money – either from structural funds or from the Common Agricultural Policy. After becoming prime minister, the Czech billionaire-turned-populist Andrej Babiš never divested himself from his businesses. Under investigation for subsidy fraud involved in one of his earlier projects, Stork's Nest, Babiš' conglomerate Agrofert received €37.7 million in agricultural subsidies the year he became prime minister, 2017.[24] In the following years, Agrofert raked in more than €29 million annually, making it the largest recipient of the EU's agricultural subsidies in the Czech Republic.[25] According to OLAF, Romania was the main committer of fraud for EU agricultural funds in 2018 and 2019. In conjunction with Romania's "National Anticorruption Direction," authorities found more than €100 million in fraud, of which "almost 90 percent is related to EU funds" and the European Commission ordered the return of €71.3 million from the years 2015–17.[26] The list could go on. The point, however, is that membership in the EU created an incentive structure for political elites that has had, at best, an ambiguous effect on the quality of institutions and rule of law in the new democracies of Central and Eastern Europe.

Patronage and corruption are only one part of the broader problem of institutional weakness. Another, even more serious one, is the de-democratization of several post-communist countries over the course of the 2010s, which defied the earlier expectation that democracy had taken strong roots in Eastern Europe since much of the region had moved without turbulence through several electoral cycles. In the late 1990s, the influential work of the Polish-American researcher Adam Przeworski demonstrated on data going back to 1950 that above a certain income level, comfortably met by post-communist countries on track to join the EU, the odds of a democracy's collapse was negligible.[27] Today, in the face of the 'third wave of autocratization' across the world, including among the EU's 'new' member states, those findings need updating.[28] The case of Hungary tends to receive the most attention, for good reasons. Besides worsening scores on Worldwide Governance Indicator (WGI) metrics, since 2019 Freedom House classifies Hungary as only "partly free." The country has seen a similar decline in performance on other metrics of democracy, including the Economist Intelligence Unit's Democracy Index, V-Dem Liberal Democracy Index, and numerous other measures of institutional quality and rule of law.

The bulk of Hungary's de-democratization came as a result of FIDESZ's "revolution through the ballot box," as Viktor Orbán called the victory of his party in the parliamentary election of April 2010, in which FIDESZ secured a constitutional majority.[29] The victory came on the back of years of growing political polarization and distrust in institutions. Shortly after the 2006 election, already contested as illegitimate by FIDESZ and far-right groups, a leaked recording surfaced, featuring the then prime minister Ferenc Gyurcsány of the Socialist Party telling his colleagues that over his term in office there was no "significant government measure we can be proud of." He and his party, the prime minister confessed, "lied in the morning; lied in the evening."[30] Two years later, a financial crisis plunged Hungary into a recession much deeper than the ones seen elsewhere in the region. This was because of a previous proliferation of Swiss franc-denominated loans, particularly mortgages in the Hungarian financial industry. After the shock, Hungarian currency depreciated, leaving a large fraction of Hungarian households and firms unable to repay their debt. Against the background of such turmoil, the large mandate to the populist FIDESZ, which promised to clean the country of corruption and solve its economic predicaments, was not surprising.

Once in office, the once center-right FIDESZ proceeded with a host of unconventional economic measures targeting foreign investors and lenders. To stabilize public finances, for example, the government nationalized assets held by private pension funds, converting them into unfunded liabilities in the country's PAYG pension system. The government created retail monopolies for tobacco and alcohol products, imposed new levies on certain businesses predominantly in foreign hands (supermarkets, utility companies), and revived state ownership in banking and the energy sector.[31] The policy mix was a departure from the center-right consensus that FIDESZ had once embraced and it was later emulated by the right-populist government of Poland, which has also sought to combine a larger welfare state with a significant economic role for the state. Yet, the departure from pro-market orthodoxy pales into insignificance in comparison to democratic norms broken by FIDESZ once in power. In October 2010, new legislation restricted the ability of the Constitutional Court to review laws. On the same day that the Court struck down a retroactive 98 percent 'tax' on severance pay for civil servants leaving the public sector,[32] a constitutional amendment was introduced that allowed for this retroactive legislation and removed the jurisdiction of the Court over tax and budgetary matters. The European Court of Human Rights ruled by unanimity that the retroactive tax on the severance pay of a Hungarian civil servant indeed violated her right to peaceful enjoyment of her property and contravened the European Convention on Human Rights.[33]

Next, FIDESZ used its large parliamentary majority to draft and adopt a new constitution (Fundamental Law) which came into force on January 1, 2012. The new constitution was written by a small group within FIDESZ and was adopted on purely partisan lines – unlike the 1989 constitutional reform, which enjoyed support across parties.[34] The Fundamental Law preserved the formal attributes of the parliamentary system, but removed many constraints on the power of parliamentary majorities and left the opposition in parliament without any impact on the legislative process.[35] While in the past anyone could challenge the constitutionality of Hungarian legislation at the Constitutional Court, for example, under the new constitution the right is restricted to the government, a quarter of all members of the legislature, and to the Commissioner for Fundamental Rights.[36] The new constitution also introduced the institution of so-called Cardinal Laws, requiring only a two thirds majority to amend the constitution more easily than the traditional procedure. In 2011–13 alone, the parliament passed 32 such laws.[37]

The *Fourth Amendment* effectively annulled all Constitutional Court case law prior to 2011 and disables constitutional review of budget and tax laws passed when the debt-to-GDP ratio exceeds 50 percent – which it has throughout the post-1989 era. Even if, for example, a tax infringes on constitutionally guaranteed rights or applies selectively to an ethnic or religious minority, the Court does not get to have a say – ever.[38] Article 26 (2) of the Fundamental Law also opened the way to reducing the mandatory retirement age for judges, thus removing the most senior 10 percent of the judiciary, including 20 percent of the Supreme Court judges and more than half the presidents of all appeals courts.[39] That was declared illegal by both Hungary's Constitutional Court and the EU's Court of Justice.[40] FIDESZ also dismissed the president of the Supreme Court, who was also the president of the National Council of Judiciary, before the end of the mandate – a decision that violated the European Charter of Human Rights.[41]

FIDESZ overhauled Hungary's highly complex electoral system to strengthen its majoritarian aspects.[42] Two-round races in local constituencies were replaced by a simple first-past-the-post system and the minimum turnout threshold (for the seat to be awarded) was scrapped. Geographic boundaries between constituencies were redrawn in ways that materially benefitted FIDESZ.[43] Citizens were allowed to vote in elections only if they registered more than a fortnight in advance, either in person or online. Furthermore, ethnic Hungarians, many of whom hold dual citizenship and who live in Romania, Serbia, and Ukraine – and among whom FIDESZ enjoys high levels of support – were given the opportunity to register to vote as well.[44] The government proposed more than 18 other changes to the election law, but those changes were ruled unconstitutional by the Constitutional Court.[45] Later, new amendments to the electoral law limited the ability of smaller political parties to present national lists of candidates in parliamentary elections, effectively forcing all opposition parties to run as a single coalition and allowed same-day voter registration in any electoral district, open to Hungarian citizens living abroad – raising concerns about the fairness of the 2022 election.[46]

With a comfortable governing majority, the FIDESZ-dominated parliament ceased to be a place of legislative deliberation. Instead, it has "become a law factory, and the production line is sometimes made to operate at unbelievable speed: between 2010 and 2014 no less than 88 bills made it from being introduced to being voted on within a week; in 13 cases it all happened on the same or the following day."[47] In 2017, Hungary adopted new legislation on nongovernmental organizations (NGOs).[48] The law echoed Russia's infamous law from 2012, which required foreign-funded NGOs to register as foreign agents and be subjected to strict disclosure requirements.[49] According to FIDESZ deputy chairman Szilárd Németh, NGOs funded by George Soros "must be pushed back with all available tools, and I think they must be swept out."[50] The law was criticized by the Venice Commission, an advisory body to the Council of Europe, among others, as "[causing] a disproportionate and unnecessary interference with the freedoms of association and expression, the right to privacy, and the prohibition of discrimination, including due to the absence of comparable transparency obligations which apply to domestic financing of NGOs."[51] During the Covid-19 pandemic, the Hungarian government passed legislation that imposed a state of emergency indefinitely and gave the government the power to legislate by decree, without parliamentary scrutiny and without the possibility of an early election, empowered the president of the country's Constitutional Court to change the court's procedural rules at will, and created new categories of crimes, including "[spreading] a distorted truth in relation to the emergency in a way that is suitable for alarming or agitating a large group of people," punishable by up to three years imprisonment.[52] Repealed by parliament in June 2020, the law was replaced by legislation that continues to vest significant power in the government to declare future health emergencies – effectively preserving the law's most controversial features.[53]

Poland, too, has experienced a considerable degree of de-democratization since 2015.[54] Before arriving in power, the leader of Poland's Law and Justice Party (PiS), Jarosław Kaczyński famously promised to build a "Budapest in Warsaw." However, PiS faced more obstacles to its agenda than FIDESZ in Hungary. With an electoral system relying on proportional representation with multi-member constituencies in the lower chamber (Sejm), PiS was not able to replicate a FIDESZ-like degree of control over parliament and relied on far tighter margins, after both the 2015 and 2019 parliamentary elections. Although the party repeatedly made the case for wholesale changes to the constitutional order, it has lacked the power to implement them.[55] Instead, the bulk of the changes were directed at Poland's judiciary. Within days of arriving in power in the fall of 2015, the new PiS-run government made significant changes to the composition and procedures of the Constitutional Tribunal. The government claimed that it merely responded to the contested election of five new Constitutional Court judges just before the parliamentary election in 2015. After the election, the government and President Andrzej Duda – a PiS nominee who had been elected shortly before the parliamentary election in October of 2015 – sought to reverse the appointments made by the previous government. This flew in the face of a ruling by the Constitutional Tribunal, which confirmed that the October election of three out of five judges was valid. In December, the Sejm passed an amendment to the existing law on the Constitutional Tribunal, which would require a two thirds majority (instead of a simple majority) and the presence of at least 13 (instead of nine) of the 15 judges for a decision, as well as a mandatory latency period before it delivers a verdict on a case. The reform was declared unconstitutional by the Constitutional Tribunal operating under the old rules. For several weeks, the government refused to publish the decision in the *Official Journal*.[56]

Furthermore, a sweeping overhaul of the judicial system gave the executive (specifically, the minister of justice) unprecedented powers over judicial appointments, including at the level of presidents and vice presidents of ordinary courts. The reforms were criticized even by the Trump-era U.S. State Department, concerned over "[weakening] of the rule of law in Poland."[57] The most recent iteration of such judicial reforms was the lowering of the mandatory retirement age for Supreme Court justices to 65 years in 2018, which resulted in an instant dismissal of 27 of the court's 74 justices who would normally still have many years of service ahead of them, according to the terms of their original appointments.[58]

Besides EU funds, another effort at European homogenization has paradoxically made things worse: the system of trans-European political parties, which emerged jointly with direct elections to the European Parliament in the 1970s. Such parties are exemplified prominently by the European People's Party (EPP), the Socialists (S&D), the liberal Renew Europe, and others. The

EU's transnational parties provide their members (i.e., national parties) with training, opportunities to network and exchange ideas, and other resources, largely financed by European taxpayers.[59] However, the party secretariats in Brussels do not dictate the terms of national electoral manifestos nor vet national candidates.

Contrary to some expectations, European parties did not usher in the age of a European democracy. Instead, their existence led to unintended consequences as the EU's enlargements also opened doors of the transnational party families to post-communist newcomers. Much like with enlargements themselves, the hope was that the West would help cultivate and institutionalize standard party systems in Eastern Europe. Pan-European parties face strong incentives to maximize their number of seats in the European Parliament as those entitle them to a share of positions within the European Parliament's committees and in its leadership. As a result, they have very little reason to hold their unruly member parties to account or be particularly selective in offering membership. This perverse incentive structure was further exacerbated by efforts to further 'democratize' the EU by introducing the informal norm of EU parties running candidates for the presidency of the European Commission ahead of European elections (the so-called *Spitzenkandidaten* system) – providing an additional reason to trans-European parties to maximize their size at any cost.[60]

That explains why, in spite of the periodically recurrent theater of *almost* expelling FIDESZ, which went on for the better part of the past decade, the EPP never made the move and allowed Orbán to walk away at his leisure in March 2021.[61] Early in December 2020, the EPP's president Donald Tusk asked haplessly on Twitter, "What else should FIDESZ do for all of you to see that they simply don't fit in with our family?"[62] "If only you knew someone high up in the EPP," somebody quipped back. Tusk's tweet was responding to a comparison by a FIDESZ MEP between the Gestapo and the EPP's leader in the European Parliament, Manfred Weber.[63] Yet, as early as in 2013, Orbán likened Angela Merkel's policies to the 1944 occupation of Hungary by Nazi Germany.[64]

While Orbán was by far the EPP's greatest liability, he has not been the only one. Before he started spouting conspiracy theories about the U.S. presidential election, Slovenia's former prime minister and Orbán's friend Janez Janša had sought to tame public broadcasters and limited parliamentary oversight of the state budget during the pandemic.[65] Over the years, the EPP has also given a free pass to the grotesque kleptocracy of Bulgaria's former prime minister, Boyko Borisov.[66] The problem also extends far beyond EPP. Before 'suspending' (though not expelling) Romania's Social Democratic Party (PSD), the EU's S&D long coddled the party even as its successive governments undermined the integrity of courts and stifled anti-corruption efforts.[67] Under the watch of Robert Fico's Smer in Slovakia, also an S&D member, a journalist and his young fiancée were killed by mobsters with ties to the highest level of the police and the judiciary.[68] The Czech Republic's oligarch-populist, Andrej Babiš, meanwhile, remains a member in good standing of Emmanuel Macron's Renew Europe – in spite of his previous conflicts of interest as prime minister, frequent outbursts against the EU, and a criminal investigation into his misuse of EU subsidies.[69]

Transnational political parties have paid no price for accommodating rogue actors and their leadership would have received very little credit for trying to purge anti-democratic or corrupt parties from their midst. Few voters are even aware of their existence at the European level. Fewer still are willing to punish their national politicians for their international associations. And since the issues affect every political family, any discussion of the subject is bound to descend into a shouting match involving accusations of hypocrisy and 'whataboutism.'

NO LEGAL FIXES

It is possible that democratic declines in Eastern Europe will be reversed. After all, Hungary and Poland are holding elections, in 2022 and 2023, respectively, in which the democratic opposition retains a solid shot at winning – unlike in countries where similar processes of incumbent entrenchment have proceeded further. Yet, it is equally possible that FIDESZ and PiS will not only maintain or strengthen their current hold on power but also that the examples of the two countries will be emulated elsewhere in the post-communist world – perhaps in Bulgaria, Romania, Slovakia, or Slovenia. Thus far, the EU's response to such developments has been notoriously ineffectual. European treaties outline a formal procedure for the scenario of "a clear risk of a serious breach" of the EU's fundamental values of democracy, rule of law, and human rights.[70] For the procedure, which can be launched by either the European Parliament or the European Commission, to arrive at any sanctions against the member state in question, unanimity of all other states is required – a tall order given the growing number of possible offenders ready to stand by each other's side. Predictably, the procedures triggered by the Commission against Poland in 2017 and 2019 and the one launched by the Parliament against Hungary in 2018 went nowhere. In addition, the Commission has also challenged member states over their rule of law violations at the European Court of Justice (ECJ), with mixed success. Poland's government backtracked from its plans following a 2018 ruling by the ECJ that allowed the forcibly 'retired' Supreme judges to return to work.[71] However, the same PiS government proved intransigent following a ruling by Poland's Constitutional Tribunal which, in reaction to a previous ECJ decision invalidating the new Polish rules on disciplining and dismissals of judges, struck down several articles of the Lisbon Treaty as unconstitutional.[72] Pursuing the judicial route has thus multiplied situations in which member states simply refuse to abide by adopted legal norms and policies, in defiance of ECJ rulings,[73] and in spite of financial sanctions imposed by the Commission for non-compliance. Such stand-offs are a result of the fact that the EU's constitutional order is not hierarchical but rather involves a variety of actors who can plausibly claim constitutional authority.[74] For some of those concerned about 'backsliding' in Eastern Europe, the situation is untenable as the ECJ should "enjoy unconditional supremacy,"[75] particularly to crack down on rule of law violations by member states.

There are number of problems with this idea. For one, the visibly problematic developments in the region and attacks on 'democratic values' cannot be necessarily reduced to explicit violations of treaty commitments. Asking the ECJ to be the vehicle through attempts at incumbent entrenchment is reversed risks expanding its purview far beyond its proper role. The entire point of federalism is a dispersion, not a concentration, of political, legal, and judicial authority – even at the cost of tensions, disagreements, and mutual accommodation by different centers of decision-making. A proliferation of ECJ rulings which are then ignored by member governments makes the EU and European law a hollow shell. There are limits to the sanctions that European institutions could conceivably impose on unruly member states and coercion was never meant to be an important part of the toolbox of what is largely an honors club. The U.S. Supreme Court's rulings are taken more seriously than the ECJ's because they are backed by the power of the federal government – including, famously, U.S. Marshals who oversaw desegregation of the South in the 1960s. To expect the same *unqualified* deference to European authorities such as the ECJ, while those same authorities lack effective instruments of leverage, much less coercion, is to forget that in politics, power matters. Moreover, powers of the U.S. federal government are limited, while states enjoy residual sovereignty in areas not enumerated as federal powers by the Constitution. The EU's institutional set-up, in contrast, recognizes no limiting principle to the gradual expansion of the power of common European institutions. While Euroskeptics are often criticized for their slippery slope arguments, it is partly because of the pushback from states – including from their judiciaries – that such slippery slopes do not materialize in the European context. Introduce the idea of the EU's 'unconditional supremacy,' along with the EU's sweeping ambitions, and the slippery slopes instantly become very immediate – as does an intemperate populist reaction against them.

Finally, the ECJ's overreach risks creating irresolvable situations, such as the stand-off between the Court and Poland's Constitutional Tribunal. How can sanctioning Poland and asking it to backtrack from its Constitutional Tribunal's ruling, which invalidated the ECJ's earlier decision, be reconciled with an EU-wide commitment to the independence of the judiciary? Of course, one may object that such independence has long been destroyed in Poland to begin with, but the Polish government is not wrong to ask, albeit in bad faith, whether European institutions expect it to put political pressure on the Tribunal to reach the 'correct,' EU-friendly decision. Even more troublingly, disagreements between national apex courts and the ECJ can occur in *good faith* when top national courts simply prioritize national constitutional law over EU law, as they are supposed to. One can disagree with the 2020 decision of Germany's Federal Constitutional Court (BVerfG) to strike down the Court of Justice of the European Union (CJEU) judgments upholding the legality of the ECJ's asset purchases[76] without accepting that the BVerfG should be somehow railroaded by European institutions.[77]

That does not mean that the EU is completely powerless against rule of law violations and 'democratic backsliding' among its members. However, it means that responding to such situations is a matter of political judgment, not of legal strictures or court cases. It is perfectly legitimate, plausible even, to claim that European leaders have been far too lenient with undemocratic practices emerging in countries such as Hungary and Poland and that much stronger political steps should have been taken by other member countries to ostracize governments that blatantly ignored the shared European commitments to democracy and rule of law. European institutions and leading EU governments, furthermore, continue to exercise significant leverage over such countries by virtue of European spending, which flows disproportionately to 'new' member states – and which can be also suspended by political fiat of the main contributors. The Next Generation EU spending package, adopted in the wake of the pandemic, relies on a heavily centralized process of articulating national spending plans. Its disbursement comes also with a new rule of law conditionality[78] – and an increased willingness of European institutions and 'old' member states to turn the spigot of European funding off. To mitigate the apparent 'resource curse'-like effect of EU spending, one can imagine a restructuring of the current approach, which would grant a far smaller role to national governments of recipient countries. The European Fund for Strategic Investments (also known as the Juncker Plan), launched in 2015, provided for a much more hands-on involvement of the European Investment Bank (EIB) which engages with applicants on the ground, private and public. Recipients were subject to the EIB's standard due diligence process, verifying that the projects are economically sound, mature enough to be bankable and adequately priced – making it far less vulnerable to political capture of European spending by political parties in power. By and large, however, Europeans should beware of simple technocratic solutions to what are inherently political problems.

THE GREAT CONFLATION

There is another side to the disappointment voiced by Western liberals at developments in Eastern Europe. It stems from the expectation that post-communist countries would do more than adopt a set of political and legal institutions modeled after those that were well known to deliver freedom, democracy, and prosperity in the West. For many, joining the West was also about embracing a much wider, and growing, set of liberal and progressive norms. Consciously or not, the liberal democratic package has been broadened to include a degree of openness to immigration and an expansive conception of gender equality and rights for sexual and ethnic minorities – in other words, issues that are oftentimes not settled even in the West. The experience of cultural change is overwhelmingly one of a bottom-up process of shifts in attitudes, rather than one that is led by elites and activists. As late as 2004, Senator Barack Obama insisted that "marriage is between a man and a woman," following the dominant public opinion in the United States.[79] The periodic nagging from Western powers-that-be, furthermore, contributed to a siege mentality in socially and culturally conservative circles in the region, encouraging the worst, most irresponsible actors to double down and seek confrontation, which may well be in their political interest.[80]

In August 2011, the then U.S. Ambassador Norman Eisen, together with diplomats from a dozen other countries, including EU member states, extended his support to Prague's first gay pride march. It seemed like an opportune moment and place to do so. The Czech Republic was among the most socially tolerant countries in the post-communist bloc, having legalized 'registered partnerships' for same-sex couples in 2006, without much political controversy. "I had as big or bigger, a budget and a soapbox as any of the other ambassadors," Eisen reminisces, "so I jumped into it and thought the US embassy was first among equals."[81] Yet, the backlash against the diplomatic support was as swift as it was unexpected, and the controversy over what was seen across the Czech political spectrum as inappropriate interference in domestic affairs became a defining moment of Eisen's ambassadorship. It was not just fringe figures on the Czech right who spoke out against it; the pushback was led by the country's conservative president, Václav Klaus. Even Karel Schwarzenberg, the foreign minister and a staunch Atlanticist, pushed back, saying that "expressions of support to rights that nobody in the Czech Republic is denied are counterproductive and redundant."[82] In retrospect, Eisen admits, "like in the United States, there are really two Czechias" – a fact he might not have fully grasped at the time. "I lived and worked in Prague, so I probably did not fully appreciate the conservative element and I thought it was more of a fringe matter and I did not imagine that Prague Pride was going to be a controversial event at all."[83] Yet not everybody got the lesson. Instead of serving as a warning, the lending of support by Western diplomats to LGBTQ initiatives has become commonplace,[84] unwittingly sending the signal that certain forms of social conservatism have no place in the community of Western liberal democracies.

Just like Western diplomats, European institutions, most ostensibly the European Parliament, have repeatedly inserted themselves in national controversies over access to abortion, sex education, persistence of gender stereotypes, and many others[85] – conflating those with questions of rule of law, media freedom, or a democratic level playing field. Following years of Orbán's authoritarian entrenchment in Hungary, the European Parliament wheeled out a report compiled by a Green MEP from the Netherlands, Judith Sargentini, which lambasted Hungary for failing to "adapt working conditions for pregnant or breastfeeding workers," for the "prevalence of negative stereotypes and prejudice against lesbian, gay, bisexual and transgender persons, particularly in the employment and education sectors," and for the fact that Hungary's "constitutional ban on discrimination does not explicitly list sexual orientation and gender identity."[86]

Instead of course-correcting under international pressure, the usual suspects have since doubled down. Hungary banned legal gender changes in May 2020, stipulating that only "sex at birth" can be entered into the civil registry.[87] Since 2019, dozens of local authorities in Poland under the control of the ruling PiS have declared themselves "LGBTQ ideology-free zones," banning pride marches and other events. In October 2020, Poland's Constitutional Tribunal ruled that even in cases involving severe foetal impairment abortion was unconstitutional, prompting a wave of mass protests.[88] In 2021, furthermore, the Hungarian parliament passed a law banning a "portrayal and promotion of gender identity different from sex assigned at birth, the change of sex and homosexuality" in educational materials and in advertisements directed at persons under 18.[89] Vaguely reminiscent of Russia's much broader ban on 'homosexual propaganda,' the legislation deserves international scrutiny. There is a question of proportion, however. Leaders who had been mostly silent as FIDESZ reshaped Hungary's political landscape to its benefit over the 2010s were suddenly speaking out. The Dutch prime minister Mark Rutte was ready "to bring Hungary to its knees," giving Hungary a choice between being "a member of the European Union, and so a member of the community of shared values" and "[getting] out."[90] Likewise, German Chancellor Angela Merkel, rarely moved by FIDESZ's earlier transgressions, weighed in and asserted that there can be "no compromise on human dignity."[91]

Such grandstanding is self-defeating. If the aim of the European project is indeed to build an 'ever-closer union' and a shared European political identity, then tying that identity to a progressive cultural outlook not shared by a large swathe of Europe's population directly undercuts integration efforts. Moreover, if one cares about stopping incumbent entrenchment and de-democratization in countries of Eastern Europe, one should seek to build as broad a coalition as possible to defend democracy, rule of law, and EU membership. Conflating them with a more expansive progressive cultural agenda forces conservative voters and politicians into a choice between such values and their ideological and religious priors. At the time of writing, the outcome of the 2022 election in Hungary was not known. However, it is noteworthy that the formerly neo-fascist Jobbik has been part of the anti-Orbán coalition and yet its parliamentarians voted in favor of the government-proposed law against 'homosexual propaganda.' In fact, it is not a stretch to hypothesize that one of the purposes of the law was to drive a wedge through the Hungarian opposition, and all those who took the bait and amplified the issue helped Orbán achieve that goal.

Like it or not, historic and cultural experiences of Eastern Europeans are often different from those of the Western counterparts, including decades under the yoke of communism. In a famous 2007 study, the late Alberto Alesina and Nicola Fuchs-Schündeln compared the attitudes of citizens of the former East and West Germany. East Germans, especially their older cohorts, display significantly more favorable attitudes toward redistribution and state intervention in the economy.[92] Across the post-communist region, the populations' support for markets and democracy remains lower than in the West. Citizens of post-communist countries are also less likely to embrace gender equality.[93] Even if one assumes that those gaps in attitudes eventually close as older age cohorts in Eastern European countries, shaped by their experience of the communist regime, are replaced with younger people whose life experiences are similar to those of their Western European counterparts, such a process might take another couple of decades, at the very least.

Meanwhile, on several cultural and religious issues, most prominently abortion and LGBTQ rights, Central and Eastern European countries have seen very little convergence with the West. Most Western democracies underwent a dramatic shift in public attitudes concerning homosexuality and same-sex marriage. As recently as 2004, 60 percent of Americans opposed gay marriage and only 31 percent were in favor. In recent years, over 60 percent have been in favor, amounting to one of the most significant reversals in attitudes ever observed in polling data.[94] Western European countries, including Catholic Ireland, followed suit. Yet, no similar shift has taken place in post-communist countries. With the exception of the Czech Republic, which legalized same-sex civil partnerships without much ado in 2006, majorities in the region continue to oppose same-sex marriage.[95] In a 2019 Pew survey, close to half of respondents in Poland, Lithuania, Slovakia, and Bulgaria, and 39 percent of Hungarians, expressed the view that homosexuality "should not be accepted by society" – compared to some 10 percent in Germany, Spain, and France, and single digits in the Netherlands and Sweden.[96] At regular intervals, the issue of gay rights is brought to the forefront not only by LGBTQ activists but also, and more frequently, by conservative voices who present it as a threat to the family and 'traditional values.'[97] In 2014, for example, Slovakia held a referendum aimed at imposing a pre-emptive constitutional ban on largely non-existent legislative efforts to legalize same-sex marriage. Because of the low turnout, the outcome was not binding. Yet, the campaign bitterly divided the country and for several months crowded out all other subjects of public policy.

Of course, it is possible to find examples of influential culturally conservative and anti-immigration movements in the West. France has featured a sizeable anti-abortion and anti-gay-marriage movement ('Manif pour tous'), and in the United States, social and cultural conservatism has been an important component of the political coalition behind President Trump. While the difference between the East and the West is not one of principle, but rather of degree, it is also a difference that cannot be just wished away. Neither can it be undone by top-down legislation or, worse yet, activism of the EU's top court. European treaties assign no powers to European institutions in those areas, nor should they. Not only is there visceral disagreement on such subjects between member states but there is also nothing to be gained from common European policies in areas such as same-sex marriage, gender equality, or access to abortion since such national policies have little or no spillover effects on other countries. Yet, the ECJ has repeatedly entertained the possibility of using the principle of free movement and non-discrimination as a vehicle for forcing governments to recognize same-sex marriages and other forms of civil partnership concluded in other countries, in spite of not adopting the same institution themselves.[98]

With some qualifications, a similar story can be told about immigration and the clash that has opened between European institutions and some Eastern European capitals after 2015. Compared to Western Europe, non-European immigrant populations are largely absent in post-communist countries.[99] The degree of ethnic homogeneity in the region is a historic anomaly. Up to World Wars I and II, Central and Eastern Europe was distinctly multi-ethnic and multilingual. Unlike the West, where a large portion of the lingering diversity disappeared with the nation- and state-building efforts of the 19th century, the process of homogenization in post-communist countries involved ethnic cleansing, deportations, and genocide – including the Holocaust, which disproportionately affected Poland, the Baltic States, Ukraine, and Belarus, or the post-1945 expulsion of ethnic Germans from Czechoslovakia. The memory of ethnic and linguistic diversity in the region, Ivan Krastev argues, is overwhelmingly one of *trouble*.[100] Moreover, joining the EU meant that between 2000 and 2016, countries such as Lithuania, Latvia, Romania, and Bulgaria lost around 20 percent of their populations, due to different combinations of aging and emigration.

The backlash against a perceived threat of uncontrolled mass immigration might have been fundamentally irrational but it was not surprising. On the European Social Survey conducted in 2016 and 2017, over 60 percent of Hungarians said that no migrants should be allowed to enter "from poorer countries outside Europe."[101] This was not simply an overreaction to the refugee crisis – indeed, earlier waves of the survey note a long-standing aversion to immigration in some of the 'new' member states, which was only amplified by the events of 2015–16. On a 2019 Pew survey, post-communist countries with small or non-existent Muslim populations also had a dramatically less favorable view of Muslims than 'old' EU countries – with 58 percent of Hungarians, 77 percent of Slovaks, 64 percent of Czechs, and 66 percent of Poles holding an unfavorable view, compared to only 18 percent of British, 22 percent of French, and 24 percent of Germans. Bulgaria, a country with a native Muslim population, was an outlier, with only 21 percent of respondents expressing an unfavorable view of Muslims. The same post-communist countries also display elevated rates of anti-Semitism and unfavorable attitudes toward Roma.[102] This gap in attitudes toward immigrants was not only exacerbated by the refugee wave of 2015 and 2016, and the EU's misguided effort at a common European solution in the form of refugee relocation quotas, but itself played an important role in deepening the crisis.

In some ways, the current concatenation of cultural conflicts on Europe's Eastern periphery is reminiscent of the 19th-century history of the United States. With states bitterly divided over slavery, many on the abolitionist side saw westward expansion as a way of alleviating the conflict. In practice, the expansion exported deep conflicts over values to new territories, with least capacity to withstand them. Similarly, the EU's Eastern enlargement effectively exported quintessentially Western conflicts, driven by the clash of expansive understanding of liberalism and equality against other values, to societies that were not necessarily prepared to adjudicate them. In the United States, the Western expansion ended up undermining previous compromises that had kept the United States internally at peace despite disagreements over slavery. The 1850s Kansas territory, for example, became a microcosm of the future conflict in the United States at large, with two capitals, two constitutions, and two competing legislatures – one on each side of the slavery debate. It was in Kansas that "Americans made the pre-war transition to the dehumanization of opponents, to the preparation to wage a justified war against savages and barbarians, and the creation of a climate where verbal violence could suddenly turn into physical violence," the historian Patricia Nelson Limerick argues in her account of conflict in the American West.[103]

The similarities between the two should not be pushed too far. There are vast differences between the question of slavery and the ongoing cultural conflicts in Europe. However, one of the unintended consequences of triumphalism at the 'end of history,' bringing post-communist nations into the EU's fold, has been the projection of an expansive understanding of Western liberalism on societies that were not necessarily ready to absorb it, igniting conflict instead of accelerating progress. A related parallel with antebellum America has to do with the fragility of the EU's quasi-federal architecture. While the dispute over slavery brewed for a long time, it was only the Supreme Court's *Dred Scott* decision of 1856[104] that forced the issue and compelled the anti-slavery states to act. Infamously, the Court held that black Americans whose ancestors were brought to the country as slaves or who were slaves themselves, had no standing to sue in federal courts – that they were effectively not citizens over whom the federal law would have jurisdiction. While arguably driven by far more charitable impulses, the recurrent efforts by the activist class, by the European Parliament and other institutions to force the issue of LGBTQ and reproductive rights, or rights of asylum seekers, at the European level is not without risks. Whereas the conflict stirred by the U.S. Supreme Court's overreach was ultimately resolved by an assertion of authority of the federal government in America's Civil War, the escalating fight between the EU's progressive-liberal circles and recalcitrant social conservatives in its East risks undoing whatever is left of the Union's fraying powers.

NOTES

1. Quoted in BBC News (2019).
2. Applebaum (2020, 3).
3. *Consolidated version*, Articles 49 and 6(1).
4. Ilves (2021b).
5. Keefer (2007).
6. Kochenov (2014); Börzel and Schimmelfennig (2017).
7. *Consolidated version*, Article 7.
8. Gateva (2013).
9. World Bank (2021).
10. Sierhej and Rosenberg (2007).
11. Mohl and Hagen (2010); Dall'Erba and Fang (2017); Ederveen et al. (2006); Pellegrini et al. (2013).
12. Aiello and Pupo (2012).
13. Surubaru (2021, 204).
14. Easterly and Pfutze (2008).
15. Fazekas et al. (2013, 68).
16. Transparency International (2020).
17. European Commission (2016a).
18. Transparency International (2020).
19. Hungary Today (2018).

20. Paravicini and Posaner (2016).
21. Shehadi (2021).
22. Erdélyi (2019).
23. Ranking (2018).
24. Mortkowitz (2019).
25. Sabev et al. (2021).
26. Sabev et al. (2021).
27. Przeworski et al. (2000).
28. See Lührmann and Lindberg (2019).
29. Bogaards (2018).
30. Cited in *The Guardian* (2006).
31. Djankov (2015).
32. Hungarian Constitutional Court (2010).
33. European Court of Human Rights (2013).
34. *Fundamental Law of Hungary.*
35. Bánkuti et al. (2012).
36. Section 24, *Fundamental Law of Hungary.*
37. Kornai (2015).
38. Scheppele (2013).
39. Halmai (2018).
40. Hungarian Constitutional Court (2012); European Court of Justice (2012).
41. European Court of Human Rights (2016).
42. Venice Commission and OSCE/ODIHR (2012).
43. Kovács and Vida (2015).
44. Verseck (2012).
45. Ritterband (2013).
46. *Submission of a Bill on the Amendment of Certain Electoral Laws.*
47. Kornai (2015, 3–4).
48. *Act LXXVI.*
49. *Federal Law of 20 July 2012 N 121-FZ.*
50. Quoted in Reuters (2017).
51. Venice Commission (2017, 18).
52. *Act XII.*
53. Hungary Helsinki Committee (2020).
54. Przybylski (2018).
55. Blokker (2019).
56. Szuleka et al. (2016).
57. Nauert (2017).
58. Davis (2018).
59. European Parliament (2021).
60. Kelemen (2020).
61. Baume (2021).
62. Tusk (2020).
63. EuroNews (2020).
64. Day (2013).
65. Palmer (2020); Vladisavljevic (2020); Kukavica (2020).
66. Oliver (2020).
67. Romania Insider (2019); Timmermans (2019).
68. Walshe and Crowcroft (2020).
69. Reuters (2019a); Mortkowitz (2019).

70.   *Consolidated version*, Article 7.
71.   BBC News (2018).
72.   See Rohac (2021b).
73.   In June 2020, for example, the ECJ declared unlawful parts of FIDESZ's law on NGOs adopted in 2017. At the time of the writing, the legislation remains part of Hungary's legal system. Likewise, the ECJ pushed against the reforms undermining the independence of Polish courts, without much follow-up from the Polish government to remedy the situation. See European Court of Justice (2019a, 2020a).
74.   Bobić (2017).
75.   Kelemen (2018, 403).
76.   Federal Constitutional Court of Germany (2020).
77.   Flynn (2021).
78.   *Regulation (EC) 2020/2092.*
79.   Steinmetz (2015).
80.   Adami (2021).
81.   Eisen (2021).
82.   ČTK (2011).
83.   Eisen (2021).
84.   e.g., U.S. Embassy Slovakia (2019).
85.   See, e.g., Matić (2021).
86.   European Parliament (2018).
87.   Reynolds (2020).
88.   BBC News (2020).
89.   *Proposal for an amendment to Bill T/16365.*
90.   Blenkinsop et al. (2021).
91.   Zalan (2021).
92.   Alesina and Fuchs-Schündeln (2007).
93.   Pop-Eleches and Tucker (2017).
94.   Pew Research (2019).
95.   Pew Research (2018).
96.   Wike et al. (2019b).
97.   Mos (2020).
98.   See particularly the *Coman* ruling (European Court of Justice 2018). For context, see Bell and Selanec (2016) and Tryfonidou (2019). The ECJ's 2021 ruling in the *Stolichna obshtina* case, in contrast, was more restrained as it only required that Bulgarian authorities issue an identification document and a passport to a child born to a same-sex household in another member state. Given that Bulgaria's birth certificates require indicating the name of the mother as well as that of the father, the authorities were required to issue a travel document on the basis of a birth certificate issued by another country (Spain). See European Court of Justice (2021a).
99.   Eurostat (2021b).
100. Krastev (2017).
101. Heath and Richards (2019).
102. Wike et al. (2019b).
103. Limerick (1987, 93).
104. Supreme Court of the United States (1856).

4. What is European integration for?

In the febrile atmosphere after the Brexit referendum, the European Commission led by Jean-Claude Juncker tried to open a debate about the EU's future with the publication of its *White Paper* in March 2017. The document outlined five distinct scenarios, including prominently downsizing the EU and its full-fledged federalization, as well as two intermediate scenarios and a preservation of the status quo.[1] The succinct publication was timely. Seventy years into the integration project the sense of common European purpose was visibly missing, in spite of decades of overwrought rhetoric about 'ever-closer union.' On a recent Eurobarometer survey, fewer than 10 percent of Europeans reported feeling primarily 'European.'[2]

The question that the *White Paper* sought to address was a perennial one. In its early years, it was not obvious that the ambitious form of European integration, epitomized by the Schuman Declaration and later by Treaties of Paris and Rome, would gain dominance. While some form of cooperation between European countries appeared inevitable to prevent the resurgence of an aggressive Germany and to keep the threat of Soviet communism at bay, different options were entertained – from deindustrializing the Ruhr, through an emerging cobweb of customs unions reminiscent of the pre-war period, to a thin intergovernmental organization favored by the British and the Scandinavians. Despite the Treaties of Paris and Rome, there were many early setbacks. Most prominently, the European Defence Community and the idea of a European Political Community merging the different integration projects into a bourgeoning superstate were rejected by France's legislature. The idea of a European Counter-Cyclical Board, featuring a Europe-wide fund for public investment, was dead in the water.[3]

That did not prevent the ambitious conception of European integration ("Doing Much More Together," to use the language of the 2017 *White Paper*) from prevailing in the decades to come at the expense of more modest views of European federalism advanced by classical liberals and personalist-minded Catholic conservatives. Through landmark cases, such as *Van Gend & Loos*[4] and *Costa v. ENEL*,[5] the principle of direct effect of the Community's law and its supremacy over national law was articulated, though never quite recognized as such by all member states and their judiciaries, resulting in frequent tensions between national and European sources of law – most prominently the '*Kompetenz-Kompetenz*' problem.[6] In the 1970s, the decision was made to hold direct elections to the European Parliament – initially known as the European Parliamentary Assembly, which played a largely consultative role. Endowed with new powers over the EC's budget and deliberately organized along the lines of newly created transnational political parties, it was seen as a step toward a democratic pan-European legislature.

THE FALSE PROMISE OF 'EVER-CLOSER UNION'

Under the dominant dispensation, the EU's reach and powers gradually grew, most of the time away from public scrutiny. While at the time of the U.K.'s accession to the European Communities, the 'acquis communautaire' was merely 2,800 pages long, today it encompasses over 90,000 pages of legislation.[7] Even the single market, a distinctly ordoliberal creature, has been used as a vehicle for expanding the powers of European institutions – the application of the principle of mutual recognition has gone hand in hand with a degree of harmonization of legal rules, and there have been pressures both from big-government member states and from the Commission to move in the direction of corporate tax harmonization, labeling low-tax regimes as a form of illegal and unfair state aid.[8]

This mindset reached its high water mark in the 1990s and the 2000s with the adoption of the *Maastricht Treaty*, the creation of a single currency, the Eastern enlargements, and the Union's attempt at 'constitutional' reform. During that period, the collective belief in the Union's ability to serve as a vehicle of progress discounted any trade-offs involved in the process of economic and political integration – in spite of an abundance of warning lights. Implications of Rodrik's Trilemma were visible in the debate over the EU's service-sector liberalization, for example. In 2004, the European Commission proposed a new directive aiming to open cross-border service provision across the EU. The legislation, known widely as the Bolkestein Directive, provided a roadmap to an extension of the idea of mutual recognition underpinning the single market to the area of services, where European markets are heavily fragmented by a multiplicity of national regulations, licensing laws, and other burdens. The idea that, say, houses in Sweden could be designed by architects licensed in Greece, or that certain professions in the West would face competition from low-wage workers in Eastern Europe quickly irked interest groups and was quickly caricatured as an attack on the 'European social model.'[9] European leaders and the Commission technocrats caved in to the pressure. Under the compromise adopted,[10] the opening up has come hand in hand with significant leeway for governments to impose onerous restrictions on outsiders, thus doing very little to liberalize the service sector. Even if the idea behind the original Bolkestein Directive was a sound one, the result should not have been a surprise. Dismantling national barriers to cross-border services provision required European institutions to interfere increasingly with policymaking in areas that are considered intimately national and domestic, such as social standards, minimum wages, or licensing laws. European institutions, however, lacked the political mandate to overwrite 'social contracts' of EU countries.

The episode also highlighted the existence of a different trade-off, namely the one between 'wider' and 'deeper' integration. Perhaps a single market in services could have been sustainable between the original six founding countries of the European Communities. Throw a dozen more competitive, or low-wage, economies into the mix and it suddenly became a politically fraught proposition. Yet, officialdom hoped that even this dilemma could be overcome – indeed, *had to* be overcome – by institutional reform moving the EU closer to the ideal of a democratic European state.[11] Finalization of negotiations leading to the first wave of enlargement coincided with a 'European Convention,' echoing the memory of the United States' founding fathers. After two years of deliberations, the EU's leaders signed the *Treaty Establishing a Constitution for Europe*. Unlike the Constitution of the United States, written on five parchment pages, the European version had 484 pages, and featured an extensive list of positive rights to be guaranteed by the Union, including the right to paid leave, maternity leave, or housing assistance[12] – despite the fact that the EU itself had no tools to deliver on such commitments. More importantly, the treaty also contained a 'passerelle clause,'[13] which would enable the Council to move certain policy areas to qualified majority rule, as opposed to unanimity – something that seemed unavoidable lest the EU's growing diversity end up paralyzing the bloc. Some countries ratified the document without much ado in their parliaments. Others, however, organized referenda. In May and June of 2005, France and the Netherlands held their plebiscites, both with high turnout rates of over 60 percent. In both cases, voters *rejected* the proposed constitutional arrangement for Europe.

Yet, the ethos of 'ever-closer union' remained impervious to these warnings. "It is not France that has said no. It is 55 percent of the French people – 45 percent of the French people said yes," the Convention's president and former president of France, Valéry Giscard d'Estaing, claimed, adding that he wished that "we [would] have a new chance, a second chance, for the constitutional project." Furthermore, "if we had chosen to have a parliamentary vote last year the constitution would have been easily adopted. It is the *method* that has provoked the rejection."[14] Indeed, shortly thereafter, the so-called Amato Group prepared a re-hashed version of the Constitution for Europe. The *Treaty of Lisbon* did not replace previous European treaties but amended them in ways that were largely equivalent to the earlier 'constitution.' The Treaty created a permanent presidency of the Council and a version of the EU's 'foreign minister,' and extended the number of policy areas that were to be decided by qualified majority. It also contained the controversial 'passerelle clauses,' which would enable European leaders to reduce the scope of decision-making in the future.[15]

This time around, nobody was taking any chances. Only one referendum was held in Ireland, as required by its constitution. Yet, in June 2008, Irish voters rejected the proposal. Toughened by the precedent set by the Danish ratification of the *Maastricht Treaty* and also by the two earlier Irish referenda on the *Treaty of Nice* – in 2001 and 2002 – the EU's leadership did not blink. Then president of the European Parliament, Hans-Gert Pöttering, alleged supposed irregularities around the funding of the Irish 'no' campaign, which was organized by the Libertas movement led by businessman Declan Ganley.[16] To some public outrage, the architects of ever-closer Europe decided to ask the Irish again, until they got the answer right.[17] The new pre-referendum campaign was intense, with the EU providing funding to the 'yes' side.[18] On October 2, 2009, over 67 percent of Irish voters said yes, at a turnout rate of 59 percent.

WHAT HAPPENED TO SUBSIDIARITY?

For Euroskeptics, the *Treaty of Lisbon* illustrated everything that was wrong with the dominant approach to integration. The then president of the Czech Republic Václav Klaus, who refused to sign the Treaty into law until the second Irish referendum, warned that it would only worsen the EU's central problem – that of "a great distance (not only in a geographical sense) between citizens and Union representatives, which is much greater than is the case inside the member countries."[19] The reasons for concern were not unjustified, in the light of how the prevailing European mindset and practical policymaking had treated the principle of subsidiarity. Since 1992, the Union law has recognized that

> [u]nder the principle of subsidiarity, in areas which do not fall within its exclusive competence, the Union shall act only if and in so far as the objectives of the proposed action cannot be sufficiently achieved by the Member States, either at central level or at regional and local level, but can rather, by reason of the scale or effects of the proposed action, be better achieved at Union level.[20]

Unlike in traditional federations, which feature a clear division of powers, a vast majority of the Union's competencies are exercised jointly by both the EU and member states. The EU's subsidiarity thus does not provide a clear line of separation between powers that ought to be held by Brussels versus those in the hands of national capitals – rather, it seeks to provide guidance. *The Edinburgh Guidelines* of 1992, which provide the operationalization of the principle, stated that subsidiarity does not have a "direct effect." Instead, it is a "dynamic concept that should be applied in the light of the objectives set out in the Treaty [on European Union]."[21] The document gives three basic criteria for assessing the EU's actions on subsidiarity grounds. First, clear transnational effects must exist, which member states are unable to regulate directly. Second, absence of EU action would either result in a conflict with the Treaty or go against member states' interest. Third, and finally, common action must produce "clear benefits" relative to inaction.[22] An immediate ambiguity arises from the use of "and/or" to separate the three indents, suggesting that the three criteria can be seen either as cumulative or alternative.[23]

Protocol 2 to the *Lisbon Treaty* requires new European legislation to "contain a detailed statement making it possible to appraise compliance with the principles of subsidiarity and proportionality" and provides two avenues to challenge undesired infringement on those principles.[24] The first is a political one, known as the 'early warning system' (EWS), consisting of yellow and orange cards issued by national parliaments. A third of all national parliaments can force the European Commission to review the proposal on subsidiarity grounds ('yellow card' procedure). If more than a half of national parliaments flag the proposal, the Commission has to justify to the European Parliament and the European Council why the proposal does not infringe on subsidiarity – or withdraw the legislation ('orange card' procedure). The second avenue is a legal challenge with the European Court of Justice, which can be brought about by member states or the Committee of the Regions.

Unsurprisingly, only a small number of subsidiarity-related cases have ever been brought to the European Court of Justice in over 20 years. While the ECJ used the principle of proportionality to strike down European legislation in *Digital Rights Ireland*,[25] it never acted on subsidiarity grounds nor has it cited the Edinburgh Guidelines explicitly. If boundaries to the EU's jurisdiction were set, as in 1993 in *Keck*[26] or in 2000 in *Tobacco Advertising*,[27] they did not provide a binding check on the EU's powers. In *Tobacco Advertising*, for instance, the Court argued that the EU's power to regulate the EU's internal markets, conferred to it by member states, had its limits. It took only three years since the latter case, which did strike down EU legislation banning tobacco advertising, to introduce a new, substantively similar, directive into EU law.[28] In the *Spain v. Council* case, the ECJ established a purely procedural yardstick for assessing the EU's decisions which simply requires EU institutions to apply "adequate" reasoning and "relevant" evidence in order to justify a piece of legislation.[29] In short, as judicial review principles, subsidiarity and proportionality requirements "have been rendered essentially meaningless platitudes," as legal scholars Gabriél Moens and John Trone conclude.[30]

Notwithstanding the potential seen in the EWS by some as a possible "virtual third chamber" for the review of EU legislation, the mechanism has never placed effective constraints on the EU's actions. 'Yellow' cards have been raised by national parliaments only three times, and an 'orange' card has never been raised. Only once has a piece of legislation been stopped as a result of the 'yellow' card – and even then, the withdrawal was not a direct result of the EWS procedure but rather of the understanding that it would not find sufficient support in the Council.[31] It is also revealing that the European Commission's own 'Task Force on Subsidiarity, Proportionality and Doing Less More Efficiently' concluded that the EU adds value in every policy area in which it is present – and there are, therefore, no "competencies or policy areas that should be re-delegated definitively, in whole or in part, to the Member States."[32]

INTERGOVERNMENTALISM STRIKES BACK

However, *contrary* to Euroskeptics' fears, neither the *Lisbon Treaty* nor the disregard for the notion of subsidiarity has ushered in a new European super-state. For one, the use of the 'passerelle clause' to override dissenting member states is only possible by unanimity – making it more of a theoretical possibility than a concrete threat to national sovereignty. In fact, even in areas where the *Lisbon Treaty* envisaged the use of qualified majority voting (QMV) – say, Justice and Home Affairs – the Council has mostly sought to avoid outright clashes and seek instead negotiated compromises whenever possible, even at the cost of paralysis. One of the rare occasions when this informal principle was abandoned in favor of crude QMV decision-making, specifically the Council's adoption of refugee relocation quotas in September 2015, resulted in a spectacular political backlash.[33] Likewise, in spite of the lack of an explicit constitutional check on the EU's power in the form of a stronger version of the subsidiarity principle, member states have ample opportunities to stop or thwart European-level initiatives and to pursue joint policies outside of the EU's official frameworks.

Paradoxically, the most important innovation of the *Lisbon Treaty* might be the institutionalization of 'enhanced cooperation' between nine or more member states, allowing them to exercise the Union's non-exclusive competences, which are not being exercised by the EU as a whole.[34] That has opened doors to a distinctly intergovernmental form of European integration ("Those Who Want More Do More" as the *White Paper* puts it), as opposed to the 'community method' according to which all members must proceed at the same speed. The procedure has already been invoked numerous times. All EU countries other than Spain have agreed on a European unitary patent and a common patent court, for example, to end the practice of costly patent litigation in numerous EU countries in parallel; 17 member states have agreed to common rules guiding the divorce and separation of international couples; and 22 member states have agreed to the creation of a European Public Prosecutor Office for cases of suspected fraud against the EU budget. Likewise, there is a discussion about a possible financial transaction tax (Tobin tax) whose implementation would likely involve the use of enhanced cooperation, as opposed to joint action by the EU as a whole.

Similarly, in its legal provisions for the EU's common defense, the *Lisbon Treaty* envisages that its establishment will involve only "those Member States whose military capabilities fulfil higher criteria and which have made more binding commitments to one another in this area."[35] That is exactly what has happened with the Permanent Structured Cooperation in the Area of Defence and Security (PESCO), in which Denmark initially chose not to participate. Moreover, if PESCO is to become a meaningful defense arrangement in the future, it will have to find ways to engage with European countries outside of the EU, most notably the United Kingdom.

The most consequential forms of tighter cooperation over the past decade eschew revisions to treaties. The governance architecture of the Eurozone, built during the crisis years of 2010–12 largely through intergovernmental treaties between Eurozone members, lies outside of the scope of EU law. Not all EU finance ministers, only those from countries within the Eurozone (Eurogroup), have a final say about the fiscal and structural reforms required of member countries – though common European institutions, most notably the Commission, play a role in monitoring, reviewing, and supplying technical expertise. Aid made available to countries in financial distress does not come from the EU's common budget – the loans and guarantees are provided by Eurozone member states through the European Stability Mechanism (ESM). Moreover, Eurozone members – as well as several member states outside of the Eurozone – decided to abide by the so-called Fiscal Compact, an inter-governmental treaty tightening the provisions of the Stability and Growth Pact. Again, the arrangement exists outside of the EU's law and is intergov-ernmental in nature – though it assigns a significant role of surveillance and monitoring to the European Commission.

To some extent, European integration has always involved loosely con-nected integration projects running in parallel. Prior to the *Maastricht Treaty*, after all, the European project was commonly referred to in plural as "European Communities," comprising the European Coal and Steel Community (ESCS), the European Atomic Energy Community (Euratom), and the European Economic Community (EEC). The heart of the (now non-existent) EEC was the Union's single market. In 1994, the European Economic Area (EEA) Agreement brought together EU members with three non-members – Iceland, Liechtenstein, and Norway – securing their access to the EU-managed single market. Through a somewhat different route, Switzerland has participated in the single market too. All four EU non-members also take part in the Schengen Agreement managing passport-less travel across much of Europe – in contrast to several EU member states that do not take part in Schengen because of other obligations (Ireland) or because they have yet to meet the criteria of membership (Bulgaria, Croatia, Cyprus, Romania). Many explicit carve-outs and special accommodations exist in other areas, including the Irish protocol on the Lisbon Treaty, Denmark's opt-outs from the Maastricht Treaty, and Poland's opt-out from the Charter of Fundamental Rights.

Even more consequential than formal opt-outs, or 'derogations,' are the ones that exist de facto. Sweden, Poland, Hungary, and the Czech Republic are formally committed to adopting the Euro. In none of these countries, however, does the political will necessary for joining the Eurozone exist. Should the EU accept this reality as a potentially permanent state of affairs – or should it operate under the assumption that these countries will eventually decide to join the currency union? The question is not rhetorical. Under the latter scenario, it may make sense for Eurozone-related considerations to drive the policy agenda affecting the entire EU, for example by building new common fiscal instruments to bolster the common currency. Yet, if a considerable number of EU countries have no intention to join, then doing so might end up making those members increasingly uncomfortable staying within the EU – not unlike the United Kingdom in the run-up to the 2016 referendum.

THE PATH FORWARD

Europe's nation states are not retiring from history anytime soon. Even if one views nationhood as a fiction[36] and even if nation states result from top-down efforts at ethnic, linguistic, and cultural homogenization,[37] they have also proven remarkably resilient. Even today, many dividing lines in European politics run often along national, rather than ideological, lines. Even with a center-left government in Germany after the 2021 election, the country has not turned into an advocate of a European transfer union. Similarly, all French governments, center-right and center-left, have held a similar, largely statist view of the EU's role – and definitely not an 'ordoliberal' one. And if pro-European liberals go on a winning streak in Hungary and Poland, they will tread carefully on the subject of asylum and immigration policy.

Europeans' divergent views of contentious, values-laden questions, the national character of political life, and the high transaction costs of bargains at the EU level are not temporary bugs but permanent features. That does not mean resigning oneself to the status quo or giving up on the EU as a permanently broken or outdated institution. It does mean charting a way forward *within* the existing institutional framework, which allows for more flexibility than meets the eye, while accepting Europe's inherent messiness and imperfections. In a sense, it means abandoning the teleological understanding of the EU as an entity that is supposed to bring Europeans to a certain historic destination – namely, a federal state that is always somehow just around the corner. It also means accepting that European governance is inherently unwieldy, featuring both cooperation and competition under partly overlapping sources of political authority.

The main barrier that keeps the EU from realizing a greater degree of flexibility under which "those who want more do more" is a lack of imagination about what can be achieved by governments cooperating in smaller coalitions of the willing within the EU. Given that the EU's main strength has always lain in the articulation and enforcement of rules, rather than in real-time decision-making, adaptation, and strategizing, it is rules – particularly of the single market and of market competition – that should be the main focus of the EU's common institutions. The response to events affecting Europe, meanwhile, ought to be (and, in fact, overwhelmingly *is*) handled by coalitions of national leaders who may rely on the EU's institutions for assistance when appropriate but who do not automatically place Brussels and the entire EU-27 at the center of their considerations. Instead, they can act either individually, or by joining forces with other like-minded governments – all within the confines of existing treaties. Disaggregating the EU's operation in this way is a radical proposition insofar as it rejects the notion of a common European sense of direction toward an 'ever-closer union' in favor of a dose of agnosticism about the EU's ultimate purpose. Simultaneously, however, it is pragmatic in seeking to make the EU work better within the existing institutional constraints, instead of constantly reimagining those constraints in ways that are not politically feasible.

There is already a long tradition of sober thinking, which takes seriously Europe's pluralistic nature and complexities of its governance, "between the extremes of teleological Euro-idealism and chauvinist Euroscepticism," as British historian Timothy Garton Ash put it.[38] Differentiated integration, for example, echoes the largely forgotten work of David Mitrany who advocated a bottom-up formation of functionally specific international organizations as an alternative to what he saw as utopian schemes of international federalism.[39] Much later, the British-German sociologist and former European Commissioner for Trade, Ralf Dahrendorf, discussed the European project as

an untidy but effective combination of a core of (for the most part single-market related) policy decisions within the framework of the Treaty of Rome, a range of common actions by some though not all members of the European Union, a dense network of intergovernmental co-operation, and throughout (to quote Garton Ash again), the advancement of "those habits of permanent, institutionalized co-operation and compromise which ensure that conflicts of interest which exist, and will continue to exist, between the member-states and nations are never resolved by force." Some call this "flexible integration; others speak of the values of 'hybrid institutions,' one day, this Euro-realist vision may simply be called the European model."[40]

The tension between the EU's simultaneous processes of centralization and decentralization, particularly to subnational units, has been analyzed through means of multilevel governance theory, developed by political scientists Liesbet Hooghe and Gary Marks.[41] In a related vein, political theorists Francis Cheneval[42] and Kalypso Nicolaïdis[43] have advanced the idea of the EU as a 'demoicracy' – a polity governed not by *the people* (as in a unitary democracy) but jointly by a plurality *of peoples*, each living in a democracy organized at the level of a nation state. Understood thusly, the EU needs to rely much more heavily on coordination between member states rather than on delegation to the European institutions. The Italian political scientist Giandomenico Majone articulated a disaggregated vision of the EU in the wake of the 2008 financial crisis.[44] Majone lambasts the permanent overreach, not matched by the EU's resources and capabilities. The recurrent gap between promises and reality, together with the absence of any political or personal accountability for European officialdom, is responsible for the erosion of public trust in the EU. Instead, he argues, the EU ought to function primarily as a "club of clubs," referring to the economic theory of club goods,[45] which are non-rivalrous in consumption (like public goods) but excludable (like private goods). If collective attempts at providing club goods at the EU level tend to fail, it is preferable to allow for a pluralism of such efforts to proliferate, involving different coalitions of EU members and non-members, embedded of course within a framework of basic, shared rules – particularly those underpinning the single market.

All of these perspectives underscore the EU's reality not as a monolith or an exercise in state-building but rather as distinct integration agendas running in parallel, with only imperfectly overlapping coalitions of participants. The EU is not a 'multi-speed' union, in which different member states proceed to pool their sovereignty at a different pace. That would presuppose that all countries are moving toward the same, agreed-upon destination – which is manifestly not the case across EU countries. Instead, a differentiated integration con-sists of providing a rules-based and thinly institutionalized underpinning to groupings of governments cooperating, bargaining, and getting along between themselves in different areas of policymaking.

Making such a disaggregation more explicit would allow coalitions of member states to overcome deadlock at the EU level. If, say, the government of Cyprus decides to veto an EU-wide initiative to sanction Lukashenko's regime in Belarus – as it did after the stolen election in August 2020 – the remaining 26 member states have every right to proceed on their own, using national-level legislation and policy tools deployed in a coordinated fashion. Likewise, if a subset of EU member states wanted to join forces and go above and beyond the climate emissions targets set jointly by the EU, it is hard to see why they should not. If, furthermore, most but not all Eurozone members want to pool their public debt into a common debt instrument, why shouldn't they?

The resulting, pluralistic, or 'demoicratic,' set-up can be characterized as a 'polycentric order.' Polycentric governance involves "many centres of decision-making which are formally independent of each other,"[46] constantly adjusting to each other's actions within a shared system of rules, as the political scientist Vincent Ostrom and his wife, Elinor – the first woman to receive a Nobel Prize in economics – defined them. The two dedicated their scholarly careers to the study of polycentric systems of governance in a wide variety of settings, from urban policy, through local management of natural resources or agriculture, to global environmental problems. Few academics have explicitly connected European integration with polycentricity[47] but the framework offers a wealth of opportunities for both understanding the EU better and for deriving ideas about how the bloc could be reformed and strengthened. Polycentric orders are "open systems that manifest enough spontaneity to be self-organizing and self-governing."[48] The point of polycentrism is not simply a description of governance involving different, independent actors. Rather, its aim is to understand how sustainable self-governance can emerge at various levels of government, from the local to the inter- and transnational.[49] While most debates about the EU emphasize vertical division of power between EU institutions and member states, self-organization and self-governance relies on "intelligent deliberation to correct errors and reform themselves"[50] instead of hierarchies, domination, and top-down impositions.

A polycentric EU would place governments of member states, as well as subnational actors, firmly into the driving seat in setting the European integration agenda. However, it would not do so unconditionally. A polycentric order requires, among its "institutional essentials," the freedom and ability to enter and exit, shared rules that are enforced, and venues for peaceful contestation among different groups.[51] In a more granular fashion, Elinor Ostrom identified several 'design principles' that have been empirically associated with successful polycentric orders. Central among those is the ability of actors to set *boundaries*, excluding those which are not participating in a particular governance mechanism. That, of course, might not be possible on issues that pertain by necessity to the EU as a whole – such as trade policy or rules of the single market – or on issues that carry significant externalities, as on climate policy. Whenever possible, such questions ought to be dealt with at the European level. Yet, in many areas of policymaking, including foreign and defense policy, education, health care, public investment, and so forth, coalitions of member states opting for tighter cooperation could exclude others from reaping the benefits of their joint actions. Imagine, for example, an alternative pandemic recovery package that would exclude from the outset countries that are seen by others as failing to uphold the standards of rule of law and transparency – as opposed to the NGEU that starts from the opposite assumption and relegates the power to make such a decision to the European Commission. Likewise, it is possible to imagine a subset of EU countries moving to simplify cross-border provision of services by harmonizing their legislation or entering into mutual recognition agreements, without pursuing the more ambitious – and contentious – route of seeking to impose the same arrangements on the rest of the EU. Much like in the case of the EU's Eastern enlargements and resulting economic reforms across the EU, such initiatives would have the potential of jump-starting virtuous cycles across the continent since there would be tangible gains to economic competitiveness for countries that would jointly liberalize their service sectors.

Participating governments, Ostrom would advise based on her study of successful polycentric orders, should be able to easily modify the rules underlying their relations, without a central authority standing in the way.[52] In addition to *voice*, a polycentric order should give participants the option of *exit*. Compliance with the agreed-upon rules needs to be *monitored*, either by participants themselves, or by an entity accountable to participants (say, the European Commission). Violations of rules would lead to "*graduated sanctions*" by "other participants, by officials accountable to these participants, or by both." Moreover, in successful polycentric orders "participants and their officials have rapid access to low-cost, local *arenas to resolve conflict* among participants or between participants and officials"[53] – something that becomes increasingly difficult as the scale of cooperation is extended to the entire EU. Finally, a system of polycentric governance needs to preserve the organizational and decision-making *autonomy* of participants, that is, not reduce member states to simple units of a bigger whole but instead 'nest' them into mechanisms of international cooperation *while* preserving their ability to govern their own affairs without outside interference.

Certain areas of policymaking in the EU are more amenable to such forms of horizontal cooperation than others. In some situations, a reliance of bottom-up coalitions of member states may not seem to be a desirable alternative to an action taken by the EU as a whole – particularly when significant externalities are present. Examples include foreign policy, defense, single market and trade policy, climate change and similarly scaled environmental problems, or pandemics, where fragmentation of policymaking appears as prima facie undesirable. In fact, a 'first-best' solution to climate change requires global coordination in bringing down emissions orchestrated by a benevolent social planner. Likewise, keeping pandemics at bay is a fundamentally *global* public good, providing justification for a central global authority to address it. The same can be said about the stability of the global financial system or planning for and mitigating the effects of possible catastrophic events that could result in humankind's extinction, such as meteor impact. Yet, if such first-best solutions are not on the menu because of collective action problems involved at the global scale, then the question of whether 'bigger' is also 'better' may not have a straightforward answer.

Much like the nation state, which is as the sociologist Daniel Bell observed "too small for the big problems of life and too big for the small problems,"[54] there is nothing suggesting that the EU, as currently constituted, represents the optimal scale for policymaking in all or most areas in which it is currently involved. It is clearly too small to solve problems existing on a global scale, such as pandemics or climate change. It is simultaneously too large to govern effectively over other policy areas, which are more local in character. More importantly, the 'optimal' scale of policymaking is not a God-given or readily observable parameter and getting the scale of policymaking right is not a question of social engineering. Rather, it is a question that involves political leadership, bargaining, and experimentation – attributes that are inherently in short supply in an EU that is committed to pursuing policies at the level of 27 diverse countries. Allowing instead national governments to pursue the "art of association" in the pursuit of common goals is no guarantee of optimal outcomes. Yet, it would be wrong to compare such outcomes against those that could be attained by an idealized, well-functioning federal union of Europe simply because such a union is not a realistic option.

There are rarely any shortcuts to 'first-best' solutions to complex policy problems. For example, while climate summitry and vocal commitments by governments to reducing emissions have been a highly visible artifact of climate change policy, the idea of a truly global effort to address the problem is largely illusory. Lasting solutions are far more likely to result from the interplay of national policies – carbon taxes, subsidies to R&D, and so forth – and private initiatives leading jointly to technological change that would make a global-scale deployment of renewables feasible. The process will be almost certainly gradual and fall short of idealized fixes to the problem – the argument of this book, however, is that 'idealized fixes' abstracting away political realities and the 'crooked timber' of humanity are generally of little use – in the EU and beyond.[55] Likewise, in the coronavirus pandemic, theory would have advised that the World Health Organization (WHO) should have played a much more significant role in the initial response, as well as in the funding, production, and deployment of vaccines – a genuine global public good. To be sure, the WHO, as well as other global bodies, has not been completely absent, but their own role has been complicated – and sometimes controversial. Meanwhile, the bulk of the global response to Covid-19, from the experimentation and learning-by-doing from various restrictive policies to the development, production, and distribution of vaccines, has been an inherently decentralized and messy process. Could things have worked out better? Of course. But it is far from obvious that relying on the mantra of global solutions would have gotten humankind out of this particular predicament faster and with a smaller death toll.

The Ostroms' early work on polycentric governance dealt with public goods provision in metropolitan areas, where they noticed that the boundaries of policy problems, whether they have to do with public goods provision, mitigating externalities, or other issues, only rarely coincided with administrative borders of the relevant decision-making units. City wards, for example, were typically too small, but consolidated metropolitan areas were too big, to act effectively. Presenting cities with administrative consolidation as a solution to their woes, as progressive reformers of the 1960s did, was wrong, they argued. Instead, local actors can build governance arrangements from the ground up since "[i]nformal arrangement between public organizations may create a political community large enough to deal with any particular public's problem."[56] Polycentrism thus provides an alternative to the false dichotomy between the EU's further centralization, on the one hand, and a repatriation of competencies advocated by Euroskeptics and nationalists, on the other. It offers instead an avenue through which the scale of policymaking in different areas can be constantly adjusted through entry and exit of member states from different initiatives.

Shifting the locus of decision-making, especially in crisis situations, away from European institutions to coalitions of national governments is warranted in light of recent experiences. Whether it is asylum policy or vaccine procurement, neither the European Commission nor the European Parliament is fit to make difficult calls with sensitive political ramifications – especially not in real time. To be sure, that does not make the European Commission in particular redundant – its expertise, human capital, and ability to collect data and survey national policies have no immediate substitutes. Yet, in contrast to the 'community method' which turns the Commission, albeit largely in theory, into a European executive and an initiator of new policies,[57] it is important that such initiatives respond to demand from member states. In turn, a differentiated approach to integration would necessarily de-emphasize the role of the European Parliament, relegating it to the strictures of its narrow legal mandate.

Probably the most important role of the European Commission and of common European institutions at large, such as the Court of Justice, the Court of Auditors, or the Anti-Fraud Office, is the oversight and enforcement of common rules. A polycentric, or differentiated, approach to governance rests critically on a general framework of rules, without which the proliferation of horizontal arrangements between member states can easily degenerate into relations of domination, in which "might makes right" and in which costs could easily be imposed on hapless member states against their will. It is easy to imagine, for example, a Franco-German industrial policy initiative, without the participation of other member states, aimed at creating giant European industrial companies to rival those of China or the United States – at a price of reduced competition, higher prices for consumers, and an uneven playing field in the EU. In fact, one does not even have to *imagine* anything – that was precisely the reasoning with which the European Commission has stopped the attempted mergers of France's Alstom and Germany's Siemens, encouraged by the two governments.[58]

The Commission's most important role is thus the protection of the foundational principles of the single market and EU-wide economic competition – free movement of goods, capital, labor, and services. How far should that role extend, given the EU's expansive understanding of its own powers? It is important to note that the EU is a community of states, not of substate units or individuals. The Ostromian principle of 'nesting' thus requires that the relevant rules and their application pertain to relations between states – or perhaps between authorities of one state and citizens or commercial entities of another state – without infringing on the autonomy of domestic governance and decision-making. To be sure, there are explicit commitments to values, human rights, and standards of their domestic governance that EU member states have made either through their accession to the EU (Copenhagen Criteria) or through other venues (e.g., Organization for Security and Co-operation in Europe) and, in principle, they ought to be held accountable for upholding those. It is, however, illusory to think that such broader commitments can be reduced to specific legal obligations that the EU should or even could enforce as an automaton. The decisions about what to do about, say, challenges to the fairness of elections in individual member states such as Hungary, other forms of incumbent entrenchment and power abuse, or conceivable human right violations, are decisions that have to be made by other member states, politically – rather than invoking European values and European institutions as a 'deus ex machina'.

Even the scope of the single market and of its underlying principle of non-discrimination is bound to be a subject of constant contestation, particularly in areas where that principle clashes with legitimate scope of domestic policymaking. However, as a rule of thumb, European institutions – which do enjoy a significant degree of 'prosecutorial discretion' in picking fights with national governments – would be advised to see their own role more narrowly, while also acting more vigorously in instances when the four freedoms are blatantly under attack. Examples of European 'rules-based' overreach include the question of in-work benefits for migrant workers from other EU countries. On its face, restricting access to such benefits (typically various tax allowances) only to a country's nationals does involve an uneven treatment of domestic and foreign workers. At the same time, such benefits are also a matter of domestic social policy focused on domestic population, not a free-for-all for all EU citizens. In *Caisse pour l'avenir des enfants*, the ECJ struck down Luxembourgish legislation that sought to limit access to family allowance only to children of the cross-border worker, residing in France, excluding his spouse's child who counted among his dependents on the grounds that such law created an unequal treatment since all Luxembourgish children are entitled to such an allowance.[59] The efforts of the government of Austria to restrict access to tax benefits only to Austrian nationals as opposed to cross-border workers have faced similar legal challenges.[60] Considering the role that in-work benefits have played in creating an impasse between European institutions and the U.K.'s government ahead of the Brexit referendum, restraint would be advisable – as would the application of some version of the principle of proportionality. Whatever benefits are achieved by insisting on the exact same treatment by national tax codes of domestic and foreign workers are clearly outweighed by the damaging political ramification that such intransigence tends to have by eroding the voters' sense of being in control of domestic policies.

Strikingly, the almost casual overreach by European institutions takes place at a time when the EU's fundamental freedoms are eroded in significant ways in other areas, most visibly with the unilateral imposition of border controls, quarantines, and other travel restrictions during the pandemic. In a related context, the previously existing principles of free movement were partly rolled back, as with the amended *Posted Workers Directive*,[61] which replaced the earlier mutual recognition of rules governing the firms who deploy their workers on jobs across national borders, with a more heavy-handed approach. The new rules, which are relevant to professions such as long-distance trucking, are essentially forcing companies from poorer, low-wage jurisdictions with weaker social protections (say, Romania) to meet the standards of wealthier, high-wage jurisdictions (say, France) in which their workers are temporarily deployed, removing their key competitive advantage in order to lessen competitive pressures on incumbents in more developed parts of the Union.[62]

EUROPE BETWEEN LIBERAL MORALISM AND MODUS VIVENDI

The contrast between the EU's ambition to be a vehicle of universal social progress and its failure to deliver on far more prosaic fronts reflects a more general challenge facing liberal thought. There, too, has been a tension between thinner conceptions of political organization, focused on maintaining a modus vivendi in complex and pluralistic societies, and the increasingly ambitious variants of modern liberalism and progressivism. Not unlike in the EU's case, the underlying tension is one between understanding human society as an order, which is complicated, unwieldy, and which inevitably falls short of moral ideals – and seeing it instead as a common project moving toward social betterment. It is hardly surprisingly that those who adopt the more ambitious formulations of liberalism and progressivism may be also inclined to see the EU as a natural instrument of such progress. Bruce Ackerman's 1994 *The Future of Liberal Revolution* is a classic of this genre, elevating the EU as a solution to interstate conflicts, environmental crises, erosion of the welfare state, and as a check on localized despotism.[63]

This 'liberal moralism', which seeks to identify "free-standing moral norms and from those norms [deduce] liberal institutions as normatively privileged over other models of political life" remains the dominant form of political theorizing, represented by figures as diverse as John Rawls, Jürgen Habermas, Ronald Dworkin, and G. A. Cohen.[64] The intellectual sources of today's liberal moralism are manifold, including scientism and positivism of the early decades of the 20th century, which sought to apply the apparatus of natural sciences to political and social problems and make them thus amenable to a resolution through rational, scientifically informed means. Exemplified by President Woodrow Wilson's progressivism in the United States as well as by the creation of professional bureaucracies, industrial policy, and the welfare state in continental Europe, this meliorist view of the social world understood human society as amenable to constant progress and improvement. With the Great Depression and the Keynesian revolution in economics, which saw the market economy as being in need of corrective countercyclical policies implemented by governments,[65] social scientists started styling themselves en masse after physicists and engineers: embracing a high degree of conceptual rigor, quantitative modeling, and emphasizing precise measurement of economic variables.[66]

On the European continent, progressive meliorism chimed well with sweeping Hegelian conceptions of history as an inevitable process of resolving its internal contradictions. This view was prominently pioneered by Alexandre Kojève who coined the term 'end of history' while arguing that modernity has made conflict, violence, and the nation state obsolete.[67] The new political dispensation that grew on both sides of the Atlantic out of the ashes of World War II and the Great Depression did not resign itself to the fundamental imperfection of human society but sought to correct it through scientifically sound, rational means. That ambition, together with the promise to supersede warring nation states of the past with more peaceful international arrangements was an attractive alternative to the temptations of centrally planned, communist economies, seen in academic circles as serious contenders to Western free-market capitalism.

The mix of what was seen as rigorous social science and political thought that saw no limits to human reason proved powerful, particularly in light of the economic expansion experienced in Europe after the war. Using rational-choice tools borrowed from economics, John Rawls' ground-breaking book, *A Theory of Justice*, outlined a distinctly liberal yet ambitious paradigm for political philosophy by seeking to reconcile individual liberty with an activist state and its large-scale redistributive policies. The book's starting point is a prioritization of individual liberty, arguing that it should be maximized insofar as it remains consistent with the same degree of liberty being available to all. This principle, however, is combined with the principle of justice. Unlike classical liberals, Rawls argued that a just social contract would permit material inequality only insofar as it enhanced the well-being of the least well-off person in society (known as the difference principle) and was associated with equality of opportunity. Rawls' work was important because it represented a reconciliation of the ideal of liberty, central to liberalism, with an expansive understanding of material equality, which characterized political and policy practice after the war – with the two fused together using a rigorous social scientific apparatus. Not only that, but the rational intellectual method showed great promise in answering practically all vexing problems arising in liberal, pluralistic societies. As Portuguese writer Bruno Maçães, who received his doctoral training in political philosophy at Harvard in the final years of Rawls' life, puts it flippantly, his

> liberalism had been so extraordinarily effective at specifying the conditions of a free society that it could produce an answer to every political question. It could produce that answer *by itself*, with no need to revert to the actual people living in a liberal society. Gender relations, the workplace, abortion, religion, technology, and money: liberal theory could tell you how to think about each of these and many other difficult questions.[68]

Inevitably, liberal moralism and his preachers have grown increasingly intrusive and arrogant, generating "sweeping pronouncements from an allegedly disinterested and objective standpoint of pure theory"[69] and showing no patience with individuals and communities that decide to deviate from its prescriptions. Far from providing a guide toward ordering a free, pluralistic society, its conclusions have often made the practice of real-world pluralism more difficult – all in the name of liberty and equality.

To be fair, pluralism is a real challenge to any advocate of a free society. It is not just the state that can be a source of coercion. Corporations, local communities, churches, schools, and families – organizations that play obviously important roles in the social fabric of free societies – are also able to restrict individual choice in significant ways or promote ideas that can be inimical to the survival of free societies. Consider the (very real) radicalization in Muslim immigrant communities in Europe, which has often attracted responses that appear prima facie illiberal – bans on religious veiling or restrictions on foreign funding of 'anti-democratic' religious groups.[70] How exactly to strike the balance between individual freedom of association and protection of broader society, including of more vulnerable groups, against illiberalism of intermediate groups – families, churches, firms, local communities – is a diffi-cult question, subject to perpetual contestation.[71] For that reason, the approach taken by liberal moralism, seeking to settle such questions once and for all, is hubristic.

Just like the EU itself, liberal moralism and progressivism, which often come as second nature to the West's educated elites, suffer from a mismatch between ambitions and the tools available to them. Liberal moralists typically seek to move important policy questions outside of the space of democratic contestation by framing them as 'rights' or as supposedly self-evident cor-ollaries of the liberal principle of equality. Hence the depicting of same-sex marriage as 'marriage equality' or the popular slogan of 'women's rights are human rights.' However, even if 'rights' were once a political and constitu-tional trump card, they become necessarily devalued by their proliferation. Moreover, while bargaining and compromise involved in democratic politics can reconcile many forms of disagreements, it cannot adjudicate between con-flicting *absolutist* claims about values – say, an employee's putative right to access birth control and their employer's right to organize its private business in accordance with a given set of religious principles, which may see birth control as anathema.[72] The problem becomes intractable when existing soci-etal defaults are not set to the norms that liberals seek to establish as standing beyond politics, *at a time* when democratic majorities are not on the liberal side, either. Especially in recent years, the rise of nationalism and right-wing populism has become a formidable challenge to the liberal moralist project, threatening not only to stop what previously appeared to be an unstoppable historic progress but also to throw Western societies into an escalating cycle of polarization between ever-more ambitious forms of liberalism and ever angrier reactionary responses.[73] Needless to say, marrying a liberal moralist, or progressive, outlook to the idea of European integration is bound to make the latter a far more divisive political concept, just as seeking to define European identity in liberal moralist terms leaves out large segments of Europe's actual population – not least in its Eastern half.

The grievance-driven populist backlash against a liberal overreach on both sides of the Atlantic ought to be an opportunity to rehabilitate a more restrained form of liberal thought, which has fallen out of fashion in the postwar era. Starting with Thomas Hobbes, the main goal of political theory in its various forms was to identify institutions that enable peaceful coexist-ence in societies marked by diversity and disagreement, rather than to pursue a specific conception of collective good. The conflicts following Europe's Reformation demonstrated that reasonable people of goodwill could have profound, even irreconcilable, disagreements about basic values. Rather than seeking to engineer such disagreements away by imposing just one dominant view of the common good, the purpose of political institutions is to keep those disagreements at bay. "Torrents of blood," James Madison notes, "have been spilt in the old world, by vain attempts of the secular arm, to extinguish Religious discord, by proscribing all difference in Religious opinion."[74] America's Founders thus internalized Adam Smith's famous insight that the best remedy for religious conflict and intolerance was freedom and competition among a plurality of different religious denominations.[75] Indeed, much of the classical liberal thought of the 18th and 19th centuries addresses the challenge of managing pluralism and disagreement through institutions such as free speech, checks and balances, separation of Church and state, and freedom of religion, as well as federalism to keep values-driven conflicts from dominating national politics.

Similarly, classical liberals of the 20th century, who advocated the idea of European federalism, argued that the proper role of government consisted not in pursuing collective, social goals grounded in a shared understanding of the common good but in setting broad, general rules, enabling peaceful coexistence and cooperation between strangers. Hayek coined the notion of extended order or 'catallaxy,' which uses institutions of the marketplace to allow for peaceful cooperation and coordination of plans of individuals pursuing different and sometimes conflicting goals.[76] Hayek's mentor, Ludwig von Mises, agreed that market institutions were essential to social and political order, which could never resolve conflicts between different values and understandings of the good, both individual and collective. In 1929, he writes that classical liberalism

> does not concern itself directly with their inner, spiritual and metaphysical needs. It does not promise men happiness and contentment [...]. Liberalism has often been reproached for this purely external and materialistic attitude towards what is earthly and transitory. [...] The most serious error of liberalism has been that it has had nothing to offer man's deeper and nobler aspirations. But the critics who speak in this vein show only that they have a very imperfect and materialistic conception of these higher and nobler needs. Social policy, with the means that are at its disposal, can make men rich or poor, but it can never succeed in making them happy or in satisfying their inmost yearnings.[77]

In this view of the world, the effort to orient human societies toward shared goals is a fool's errand. Besides the challenge of pluralism and conflicts of values, the knowledge needed to arrive at and implement a more robust conception of the common good was not available to any human mind. As a result, the aim of liberal institutions is to constrain individual conduct through generally applicable, abstract rules that protect negative freedoms – and not to overstep that mandate by either seeking to guarantee *positive* rights or bring about any particular social or economic aims. In this understanding of pluralism, a competitive market plays a central role in enabling cooperation and coordination, including between strangers and people who might have sharp disagreements and dislike for each other. "It is one of the necessary conditions of the extension of human cooperation beyond the limits of individual awareness," Hayek writes in his final book, "that the range of such pursuits be increasingly governed not by shared purposes but by abstract rules of conduct whose observance brings it about that we more and more serve the needs of people whom we do not know and find our own needs similarly satisfied by unknown persons."[78]

Hayek and Mises could be criticized for what appears as a monomania with market institutions but that does not detract from their fundamental insight about the impossibility of directing pluralistic societies toward shared goals. The best a liberal political order can hope for is a modus vivendi, allowing individuals to get along, coordinate their plans, and resolve conflicts in an orderly fashion. In *Liberal Archipelago*, the libertarian philosopher Chandran Kukathas provides its formulation of a liberal solution to the problem of pluralism based on the principle of freedom of association. A pluralistic society, he argues, must allow for a vast diversity of associations between individuals to emerge, as an archipelago of islands. Yet, those will necessarily include illiberal and otherwise repellent ones, floating in a sea of begrudging tolerance – and that is just fine, as long as individuals enjoy the freedom to leave their respective 'islands.'[79] It is not just the free market doing the heavy lifting in allowing for cooperation, as in Hayek's and Mises' formulations, but rather the proliferation of shared associations and forms of governance growing organically between inhabitants of different 'islands' – not unlike in the personalist accounts of social and political life. Starting from a different philosophical tradition, John Gray (2000) also offers an influential account of modus vivendi, which eschews the Rawlsian notion of moral consensus in favor of a vision of uneasy yet peaceful coexistence of people who remain divided on fundamental moral questions.[80]

Of course, politics cannot be reduced to a maintenance of civil peace. Democratic politics does involve clashes between different conceptions of collective good – including of the liberal moralist, progressive, or technocratic varieties. There are good reasons, however, for why seeing European politics also as an instrument of liberal or technocratic meliorism, instead of prioritizing the role of the European project in facilitating coexistence between European nations, might become perilous. Consider the European Commission's proposal to extend the list of "EU crimes" to include hate speech and hate crime.[81] Consolidated democracies have potent outlets for peaceful contestation of political ideas which allow a prevailing orthodoxy to be legitimate – most importantly the ballot box. In the EU as a whole, such democratic contestation is far more limited given the political organization of the European Parliament and the confusing role of the European Commission as both an executive political body and as a civil service. Inevitably, the bulk of such contestation and compromising takes place between (democratically elected) governments within the Council. As a result, clashes between different ideologies, ideas, and interests – which are commonplace within countries – take on the form of clashes between national governments. If not tempered by prudence and the recognition of the EU's original purpose as a *peace project*, they risk turning the EU into an arena of conflict instead of a mechanism of interstate modus vivendi. Former Chancellor of Germany, Angela Merkel, understood this well although her own two-pronged answer to the challenge left a lot to be desired. On the one hand, she sought to use European rules to avoid open clashes of different visions for how the EU's crises ought to be resolved, presenting typically technocratic solutions as being an alternative. On the other hand, once the politics of rules exhausted itself, she was ready to strike last-minute bargains that departed from the established rules – think of bailouts for countries in financial distress, or the 2015 suspension of the Dublin rules on asylum – whose success rested on the immense clout that Germany wielded over the integration project.[82]

Conflict is not going to disappear from Europe. But it is important that the EU moves beyond the naïve liberal-meliorist view of seeing the EU as an instrument of unstoppable historic progress – as well as the two-faced Merkelian approach, cloaking power politics into a language of technocracy. The main promise of the differentiated, polycentric answer to the challenge raised in the Commission's *White Paper* is a much easier possibility of exit from arrangements that are unsatisfying or that risk igniting needless conflicts – in contrast to the all-or-nothing approach that characterizes the view of the EU as constantly evolving toward an 'ever-closer union.' A polycentric vision of the EU does entail abandoning some of the intellectual commitments common among the West's political and intellectual elites – most notably the wish to use common European institutions as tools for betterment for Europe, its democratic societies, and of humankind at large. One may wish, for example, for a reversal of the de-democratization taking place in countries such as Hungary and Poland and for a bridging of the deep differences that exist between member states. Yet some of those afflictions are not problems that can be solved by clever top-down policies or new rules. Instead, they are conditions that Europeans must live with. As the example of antebellum America illustrates, it is precisely due to the rationale of a decentralized, federal constitutional set-up, as opposed to that of a simple unitary state, that deep moral disagreements exist between different parts of the federation – and yet that there are also gains from formalized cooperation in areas of mutual interest, such as foreign and defense policy or trade.[83]

The United States ended up fighting a civil war over its internal moral disagreements and the power of the federal government was eventually required to end slavery. Fortunately, whatever one thinks of the current culture wars on the European continent, the salience of Europe's divisions does not rise quite to the same level. There is another reason for optimism about Europe's version of unity in diversity. Unlike the North–South divide in antebellum America, the EU's disagreements cut in different ways. There might be an East–West fissure on issues of LGBTQ rights, immigration, and cultural matters, but there is an equally, if not more important, North–South divide on questions of economic governance. Foreign policy issues – say, policies toward China or Russia – cut across many European societies and can conceivably lead to different coalitions of European actors working together. The multiplicity of such sources of tension and of the possible coalitions of countries is a good thing, even if they project the image of instability and seeming chaos. Cross-cutting conflicts facilitate bargaining and compromise – again, unlike in antebellum America where both the issue of slavery and of protectionism united roughly the same, similarly sized, coalitions of states.

Most importantly, wishful thinking about European unity is no substitute for a practical form of politics and institution-building that enables the EU to function and even thrive on a continent that is and will remain divided – and which also may feature flawed democracies. A differentiated approach to integration, in contrast, offers precisely that: avenues for bargaining and ad hoc collaboration between member states, provisional solutions, and muddling through – without the bitterness of perceived domination by others. It may not be a panacea, nor history's final station. It is simply a path along which groups of EU members and their partners outside of the EU, such as the U.K., can work around the constraints posed by the imperfections of the EU's institutional design and by the continent's inherent diversity. And that is no small feat.

NOTES

1. European Commission (2017a).
2. Cheneval (2019, 75).
3. Dyson and Maes (2017, 13).
4. European Court of Justice (1963).
5. European Court of Justice (1964).
6. In a nutshell, the challenge consists of determining whether the ECJ and/or national apex courts have the power to define their own jurisdictions – and what happens if those jurisdictions overlap.
7. Anderson (2021).
8. In recent cases, the ECJ rejected the reasoning. See European Court of Justice (2021b).
9. Grossman and Woll (2011).
10. *Directive 2006/123/EC.*
11. For a conceptual version of that argument, see Kelemen et al. (2014).

12. *Treaty Establishing a Constitution for Europe*, Articles II-93 and II-94.
13. *Treaty Establishing a Constitution for Europe*, Article IV-444.
14. Quoted in Beunderman (2006).
15. See particularly *Consolidated version*, Articles 31 and 312.
16. Smyth (2008).
17. Collins (2008).
18. Waterfields (2009).
19. Klaus (2009).
20. *Consolidated version*, Article 5(3).
21. European Council (1992, 17).
22. European Council (1992, 20).
23. Öberg (2017a, 393–4).
24. *Protocol 2*, 206–9.
25. European Court of Justice (2014).
26. European Court of Justice (1993).
27. European Court of Justice (2000).
28. *Directive 2003/33/EC.*
29. European Court of Justice (2006). For an argument for why some actually see such tests as appropriate, see Öberg (2017b).
30. Moens and Trone (2015, 65).
31. European Commission (2021f).
32. Reho (2019, 9).
33. See Novotný (2021).
34. *Consolidated version*, Article 20.
35. *Consolidated version*, Article 42(6).
36. Anderson (2016).
37. Gellner (1983).
38. Quoted in Dahrendorf (1996, 10).
39. Mitrany (1943); see also Ashworth (2013).
40. Dahrendorf (1996, 10).
41. See, e.g., Hooghe and Marks (2001).
42. Cheneval (2011).
43. Nicolaïdis (2013).
44. Majone (2014).
45. Buchanan (1965).
46. Ostrom et al. (1961, 831).
47. The most important exception is the edited volume by van Zeben and Bobić (2019).
48. van Zeben and Bobić (2019, 35).
49. van Zeben and Bobić (2019, 35).
50. Ostrom (1991, 243).
51. van Zeben and Bobić (2019, 40).
52. McGinnis and Ostrom (1992, 9).
53. McGinnis and Ostrom (1992, 9).
54. Bell (1977, 132).
55. For a discussion of the extent to which the existing climate policies are already polycentric, see Jordan et al. (2018).
56. Ostrom et al. (1961, 836).

57. Contrary to frequent promises of a 'political' Commission, the EC appears to have grown less political in its rhetoric and communication. See Pansardi and Tortola (2021).
58. European Commission (2019d).
59. European Court of Justice (2020b).
60. Strban (2020).
61. *Directive 2018/957.*
62. Trzeciakowski (2017).
63. Ackerman (1994). More recently, the historian Konrad H. Jarausch has sought to revive the notion that the EU and the European social model provided a compelling alternative to "military adventurism and rampant inequality of plutocratic capitalism and right-wing authoritarianism." See Jarausch (2021).
64. McCabe (2021, 2).
65. Keynes (1936).
66. In the United States, this change was illustrated by the Cowles Commission at the University of Chicago and later at Yale, many of whose associates went on to receive Nobel Prizes in economics. See Christ (1994).
67. Rech and Grzybowski (2016).
68. Maçães (2020, 130).
69. McCabe (2021, 4).
70. Ministry of Immigration and Integration (2021).
71. Levy (2017).
72. For a discussion of the strains that the growing inclusiveness of political life in the United States, accompanied with a rights-based understanding of politics, places on the U.S. constitutional architecture, see Orren and Skowronek (2017).
73. See Mounk (2019).
74. Madison (1785).
75. "The interested and active zeal of religious teachers can be dangerous and troublesome only where there is either but one sect tolerated in the society, or where the whole of a large society is divided into two or three great sects; the teachers of each acting by concert, and under a regular discipline and subordination. But that zeal must be altogether innocent where the society is divided into two or three hundred, or perhaps into as many thousand small sects, of which no one could be considerable enough to disturb the public tranquility." Smith (1904, Book V, 314).
76. Hayek (1978, 108–9).
77. Mises (1985, 4).
78. Hayek (1988, 112).
79. Kukathas (2007).
80. For a discussion of the different strands of modus vivendi theorizing, including contributions by John Horton and Enzo Rossi, as well as some of the pressing philosophical challenges facing the approach, see McCabe (2021).
81. European Commission (2021b).
82. See Auer (2019).
83. See Reho (2019, 9).

5.   Out of the Euro trap

The introduction of the common European currency was a triumph of politics over economics. Specifically, it represented a victory of an ideological commitment to moving the integration machine forward, epitomized by the Commission's slogan of "One Market, One Money," over warnings of economists across the political spectrum.[1] Whatever benefits to cross-border trade could have been generated by a single currency as opposed to a system of national currencies with flexible exchange rates, the economic theory of optimum currency areas[2] suggested that the move was highly problematic,[3] especially considering the enormous differences in economic performance between the original, founding members and the 'Southern' countries that joined the EEC in the 1980s. Forcing a common European currency on vastly different economies, without a much higher degree of labor market integration, price and wage flexibility, or fiscal transfers was bound to become a source of macroeconomic instability.

Already in the 1970s and the 1980s, Europe saw attempts at setting fixed exchange rates between European currencies ('snake in the tunnel' and the European Monetary System, respectively). Those proved untenable since different countries neither pursued coordinated monetary policies nor underwent much economic convergence. Past setbacks did not matter for the bargain struck in the early 1990s – the assumption behind the Euro's creation was that the introduction of the common currency would sooner or later create pressure to complement it with appropriate fiscal and structural reforms: a pan-European system of fiscal transfers, a higher degree of labor mobility between countries as European nations come more closely together, and an added boost of economic flexibility.[4]

Without such reforms, the common currency was going to increase interdependency between European economies and the downside risks of financial shocks, without tools to manage such risks in an effective and democratic way. Anticipating some of the political blowback against the idea, architects of the Euro laid down rules for sound administration of public finances at the national level (Stability and Growth Pact),[5] and an explicit no-bailout clause in the *Maastricht Treaty*,[6] to prevent irresponsible fiscal behavior by governments that might otherwise expect that other members of the monetary union would come to their rescue in financial difficulties. The set-up of the European Central Bank, moreover, emulated the example of Germany's Bundesbank by heavily prioritizing price stability over employment and growth, remaining detached from politics – *and* setting up its headquarters in Frankfurt.[7] Yet, the fears were not assuaged. As early as in 1992, 62 German economists wrote an open letter criticizing the "lax" character of convergence criteria and the "overhasty" introduction of the Euro.[8] The letter generated a debate, with chief economists of leading financial institutions providing a rebuttal, and the subject remained hotly debated throughout the 1990s. As late as 1998, 155 German economists pleaded for a delay in light of the unsatisfactory progress in terms of economic convergence and fiscal and financial stability. The stern response from European institutions noted that the introduction of the Euro was "totally irreversible."[9]

Today, there is no question that the critics were right. Shortly after the Euro's creation, Greece joined without even meeting the fiscal and financial stability criteria for membership.[10] The fiscal rules themselves were not only vague and summarily ignored by larger countries, but they also encouraged the exact opposite of prudent fiscal behavior. The rules encouraged a pro-cyclical fiscal policy, running larger deficits in good economic times and resorting to painful budget consolidations only in recessions – amplifying thus the size of both economic booms and busts, rather than acting as macroeconomic stabilizers.[11] For the EU's Eastern European 'newcomers,' formally committed to joining the Euro and generally enthusiastic about integration, perceptions of the common currency's downside risks became an early dividing line, which balanced the political benefits of tying oneself to the EU's integration core against the costs of losing control over domestic monetary policy. Slovenia, the Baltic States and Slovakia joined the Eurozone through the conventional, official channel at the first possible opportunity after becoming members (Slovenia in 2007, Slovakia in 2009, Estonia in 2011, Latvia in 2014, Lithuania in 2015), notwithstanding the challenging circumstances in which the Eurozone found itself at the time of their accession. Yet, a sizeable contingent among the 'newcomers' – Poland, the Czech Republic, and Hungary – have never really had much of intention to do so and whether they will ever join after witnessing the crisis of the 2010s remains an open question.

The introduction of the Euro went hand in hand with the rollout of the *Lisbon Strategy* to encourage EU-wide economic reforms that would turn the EU over the following decade into "the most competitive and dynamic knowledge-based economy in the world, capable of sustainable economic growth with more and better jobs and greater social cohesion."[12] A dose of economic flexibility would have mitigated some of the risks of introducing a single currency to a number of diverse economies. It was quickly apparent, unfortunately, that the ambitious goals of the new program would not be met. By 2010, per capita ncomees in the EU, expressed in purchasing power parity terms, were roughly two thirds of those in the United States. While R&D

in the EU had gone up from 1.75 percent of GDP in 2000 to 1.96 percent
in 2010, it was still a far cry from America's 2.74 percent of GDP spent in
2010.[13] Keeping an awkward silence about the *Lisbon Strategy*'s failure in
2010, the European Commission launched another competitiveness agenda
featuring new ambitious goals – though less ambitious than overtaking the
world's more dynamic economies, such as the United States. The results were
not dramatically different. According to the *Europe 2020* strategy, 75 percent
of Europeans aged 20–64 should have been employed by 2020. While the
EU tends to outperform the United States on this metric, it missed the target
with only 72.4 percent employed.[14] Among other ambitions, 3 percent of
the EU's GDP should have been invested in R&D (by 2018, the figure was
only 2.2 percent[15]), and at least 40 percent of the "younger generation should
have a tertiary degree" (a goal that was actually met).[16] The EU's economic
ambitions received a further hit with the Covid-19 pandemic. While the U.S.
economy contracted by 3.5 percent in 2020, the virus shaved off 6.1 percent of
the EU's GDP, according to the estimates by the IMF.[17] After these somewhat
embarrassing episodes, the EU today lacks an explicit strategy aimed at promoting economic competitiveness. As Dzurinda puts it pithily, "as died Kohl,
so did economic reforms. During my era one would hear mentions from [Dutch
PM] Balkenende or [Spanish PM] Aznar but today's Europe seems happily
complacent."

Neither did financial distress, which met Greece, Italy, and other countries
on the Mediterranean periphery after 2009, result, as some had hoped, in
complementing the monetary union with a fiscal one. The idea of mutualizing
the debt of Eurozone countries or of permanent redistribution schemes to
help countries in economic hardship proved unpalatable to political leaders
in the 'frugal' countries of the North, not to speak of recent Euro adopters
such as Slovakia, where bailing out much wealthier countries was an obviously unattractive political proposition. In firefighting, the European Central
Bank (ECB) was determined to do "whatever it takes" to keep the Eurozone
together.[18] In practice, that meant massive purchases of government bonds by
the ECB, particularly those issued by governments that faced high financing
costs – a haunting scenario for Germany's sound money advocates.

The crisis led also to the creation of an ad hoc mechanism of financial
assistance, complemented with new tools for micromanaging the public
finances of affected countries by the European Commission. The ESM was
set up with strict conditionalities in order to get around the 'no-bailout' clause
of the Maastricht Treaty[19] – and also to assuage fears of the Eurozone's
core governments that they would be on the hook for the profligacy of the
periphery. The Stability and Growth Pact, meanwhile, was transformed into
the Fiscal Compact, with rules guiding acceptable levels of deficit and debt,
which depend on economic circumstances and underlying debt dynamics in

order to mitigate the pro-cyclical effect of previous fiscal rules. The new, highly complex system accords a prominent role over national fiscal decisions to experts at the European Commission or at the European Fiscal Board, an autonomous fiscal watchdog.[20]

The resulting arrangements were unpopular both in countries that were net contributors to the system and in those that were being helped. In Germany, the bailouts and the concerns over the ECB's role in monetizing the periphery's debt in violation of its own mandate were proximate causes for the rise of a populist far-right movement, the Alternative for Germany – a first in the postwar era. In Ireland, which received a €67.5 billion EU bailout in 2010, an *Irish Times* editorial asked: "[Is this] what the men of 1916 died for?"[21] In Slovakia, an early post-communist adopter of the Euro, a clash over the Greek rescue package brought down a reformist, pro-EU government and helped install a populist one. The staunchly pro-European government of Iveta Radičová, which arrived in office in June 2010, was unable to make the case for why Slovak taxpayers ought to be picking up the bill for profligacy of political elites in a wealthier member state. Very quickly, the post-communist newcomer was dubbed the 'enfant terrible' of the Eurozone[22] with tensions in Slovak politics at their peak; the condescension of European officials was palpable. In September 2011, the Commission's president José Manuel Barroso quipped that "sovereignty is fine, but you cannot allow a small stakeholder in the community [Slovakia] to slow down all the others."[23] By then, Radičová's opposition had softened as the debate in the Eurozone shifted away from assisting Greece toward more systematic efforts at building institutionalized financing facilities for countries in distress (European Financial Stability Facility (EFSF), ESM) with stricter conditionalities attached – yet the continuing disagreements over this question led to the collapse of her coalition government in October 2011.[24] The dispute also created a new fault line in Slovak politics, leading to years of recriminations and distrust among leaders and parties that were otherwise ideologically very close.

In all three of these, traditionally pro-EU nations, the crisis saw "their European projects put on a collision course with their political traditions, expectations and material interests."[25] On the debt-ridden Mediterranean periphery, meanwhile, populist movements both on the right and the left thrived on lambasting what was seen as unacceptable foreign domination – "Teutonic Yoke," as the ECB's former chief economist put it[26] – in intimately domestic areas of policymaking, including taxation and the generosity of pensions and social safety nets.[27] In 1997, Harvard University's Martin Feldstein wrote presciently that the Euro, which would lead to "a much more centralized determination of what are currently nationally determined economic and social policies," is "often advocated as a way to reduce conflict within Europe." However, he predicted, "it may well have the opposite effect. Uniform monetary policy and inflexible exchange rates will create conflicts whenever cyclical conditions differ among the member countries. Imposing a single foreign and military policy on countries with very different national traditions and geographic circumstances will exacerbate these economic conflicts."[28] The question, twenty years into the common currency's existence, is how these structural flaws can be overcome without unraveling the entire construction, which would have far-reaching economic consequences.

'FEDERALIST' FOOL'S ERRANDS

Proponents of closer integration have been advancing a seemingly obvious solution: to complement the monetary union with a fiscal one. A pan-European system of transfers directed at regions and populations facing economic hardship – an EU-wide unemployment insurance scheme, for example – would help align business cycles across different Eurozone economies and take the pressure off national governments facing financial distress. To pay for the new spending, EU-wide taxes and European sovereign debt could be introduced, creating an additional layer of macroeconomic stabilizers.

That is, such 'federalists' claim, what the United States has done in order to become the most successful federal state in history.[29] In the 'Hamiltonian Moment' of 1790, the federal government took on the debt of the newly independent American colonies as well as a substantial fiscal policy role, which has since grown dramatically, particularly during the 20th century. The decision to federalize the debt of American colonies was a response to a one-off debt problem, which arose out of a shared existential struggle for independence. In the words of one of the Founding Fathers, the fledgling United States faced the stark choice between 'hanging together' or being 'hanged separately.' Today, U.S. federal spending exceeds that of individual states and provides a substantial buffer against local economic shocks. When Michigan's economy, for example, is hit by a slump in global demand for automobiles, it will be overwhelmingly the federal government that cushions the shock through unemployment benefits and other assistance. In contrast, however, should a similar shock hit Germany or Central Europe, it will be mostly national governments that will be expected to help. With a little more European solidarity, the conventional wisdom goes, the EU could become far more economically healthy and politically cohesive.

There are several reasons why the 'Hamiltonian Moment' is the wrong metaphor for Europe's current situation. For one, the grand bargain of 1790 included an explicit commitment by the U.S. government *not* to bail out states again.[30] In its early history, the U.S. federal government managed to stick with the principle, most prominently during the banking crisis of the late 1830s and early 1840s when several heavily indebted states became insolvent.

Notwithstanding the clamoring for federal assistance, the administration *did* allow state governments to fail. States then had to negotiate with creditors, and after a while most were able to return to financial markets. The experience also prompted almost all U.S. states to pass balanced-budget amendments to their constitutions. That is most certainly not the form of fiscal federalism that proponents of 'ever-closer union' and European solidarity have in mind. Furthermore, the contemporary, 21st-century version of American federalism, in which the federal government plays a massive fiscal role and in which the states' largest spending programs – education, health, and social services – are underwritten in various forms by federal funding, remains a political impossibility.

One reason is that, given the differences in the size of public debt or unemployment rates across the Eurozone, the winners and the losers of a fiscal union are easy to identify. And judging by the resistance in the EU's more 'frugal' countries to the emergency loans to the periphery and the ECB's de facto monetization of its debt, it is unrealistic to expect that either a massive one-off federalization of national debts, benefitting the Eurozone's periphery at the core's expense, or an open-ended commitment to decades of transfers which would flow from the core to the periphery could suddenly become attractive political propositions. There is also the question of magnitude. The U.S. federal budget exceeds 20 percent of GDP, compared to some 1.5 percent in the case of the EU. Plausibly, a European unemployment insurance scheme – a frequently proposed European 'stabilizer' – could add several percentage points. Compare that to the average size of the economic contraction observed during the Eurozone crisis across 'old' member states: 7.6 percent. Greece, moreover, lost over 40 percent of its nominal GDP between 2008 and 2014. In short, in order to make a meaningful macroeconomic difference, the bargain that would be required of European governments would consist of an unprecedently *dramatic* fiscal centralization, going far beyond any realistic proposals.[31]

In April of 2020, German Chancellor Angela Merkel announced that she was ready to support the creation of common European debt instruments to finance the EU's recovery. The announcement and the subsequent tentative compromise hammered out with President Macron of France was hailed as a major breakthrough, not just for the EU's economic response to the pandemic but also for the Eurozone's architecture. Echoing America's 'Hamiltonian Moment', NGEU and its 'Recovery and Resilience Facility' are being funded by the issuance of bonds by the European Commission on behalf of the EU's 27 member states. The program has been phased over the seven-year period starting in 2021, in conjunction with the EU's budget, the 'Multiannual Financial Framework.' Together, the two amount to over €1.8 trillion through various spending channels. However, close to €1.1 trillion of that amount was the EU's regular budget, the MFF, while the NGEU's addition was a 'mere' €750 billion. Compare that to the CARES Act, worth $2.2 trillion, which was both adopted by the famously deadlocked and dysfunctional U.S. Congress and signed into law by President Trump before the end of March of 2020 – on top of the gargantuan federal budget. Not only was the U.S. recovery package out of the door almost immediately, but much of the CARES Act funds had also been spent by the time the EU concluded its own deliberations. Even if the creation of a common debt instrument appears as an advance, less than half of NGEU spending (€360 billion) takes the form of grants. The rest has to be repaid by national governments, adding to their debt burdens and potentially escalating their costs of financing – thus defeating the entire purpose of debt mutualization. Even this arguably minor spending project was met with gnashing of teeth in countries such as the Netherlands, resulting in protracted negotiations, particularly over conditionalities that would allow EU institutions to hold off disbursement to countries not complying with EU law, such as Hungary and Poland.

THE REAL LESSONS OF AMERICA

It is possible that NGEU's success will encourage more fiscal integration in the future. But making this rather remote possibility an article of faith betrays a degree of naivete and a disregard for the EU's actual history, which rarely followed the neat logic entertained by Jean Monnet and his ilk. Rather than a model for fiscal integration that is unlikely to ever materialize, the United States could serve as a source of different lessons for the EU, leveraging the strengths of the single market in coordinating fiscal and financial behavior of governments and banks. It is well known that the U.S. economy offers a higher degree of overall price and wage flexibility than European economies.[32] Notwithstanding the EU's freedom of movement, cultural, logistical, and language barriers to movement of labor between U.S. states are far less significant than in the EU. As a result, the U.S. economy is far more adept at absorbing asymmetric economic shocks. Importantly, America's financial and capital markets are also better integrated. As a result, individual Americans, companies, and financial institutions are far better insulated from the vagaries of local economic conditions. Most Michiganders, or Michigan-based financial institutions, are not disproportionately exposed to risks facing the economy of Michigan. Yet, the same cannot be taken for granted in European economies. A report on Europe's financial integration by the European Central Bank reveals a significant 'home bias': "Investors in Spain, Austria, Portugal and Finland hold a portfolio which is more than ten times more exposed to bonds issued by domestic firms than the benchmark portfolio [...], while those in Belgium and Italy only have a portfolio bias of about four times."[33] This bias affects banks more than other financial institutions, such as investment funds, which are generally less developed in Europe than in the United States.

The excessively national character of banking and financial markets in Europe creates a twofold risk of a 'doom loop,' which is precisely what brought the Eurozone to its near collapse. The first mechanism of the doom loop revolves around the fiscal stress that the failure of large financial institutions in member states poses for governments which take on the costs of resolving the situation to protect depositors and creditors, or to prevent wider failures of financial intermediation. To be sure, the German government's decision in October 2008 to assist German banks exposed to U.S. mortgage markets with an emergency package worth €500 billion did not lead anyone to question Germany's solvency.[34] However, many other countries were in considerably weaker starting positions. In Spain and in Ireland, for example, government interventions aimed at protecting their banks' solvency quickly transformed a banking crisis into a fiscal one.[35]

A reverse mechanism has also been at play. Sovereign defaults are more economically damaging if 'home-biased' banks and other financial institutions become overly exposed to domestic sovereign debt. If an insolvent government imposes a haircut on its creditors, financial institutions that hold large amounts of government debt may fail as well. And if banks are interconnected or hold similar portfolios, financial contagion ensues, with dramatic downsides for the real economy, at home and internationally. It was partly for this reason that the prospect of Greece's uncontrolled default in the early phases of the financial crisis appeared intolerable to European leaders. Much like the collapse of Lehman Brothers in the United States, which had repercussions far beyond the confines of the ill-fated Wall Street firm, a prospective sovereign default by Greece risked bringing down financial institutions holding significant amounts of Greek debt.

The common currency and the partial integration of financial systems thus give rise to a collective action problem – a misalignment of incentives facing national governments and banks with the collective interest of the Eurozone and the EU. Compared to the deeper, culture- and politics-driven causes of the Eurozone's lack of economic integration, further consolidation of the financial sector and its subjecting to a shared system of rules seems like low-hanging fruit. Weakening the nexus between banks and national governments enables banks to diversify away from local sources of financial risk and to make prospective defaults by Eurozone governments a far less dramatic occurrence than how they loomed between 2008 and 2012. More importantly, the EU's no-bailout policy can only become credible if the risk of contagion across borders is reduced. Otherwise, as long as banks or governments understand that they are 'too big to fail,' they can reasonably expect that taxpayers from across the Eurozone will eventually come to their rescue.

How would a fully integrated market in banking services address that collective action problem? At the level of banks, common European rules for bank resolution would curb moral hazard driven by the expectation of some domestic banks that the national government would step in to help in case of distress. It would also ensure that bank crises do not grow into national fiscal crises. Common rules against the banks' home bias and the banks' treatment of government bonds based on their riskiness, in turn, would limit the financial sector's exposure to unsound domestic (or foreign) government debt, limiting the danger of financial contagions triggered by government insolvency. Subject to consistent capital rules, decentralized market mechanisms would diversify risk and serve also as a disciplining device for governments and financial institutions, while allowing Eurozone governments to pursue diverse fiscal and economic policies – without the need for costly and politically contentious fiscal unification or forms of fiscal micromanagement practiced at the present time. Relative to the status quo, a 'banking union' should aim primarily at extending the principle of non-discrimination to banking.

Unfortunately, one of the side effects, as well as contributing factors, of the Eurozone's economic crisis has been a disintegration of banking markets. Since the crisis, banks have become less willing to lend (primarily) to other banks across borders. From the peak prior to the financial crisis, total cross-border lending in the EU fell by almost a third by 2014, and it has never quite recovered since.[36] What the Eurozone thus needs far more urgently than pipe dreams about a fiscal union is a reversal of that trend. Some efforts have been made, in a characteristically heavy-handed, top-down way, under the buzzword of a future 'banking union,' announced in 2012. The plan involved three connected elements: a single supervisory mechanism (SSM), a single resolution mechanism (SRM), and a European Deposit Insurance Scheme (EDIS). Participation in these structures is mandatory for Eurozone members but open to EU countries outside of it and, since 2020, Bulgaria and Croatia have taken part, jointly with their accession to ERM II. However, out of the three mutually supporting 'pillars,' only the first two have been built. The third one, EDIS, remains highly controversial since a common deposit insurance scheme is redolent of a fiscal union, particularly if some countries' banking sectors are in a clearly worse shape than others.

Yet some important complementary elements remain off the table – most importantly the rules surrounding the treatment of sovereign bonds by the ECB. Those are currently accepted at equal terms as collateral, creating a perverse incentive for banks not to discriminate between higher- and lower-quality debt. Yet, one of the purposes of a well-functioning financial market is precisely to price the risk of different assets accurately, including of sovereign debt. While being arguably the least important part of the entire edifice, the common supervision of banks under the SSM is also the most advanced element of the banking union currently in existence. However, unlike the enforcement of rules of the single market, held firmly in the hands of the European Commission, the SSM is not really a *single* mechanism. The ECB oversees the system and directly monitors "significant" banks, but it does so in conjunction with national authorities, which are responsible for monitoring financial institutions deemed less significant.[37] Setting aside the fact that financial crises seldom emerge in those segments of the economy where they are expected, which raises a question about the wisdom of segmenting European banking into a two-tier regulatory regime, the system is flawed in a number of other ways. One, since monetary policy affects many aspects of banking, the interests of the ECB as a monetary authority and the interests of the ECB as a bank regulator might diverge. It might become tempting for the ECB to prop banks' balance sheets with a policy of low interest rates, for example, even if doing so comes at the cost of inflation, of stretching the bank's mandate, and of damaging its credibility.

Two, the usefulness of a supposedly shared system of banking rules is limited without a common understanding of how failing banks are to be wound down. The credibility of any bank regulator hinges on the question of what they can be expected to do in case of a bank failure. Under a clear no-bailout regime, banks are incentivized to act cautiously; if taxpayers are supposed to take on any losses, bankers might lose any inhibitions. With a muddle between the SRM and national policies, the reality of bank resolution in the EU lies somewhere in between – yet its muddled nature is itself a source of ambiguity and a reason for miscalculations.

The SRM's procedures of bank resolution foresee the process to take place under the direction of the EU's single resolution board, jointly with national authorities, and using funding from the single resolution fund. But that set-up risks replicating the doom loop as it opens the possibility of national governments stepping in to rescue banks important for political reasons. In 2017, as two banks in the Veneto region of Italy, Veneto Banca and Banca Popolare di Vicenza, were closed down, the Italian government acted on its own and set up a fund worth €20 billion to provide assistance to other distressed banks and to help move assets of the two failed banks to other financial institutions.[38]

Finally, the efforts to replace national deposit insurance funds with a single European one, EDIS, have gone nowhere, despite the repeated calls of the European Commission and a supposedly shared commitment to move ahead.[39] Particularly in the more 'frugal' member states, the creation of such a fund would be seen as tantamount to setting up a de facto European system of transfers, using taxpayers' money from countries with well-managed banking systems to help the poorly run ones, while encouraging moral hazard. Compromise solutions debated recently sought to establish a hybrid system with national and European deposit insurance schemes co-existing, with EDIS simply providing liquidity to national systems when necessary.[40]

The EU finds itself in a chicken-or-egg type of situation. The core countries fear that a common deposit insurance scheme would be a blank check for fiscal transfers to the periphery. Yet, without a common deposit insurance and an agreed-upon orderly bank resolution regime, there is uncertainty about how bank failures will be resolved, which incentivizes banks to take on reckless risks – especially if they perceive that their national governments have their back. To get out of this trap, a prominent group of seven French and seven German economists ("7+7") argued that several steps had to be taken at once.[41] One, the introduction of deposit insurance ought to go hand in hand with the introduction of supervision that would penalize banks for their 'domestic bias' (i.e., excessive exposure to the sovereign debt of their home governments). That way, the bank–government nexus could be broken, while ensuring that deposit insurance does not become a one-way transfer machine to the Eurozone's periphery. At the same time, the bloc needed predictable rules guiding sovereign insolvency to ensure that a possible default by Eurozone members does not grow into a systemic threat to the financial stability of the monetary union. For the investors, knowing ex ante the risks they are exposing themselves to by investing in the debt of a particular country would also lead to more prudent decisions.

The 7+7 group makes a number of additional proposals, some of them controversial – particularly setting up a joint fund to provide financial assistance to countries facing large economic disruptions. Again, to prevent the system from becoming a redistribution scheme to the periphery, the authors want national contributions to the fund to be higher for countries that are more likely to draw on the fund – and gradually adjusted over time to reflect reality.[42] Finally, together with rules against domestic bias, banks need access to a safe European asset. That last point has been used as an argument for common European bonds, issued and guaranteed by the EU as a whole – something that has been seen with great suspicion in core Eurozone countries, for whom this would represent yet another transfer scheme to the periphery. However, a safe European asset could be created synthetically from a GDP- or risk-weighted portfolio of sovereign debt of the EU or Eurozone countries, which would then be accepted as collateral by the ECB (instead of any EU sovereign debt, as is currently the case).

Jointly, an EU-wide commitment to a common process of bank resolution, stopping governments from helping their national champions, and the rules against home bias, particularly regarding sovereign debt, are logical corollaries of the single market's founding principle of non-discrimination. In fact, that is precisely what is irking some of its critics, who see the governments' ability to use 'credit policy' to help 'national champions' as something desirable.[43]

Critics have argued that tightening market discipline risks making countries with already large public debts more vulnerable – in part because the proposed rules would prevent national banks from acting as de facto lenders of last resort, either under pressure from the government or by necessity (due to their already large exposure to national debt).[44] But that objection simply means that the currently existing levels of public debt among Eurozone countries are unsustainable and need to be brought down. Indeed, history offers no example of viable monetary unions in which its constituent parts would be similarly indebted. But gradual debt reduction can be pursued without transfers to the periphery or federalization of national debt – and not only through painful austerity measures. Following a predefined rule, the ECB could acquire a proportion of national debts in exchange for its own debt to avoid inflationary pressures. Countries participating in the scheme would forego seigniorage, which would be used instead to repay the countries' debts to the ECB.[45] Note that this scheme would not be dramatically different from quantitative easing, through which the ECB has already purchased a significant proportion of the Eurozone's debts.

Polycentric orders work best, the Ostroms noted, when they involve rules that prevent participants (or external actors) from simply imposing costs on others. The point of extending the logic of the single market and its underlying principle of non-discrimination is precisely to curb such irresponsible behavior that ends up having spillover effects through the vagaries of interconnected though unevenly managed and unevenly diversified financial systems. Easier cross-border banking, rules on insolvency resolution, capital, and home bias, would help place the responsibility for fiscal decisions with the actors who take them (national governments) and that responsibility for banks' risk management decisions with banks and their shareholders. To be sure, the focus on a tighter integration of banking and financial sectors does not preclude joint action in other areas. If a group of Eurozone countries, or perhaps the entire Eurozone, desire to move ahead with debt mutualization or other forms of fiscal integration, they ought to be free to do so. However, it does the EU a disservice to bet the Eurozone's future financial stability on that move, which seems increasingly elusive.

NOTES

1. Krugman (1990); Levy (1992).
2. For the original formulation, see Mundell (1961).
3. See also Maes (2002).
4. See Masini (2017, 209).
5. *Consolidated version*, Article 126.
6. *Consolidated version*, Article 125.

7.   On the tension between the Eurozone's founding rules and the discretion and improvisation involved in managing the crisis post-2008, see Auer (2019).
8.   For context, see Hoekstra et al. (2007).
9.   Blocker (1998).
10.   Hanreich (2004).
11.   Bilbiie et al. (2021).
12.   Wyplosz (2010).
13.   World Bank (2021).
14.   Eurostat (2021d).
15.   World Bank (2021).
16.   Eurostat (2021e).
17.   International Monetary Fund (2021b).
18.   Draghi (2012).
19.   Sustainability of public debt is one of the conditions for ESM financing, according to the ESM's charter – which both distorts reality and risks fueling extreme policies to move debt and deficit metrics on a sustainable path when a government needs assistance.
20.   The European Fiscal Board itself warned against a further proliferation of fiscal rules in its 2018 annual report: "The current system of EU fiscal rules has reached its limits, and new attempts to fix the many issues in isolation without taking into account the more general architecture of the rules would make things only worse." See European Commission (2019c, 70). Instead, the Board calls for a streamlining of surveillance and strengthened sanctions – but such objectives can be achieved precisely by relying on financial markets while curbing the banks' domestic bias.
21.   Auer (2014, 325).
22.   Mesík (2020).
23.   Cited in Auer (2014, 325).
24.   See Auer (2014) for a discussion of the effect that the Eurozone crisis had on Slovakia and on another traditionally pre-European member state, Ireland.
25.   Auer (2014, 332).
26.   Dyson (2017, 169).
27.   Fabbrini (2014).
28.   Feldstein (1997, 41).
29.   Simms (2012).
30.   Sargent (2012).
31.   See Wyplosz (2018, 10–11). A complete redrawing of the fiscal balance between states and the EU is of course unpalatable to voters on a continent where parliaments were created specifically to hold the power of the purse. On that point, see Congleton (2010).
32.   For a discussion of the competitiveness and flexibility of the EU economy, including from a comparative standpoint, see Aslund and Djankov (2017).
33.   European Central Bank (2018, 106).
34.   Sobolewski and Carrel (2008).
35.   For a model of the mechanism through which the banking crisis led to a fiscal one, see Acharya et al. (2014).
36.   Hoffmann et al. (2019).
37.   European Commission (2017b).
38.   Zampano (2017).
39.   European Commission (2017c); Reuters (2019b).

40. Valero (2020).
41. Bénassy-Quéré et al. (2018).
42. Like many similar proposals, the main weakness of the idea lies in its macroeconomic insignificance.
43. Avaro and Sterdyniak (2014).
44. Tabellini (2018). See a response from two of the co-authors of the original 7+7 group report in Pisani-Ferry and Zettelmeyer (2018).
45. Wyplosz (2018, 22–3).

6. Shared challenges, divergent interests, decentralized solutions

Can ad hoc cooperation by the EU's member states and their coalitions, under the aegis of four freedoms, be a substitute for coherent policy action at the EU level, which has been often difficult to come by? This chapter looks at two areas of policy which have been characterized by sharp disagreements between member states and also by the presence of large externalities from uncoordinated national policies: energy policy and immigration and asylum. Energy policy decisions of individual member states have implications for others in areas from security to climate change. Likewise, immigration policy decisions of individual EU countries affect others too, as the EU learned the hard way in 2015 when the relative generosity of the asylum system in Germany, among other countries, fueled uncontrolled inflows of migrants and asylum seekers to countries at the EU's external border. In both cases, devising common European solutions has proven difficult. In contrast, under the right conditions, decentralized, polycentric solutions can reconcile different interests better than a one-size-fits-all approach – and in fact are already doing so in practical ways.

LETTING A THOUSAND ENERGY POLICIES BLOOM

European countries have not always seen eye to eye on questions of energy. While climate change has traditionally led the list of considerations guiding energy policy choices in the EU, there is a considerable East–West gap on the issue. In many 'old' member states, sizeable pluralities – 43 percent of Swedes and 35 percent of Danes, for instance – see climate change as "the single most serious problem facing the world as a whole." That percentage drops to much lower levels in the post-communist world (8 percent in Croatia, 7 percent in Romania, 5 percent in Bulgaria).[1] In 2019, the president of the European Commission, Ursula von der Leyen, announced that the EU was committing itself to bring down carbon emissions to 55 percent below 1990 levels by 2030[2] and to "[become] the first climate-neutral continent by 2050"[3] – an ambition that had been pointed to already in the Commission's European Green Deal of December 2019.[4] Over the current seven-year 'financial framework,' the EU is planning to spend over half a trillion Euros reducing its carbon footprint, building 'hydrogen valleys,' increasing the energy efficiency of its housing stock,[5] and creating a new electric charging point infrastructure. To that end, the EU is using a significant part of its post-pandemic recovery fund (NGEU), worth €750 billion in loans and grants to member states, and an increased seven-year MFF for 2021–27 of €1.0743 billion to finance the investment into emission reductions.[6]

Unsurprisingly, not everyone has been fully on board. Poland in particular, whose electricity supply relies heavily on coal and lignite, openly defied the bloc's ambitious emissions goals.[7] The reasons are economic, political, and strategic. Renewables are expensive to deploy at a scale at which they could make a substantial difference to the country's energy mix. Yet, while Poland's coal and lignite mining industry is not profitable either, it employs a significant number of workers who would find transitioning into other professions difficult and whose support is needed by the governing Law and Justice Party.[8] Furthermore, switching to less polluting natural gas, Polish elites fear, could make Poland vulnerable to Russian influence since most of the natural gas supplies in the region are still coming from the East. In the absence of cheap and plentiful renewables, the prospect of being vulnerable to Russian extortion by switching from coal to natural gas is understandably an unappealing proposition for most Poles, particularly after Russian aggression against Ukraine.

Governments across the EU differ also on the desirable paths toward decarbonization. While nuclear energy is an obvious clean alternative to carbon-reliant energy sources, for a number of countries it is a no-go. Austria, Germany, and Italy, for example, have respectively never built nuclear energy capacities or are phasing them out. In fact, for decades, Austrian activists and the political class have voiced loud protests against the reliance of neighboring countries on nuclear energy. Meanwhile, Austria's post-communist neighbors, the Czech Republic, Slovakia, and Hungary have expanded, not reduced, their nuclear power capabilities.[9] The Czech Republic is planning to build a new reactor in Dukovany.[10] Romania, which recently scrapped its partnership with China, is planning to build nuclear reactors 3 and 4 at Cernavoda. Hungary is proceeding with the construction of the Paks II reactor by Rosatom. Nuclear power constitutes over 70 percent of France's energy mix – notwithstanding the pledge made initially by President François Hollande and later by Emmanuel Macron to reduce its share to 50 percent by 2025.[11] In fact, in February 2020, President Macron correctly called nuclear power "the most decarbonized non-intermittent production of energy in the world."[12] France's hydrogen strategy relies primarily on the electrolysis of clean hydrogen using nuclear power – not solar and wind as in Germany.[13] In Sweden, where nuclear power accounts for over 30 percent of the overall energy mix, public opinion has gradually moved in support of it, and the main center-right party, Moderaterna, opposes the phasing out of existing capacities.[14] In Finland, a Finnish–Russian consortium is going ahead with expansion at Olkiluoto 3.[15] Former prime minister of the Czech Republic, Andrej Babiš, was among the early voices calling for nuclear power to be categorized as a 'clean' energy source, eligible for funding under NGEU[16] – a move that the Commission has finally taken in 2022.[17]

Other carbon-free sources of energy, particularly solar and wind, face important questions about their scalability, intermittence, and battery storage. Those, at the very least, warrant significant investment into research and development, both private and public. On that front, unfortunately, the EU has not positioned itself as a global leader. While 35 percent of spending under the EU's flagship R&D program Horizon Europe is dedicated to climate issues, the R&D budget itself was slashed from the original proposal from last year of €100 billion[18] to €75.9 billion.[19] However, even if solutions to the technological challenges come from elsewhere – say the United States or Asia – their diffusion in Europe will depend critically on the presence of competitive and well-integrated markets. If energy companies can offer their profit-making innovations to 500 million customers, they will act very differently than if they face 27 segmented national markets.

For a long time, energy security has been an important source of the EU's divide on energy policy, traditionally pitting post-communist countries fearful of Russia's leverage over them against their more complacent neighbors to the West. Small post-communist countries had their energy mixes long attuned to the realities of the Cold War era, during which they imported natural gas from the Soviet Union. Soviet technology was also used to build nuclear power plants across the region, with decades-long contracts guiding their maintenance and disposal of nuclear waste. Building on those legacies, Putin's Russia structured its energy relationships as instruments of power politics to give itself maximum leverage over much smaller and more vulnerable geopolitical players. Gazprom's natural gas contracts bundled sales and commitments regarding the use of gas transit infrastructure. Contracts were set for long time periods, with guaranteed annual supplies to ensure steady revenue, and restrictions on reselling in order to achieve a segmentation of national markets that would provide Russia with scope to price discriminate.[20]

The Russo-German project Nord Stream 2, a pipeline bypassing Eastern Europe, caused significant consternation in countries that believed that its completion would provide the Kremlin significant controls over their own natural gas supplies, which could be turned off without limiting supplies to Germany. The fear was particularly significant in the case of Ukraine, which would cease to be a significant transit country. The Trump administration decided to impose far-reaching sanctions on the project, without dissuading the German government from its pursuit. The Biden administration has voiced its concerns too but waived the sanctions authorized by Congress to remove what had been a vexing pressure point in the U.S.–German relationship.[21] The project was scrapped only after Russian invasion of Ukraine in 2022, which has also brought the issue of energy security and dependence on Russian oil and gas to the forefront.

The divergent interests of countries and the costs that their policies might impose on other member states cannot be wished away, nor are they going to disappear under the umbrella of common EU policies. However, one important mechanism that helps dull the edges of existing disagreements, whether they concern energy security or climate change, is a competitive single market in energy. On the energy security front, competition gives countries, including small ones, a greater array of options and weakens the leverage that any large supplier may have over them. A competitive energy market is also essential to the diffusion of carbon-free energy technologies and makes wasteful and highly polluting national policies, such as subsidizing coal mining, more difficult to sustain.

In 2009, the EU introduced the so-called Third Energy Package,[22] which set standards for the independence of national regulators[23] and delegated to them new responsibilities to oversee the protection of consumer choice and competition at retail level. More fundamentally, the Package introduced the legal requirement to separate the ownership of transmission networks and of energy suppliers, unbundling the question of gas transit from actual purchases. Russia unsuccessfully challenged the move as discriminatory with the World Trade Organization, but the complaints were dismissed as unfounded. In 2015, furthermore, the European Commission struck down as illegal Gazprom's contractual restrictions on cross-border resales of natural gas through which the Russian monopolist sought to 'divide and conquer' individual gas markets in the region and price discriminate.[24]

Under the umbrella of the Three Seas Initiative (3SI), Central and Eastern European countries have invested significant resources into building new gas connectors in order to facilitate the flow of natural gas between countries and keeping Russia from exercising undue influence over energy supplies to countries whose relationships with Moscow have mostly deteriorated over the past years. The 3SI involves 12 countries along the north–south corridor from the Baltic to the Adriatic and Black Seas, echoing the interwar project of Intermarium. Connections have been built between Poland and Lithuania (GIPL), Latvia and Lithuania (Klaipeda-Kiemena), Greece and Bulgaria, Romania and Hungary, Bulgaria and Serbia, Slovakia and Hungary, Poland and the Czech Republic, and others. Many of those allow for 'reverse flow' of natural gas – a mechanism that allows the network to send Russian gas back East to a country that might have been affected by cuts in Russian supplies, as was Ukraine in 2014.[25] The 3SI also financially supported the construction of a liquefied natural gas (LNG) terminal in Krk, Croatia, opening up the region to LNG imports from the United States and Canada.

With new gas interconnectors[26] and the deepening integration of the electrical grid, the EU has been moving in the right direction, albeit slowly. Electricity prices have been converging, especially between Austria, Belgium, France, Germany, Luxembourg, and the Netherlands. Yet, the volume of cross-border trade in electricity remains limited.[27] A similar price convergence, benefitting final consumers, exists on the natural gas market.[28] Imports of LNG via seaborne routes have also helped to erode the oligopoly of a small number of European, including Russian, suppliers. More needs to be done, however, to make European energy markets more competitive and eliminate the EU's dependence on Russian energy sources. Most importantly, the rules on the unbundling of energy production and distribution should be tightened. While the Third Energy Package foresees ownership unbundling as the default option for transmission, it contents itself with mere legal unbundling for distribution networks, and the rules are further relaxed for small-scale producers and distributors.[29] That is, however, highly problematic since it allowed a project such as Nord Stream 2 to be controlled by Gazprom, a company that also stood to benefit from a pipeline design that not only excluded alternative suppliers but also diminished the bargaining position of Ukraine. Besides weaning Europe off Russian oil and gas, an independent Ukraine must be made as soon as practicable into the EU's energy market, both on a regulatory level – where most of the heavy lifting would need to be done by Ukrainians themselves – but also through investment into new interconnectors with EU countries, which could be spearheaded by countries of the 3SI.

Again, strengthening the single market in energy and making it more competitive is not a panacea. It does not cut Europe off from supplies of Russian oil and gas – something that would require a discrete political decision. Neither does it, in itself, do much to speed up decarbonization – an issue that has been central to the Commission's Fourth Energy Package of 2019, which explicitly sets as its main goal to facilitate the transition away from fossil fuels toward cleaner energy.[30] Yet, proponents of top-down efforts to decarbonize often forget that a well-functioning European market in energy is a necessary condition both for weaning the EU successfully off Russian energy *and* for addressing climate change. After all, climate-friendly energy policy will be always bound to fail, unless it leads to the deployment of non-carbon energy supplies, which will be able to compete, unsubsidized, with fossil fuels. With well-functioning energy markets, such climate-friendly innovations are likely to spread more rapidly, primarily because they carry advantages for their adopters. The same mechanism will also put pressure on reluctant governments to decarbonize, simply under the pressure of consumers switching to cleaner sources of energy – as long as those are also cheaper and more reliable.

IMMIGRATION, SCHENGEN, AND ASYLUM

With over 1.8 million people crossing the EU's borders illegally and more than 1.2 million applying for asylum in 2015,[31] the refugee crisis was the largest movement of population on the continent since the tumultuous displacements of World War II, to be trumped only by the arrival of millions of Ukrainian refugees following Russia's invasion in 2022. Thousands drowned in the Mediterranean Sea having boarded cramped overcrowded vessels operated by criminal gangs. In the minds of Europeans, however, the real humanitarian tragedy was quickly replaced by a sense of threat, compounded by terrorist attacks in Paris in November 2015 and in Brussels in March 2016. The global political repercussions of a migration situation that was visibly out of control were immense, starting with the salience of immigration and asylum in the campaign leading to the Brexit referendum as well as its use by the Trump campaign.[32] Central to the chaotic nature of immigration flows in the EU were the different views of member states about how generous asylum policy should be. Upon arrival on Europe's shores, asylum seekers thus faced strong incentives to move to countries such as Germany or the Nordic states, where chances of obtaining asylum were high and where living conditions for asylum seekers and refugees were far more favorable than in the oftentimes improvised facilities in Greece, Italy, and Spain. In the ensuing chaos, both larger human caravans and smaller groups were moving across the EU, oftentimes on foot and under appalling humanitarian conditions. Secondary migration also proved to be highly politically disruptive, particularly as some countries – most notably Hungary – insisted on the literal application of the de facto suspended Dublin system, which stipulated that those seeking asylum ought to file their claims and remain in the first EU country that they reach.

To remedy the situation, the European Commission proposed a system of relocation quotas, which would have required all countries to bear a fraction of the overall burden, including post-communist member states. The proposal immediately inflamed passions, especially in Central and Eastern Europe, where the rejection of 'immigrant quotas' quickly became a rallying cry for politicians of all political stripes, not just far-right populists. The proposal was adopted by QMV at the European Council in September of 2015, against the protests of the Czech Republic, Hungary, Slovakia, and Romania. The use of QMV to get such a politically sensitive matter through was unprecedented. Although questions of immigration and asylum did fall technically under QMV, there had long been an understanding that consensual decisions were preferable to a crude overriding of a coalition of member states. Yet, QMV was not the get-out-of-jail card that proponents of a common European response often assume. Post-communist countries, including those that previously supported the proposal (Poland), simply refused to implement it, making duly adopted European legislation a dead letter.[33] Not unlike the crisis in the Eurozone, which introduced a new fissure into European politics, immigration had the same though much larger effect across the EU as a whole, bringing previously unthinkable political rhetoric into the mainstream conversation, hardening anti-EU postures across the population, and pitting 'new' members against the 'old' ones. In October 2015, Czech president Miloš Zeman warned, for example, that the inflow of refugees will lead to the stoning of "unfaithful women" and forced veiling.[34] While similar excesses could be observed in Western Europe, in post-communist countries, the crisis of 2015 and 2016 was the first time that immigration, previously a largely abstract consideration, became a subject of heated political debate.[35]

The crisis had also a straightforward structural reason: namely, combination of the EU's freedom of movement with absence of a shared approach to border protection and asylum. In 1985, the Schengen Agreement abolished internal border checks between most EEC countries. Rightly celebrated as a major achievement, it led to the creation of a common visa policy, but it left, for the most part, the protection of the EU common border to its members.[36] Instead of a federally run Customs and Border Protection agency patrolling the U.S. border with Mexico, imagine the U.S. government assigning the task to Texas, Arizona, and neighboring states, while Montana, New York, and other 'northern' states were made responsible for guarding the northern border. That is precisely the nature of the so-called Dublin system,[37] under which asylum seekers are required to apply for asylum in the first EU country that they reach and wait there for the outcome of the asylum proceedings – at the expense of host governments (say, Greece, Italy, or Hungary). The amount disbursed from 2008 to 2013 by the European Refugee Fund covered only 14 percent of the asylum costs in the EU for just one year.[38] However, despite efforts to harmonize the asylum system in the EU,[39] a common legal framework for determining eligibility for asylum is absent.[40] Even today, a Syrian asylum seeker would stand a much higher chance of receiving asylum in Germany or Sweden than in Greece or Hungary. In the run-up to the crisis, the former countries also offered significantly better treatment of asylum seekers, better economic opportunities, and already existing diaspora communities, all attracting further migration. Countries on the EU's border, meanwhile, had very little reason to bear the grunt of asylum costs and allowed migrants to continue in their journey through the EU – hence the scenes of chaos across the EU witnessed through much of 2015.

Given that European countries continue to disagree vociferously on how generous and open their immigration and asylum policies should be, it would be very bad news if the future of the Schengen Area hinged on the creation of a single, centralized system such as the one existing in the United States.

Fortunately, far less demanding polycentric solutions can work – as long as the EU's external borders are not porous. After all, the acute phase of the 2015 refugee crisis was brought to an end with the EU–Turkey agreement negotiated primarily by German Chancellor Angela Merkel in 2016, which incentivized (bribed) the Turkish government to stop the flow of migrants and asylum seekers. The deal was akin to sealing a leak in the EU's borders, only from the other side. In all accounts of polycentric governance, the ability to exclude third parties from the enjoyment of common-pool resources is a critical condition for the sustainability of governance structures that can manage those resources. The same logic applies to asylum policies. In fact, individual member states have already taken significant strides themselves, and the numbers of third-country nationals present illegally in the EU have come down considerably, from over two million in 2015 to pre-crisis levels. The importance of a secure and orderly external border has started to sink in in Brussels and in national capitals that were previously relaxed about the subject. The EU's border protection agency, Frontex, has been beefed up significantly, with a budget that has increased from €143 million in 2015 to €543 million in 2021.[41] By 2027, Frontex has been tasked with hiring a 10,000-strong Standing Corps to complement national border protection agencies and be deployed, particularly in crisis situations, though as of 2021, the hiring process appeared to be lagging far behind schedule. In October 2021, 12 European governments – including Eastern European ones as well as Austria, Denmark, Greece, and Cyprus – have urged the European Commission to provide funding to new border barriers under construction by governments on the EU's external border, most prominently Lithuania, which had been at the frontline of illegal immigration flows encouraged by Lukashenko's regime in Belarus. The interior ministers also asked the Commission to reconsider the excessively restrictive rules that keep governments from returning illegal migrants to the country from which they have entered the EU under the non-refoulement principle.[42] As in other contexts, the choice between European solutions and those spearheaded by coalitions of the willing is not a binary one. Clearly, some countries will have more interest than others in setting up effective coastguard capabilities. The 2014 Joint Operation Triton policing the Mediterranean, for example, was conducted with the support of Frontex, under Italian command, with a coalition of 15 countries, including some non-EU members.

Ensuring that immigration is under control does not necessarily mean a restrictive immigration policy. In Canada, a tightly controlled immigration and asylum system is combined with high immigration rates, in a politically sustainable fashion. Likewise, given the continent's aging population and economic sluggishness, there are good reasons for European labor markets to be open to foreign talent, as well as unskilled labor. In fact, for all the anti-immigration rhetoric, Poland has long been the largest importer of non-EU labor and its economy has benefitted from the inflow (particularly from Ukraine and Belarus) substantially. Along with other post-communist countries, Poland also proved to be extremely generous toward refugees fleeing Russia's aggression against Ukraine in 2022. However, a welcoming immigration regime is sustainable only when combined with a shared sense that immigration rules exist, that they are fair, and that they are being enforced. Any number of factors, from regional conflicts in the EU's neighborhood and the Taliban's takeover of Afghanistan, through destabilizing effects of climate change, to the simple fact of rising incomes in the countries of sub-Saharan Africa, are susceptible of further accelerating the flow of migrants and asylum seekers again. The 2015 crisis heralded also a significant widening of the institution of asylum, not as an exceptional tool, but rather as an alternative to normal channels of immigration. In 2011, only some 59,000 positive asylum decisions were made in all EU countries, either on humanitarian or Refugee Convention grounds – a number that skyrocketed during the refugee crisis to over 307,000, 672,000, and 437,000 in 2015, 2016, and 2017, respectively. Even though the acute phases of conflicts that fueled the crisis are largely over, the number of asylums granted has never since fallen below 200,000.[43] There are, moreover, insistent calls to broaden the asylum and refugee status relative to the 1951 Convention to include "climate refugees,"[44] women fleeing forced marriage and domestic violence,[45] or to LGBTQ persons fearing not just for their life or freedom but also facing "lesser forms of harm [that] may cumulatively constitute persecution," as UNHCR guidelines put it.[46] There is no denying that climate change is capable of imposing significant hardship on people, particularly in poorer parts of the world, and that the treatment of women and minorities, including sexual ones, often falls short of standards taken for granted in Western liberal democracies. Yet, precisely because the world is replete with suffering, injustice, and intolerance, the relevant question is whether it is reasonable to expect that the EU, or Western democracies at large, should extend open-ended protection to anyone falling into such sweepingly broad categories – particularly in the light of ample evidence suggesting that voters do not wish that to be the case. Even if an expansive view of asylum is adopted by some EU governments, it would be counterproductive and irresponsible to seek to impose it on all member countries or to use it as a pretext for a relaxation of the external border regime with regard to illegal crossings.

Assuming that the consensus on the need to keep the borders secure is translated into effective policies that prevent illegal entries into the EU, how much of a problem does the lack of agreement on a common immigration and asylum system represent? Doesn't a diversity of approaches between EU countries, from restrictive to lenient ones, encourage *precisely* the kind of secondary migration that disrupted European politics in 2015 and 2016? Not necessarily. For one, the current existence of different policies regarding work and long-stay visas issued to third-country nationals raises no such problems. While the Schengen Area is open to passport-less travel, work visas issued by individual EU countries provide limited options for migrants to move to other EU countries without undergoing a separate legal process. In contrast, what made the refugee crisis unique was the combination of the sheer volume of illegal crossings *and* the Dublin system's misalignment of preferences of both asylum seekers and national governments, which resulted from insisting that asylum procedures take place in countries selected purely by an accident of geography. Mandatory relocation quotas, as the EU learned the hard way, could not resolve the problem. Not only are such quotas inoperable without the governments' consent and risk compounding the backlash against both the EU and immigration at large, but they also ignore the agency of asylum seekers themselves who may have good reasons to seek specific EU countries, as opposed to others.

Fortunately, there are alternative approaches, which could be operated on a decentralized, voluntary basis either by all EU countries or by coalitions of its members. Some or all EU countries could agree on a total number of asylums that they are collectively willing to accept, agree on an initial assignment of quotas between countries, and then trade such quotas on an open market.[47] Tradable quotas would enable countries that do not want to accommodate refugees – such as Slovakia, Poland, or Hungary – to pay others to step in. Of course, even that system of burden sharing would require a prior agreement about the total level of asylum seekers or refugees that the EU is willing to accept and, more controversially, the initial assignment of quotas. A critic could point out that such a system would sidestep the agency of asylum seekers and would risk fueling secondary migration and chaos within the Schengen Area. To align preferences of national governments and asylum seekers, a two-sided matching market could be set up either by all EU countries, or a subset of them, as developed by political scientist Will Jones and economist Alexander Teytelboym.[48] A matching market would enable refugees to apply for protection in several EU countries, ranked by order of preference. It would also enable states to compete for particular groups of refugees. In addition to reflecting countries' preferences over the characteristics of refugees, the system would enable member states to set the minimum and maximum quotas of refugees they would be willing to accept. Of course, for the matching market to make a meaningful difference in the past crisis, the minimum quotas set by individual countries would have to add up to a number commensurate with the numbers of asylum seekers coming into the EU.

The system, from which members could opt out, would operate on a voluntary basis and would accept the preferences of governments over the number of asylum seekers and their characteristics at face value. As such, a matching market would allow for a degree of free-riding, which would be politically one of the scheme's selling points for countries averse to receiving large numbers of asylum seekers. As long as other governments (particularly those in asylum seekers' favorite destinations) were willing to pick up the slack, the matching market would not be jeopardized if a number of EU countries decided to accept no asylum seekers or not participate in the scheme at all – after all, very few of them are seeking asylum in countries that are explicitly unwelcoming, such as Hungary. Another appealing characteristic of this proposal is that it puts national governments in control of the refugees' characteristics, potentially including their qualifications, language skills, or country of origin. The matching mechanism would thus attenuate the incentives for uncontrolled movements of asylum seekers and migrants, which drove much of the chaos of 2015 and 2016. That is because arriving in any particular destination country would become much less important from the perspective of individual asylum seekers. Applications to the joint matching mechanism could be submitted from any EU country, or even from outside the EU. To be sure, the matching market is not, in itself, a technocratic silver bullet. However, its performance should not be compared against a well-functioning asylum system for which there is no political agreement across the EU. Together with a credible border policy, it can be a partial, politically feasible solution that would be vastly superior to the chaos-prone status quo.

Polycentricity, unbundling, and the fostering of horizontal and market relationships as a main instrument of European policymaking is no guarantee of perfect policies. It is, however, the most promising method through which European democracies can work together and accommodate their differences on subjects that do need some form of collective response, without repeating the failures of the top-down forms of overreach that were the norm in the past. The fact that progress on three of the most pressing and divisive issues facing the EU today – economic governance in the Eurozone, energy policy, and asylum and immigration – does not require ambitious and far-reaching centralization to which member states are unlikely to acquiesce should be a reassuring one. Counterintuitively, it suggests that the EU's growing reliance on coalitions of the willing is moving the bloc down the right path, although the official rhetoric is often out of sync with underlying realities. It should be clear, at this juncture, that the EU does not need a proliferation of new rules, agencies, or grandiose schemes to solve either its energy or immigration challenges – or any number of other woes it is facing. For domestic policy solutions to emerge, the bloc as a collective whole and its governing institutions should have only one overriding task, namely, to stick firmly with its foundational principles – the four freedoms – and to follow their logic consistently.

NOTES

1. European Commission (2021a, 10).
2. European Commission (2020a).
3. European Commission (2020a).
4. European Commission (2019e).
5. Rohac (2020).
6. European Council (2020a).
7. Al Jazeera (2019).
8. Brauers and Oei (2020).
9. See Eurostat (2021c).
10. Jakubcová (2020).
11. Sénécat (2017).
12. Gay-Padoan (2020).
13. Feitz (2020).
14. Analysgruppen (2019).
15. Kauranen (2019).
16. Zachová (2020).
17. Abnett and Jessop (2022).
18. European Commission (2020b). In comparison, in 2020 the U.S. Department of Energy (DOE) is spending $2.3 billion to secure energy independence and fund innovations and $5.5 billion in science funding for R&D and DOE's National Laboratories.
19. European Council (2020b).
20. See European Commission (2015).
21. BBC News (2021).
22. Two directives, one concerning common rules for the internal market in gas (2009/73/EC), one concerning common rules for the internal market in electricity (2009/72/EC) and three Regulations, one on the conditions for access to the natural gas transmission networks ((EC) No 715/2009), one on the conditions for access to the network for cross-border exchange of electricity ((EC) No 714/2009), and one on the establishment of the Agency for the Cooperation of Energy Regulators ACER ((EC) No 713/2009). See *Directive 2009/73/EC of the European Parliament*; *Directive 2009/72/EC of the European Parliament*; *Regulation (EC) No 715/2009 of the European Parliament*; *Regulation (EC) No 714/2009 of the European Parliament*; and *Regulation (EC) No 713/2009 of the European Parliament*.
23. European Union Agency for the Cooperation of Energy Regulators (2021).
24. European Commission (2015).
25. Somewhat reluctantly, the Slovak government then opened the reverse flow of gas to help. See Deutsche Welle (2014).
26. Rqiq et al. (2020, 9).
27. European Union Agency for the Cooperation of Energy Regulators (2020).
28. Chyong (2019).
29. Rossetto (2020). See also Eikeland (2011).
30. European Commission (2019a).
31. Frontex (2019).
32. Garrett (2019); Hall (2016).
33. Auer (2019).

34.   Quoted in Britské listy (2015).
35.   Krzyżanowski (2018) has a discussion of the events that forced a major transformation of the debate over migration in Poland.
36.   Hobbing (2005).
37.   The most important ones are the Dublin Convention and the Dublin Regulation (Dublin II). See *Convention Determining the State Responsible for Examining Applications for Asylum* and *Council Regulation 343/2003*.
38.   Matrix Insight et al. (2010, 47).
39.   See *Convention Determining the State Responsible for Examining Applications for Asylum* and *Council Regulation 343/2003*.
40.   Moraga and Rapoport (2015). For more detail, see Jaillard et al. (2010).
41.   Frontex (2020).
42.   See Nehammer et al. (2021).
43.   Eurostat (2021a).
44.   Berchin et al. (2017).
45.   Cheikh Ali et al. (2012).
46.   UNHCR (2012).
47.   See Moraga and Rapoport (2015); Schuck (1997).
48.   See Jones and Teytelboym (2017).

7. The superpower that wasn't

Remember predictions of the EU's rise to geopolitical prominence? "Europeans [...] have been developing a new kind of power that cannot be measured in terms of military budgets or smart-missile technology," Mark Leonard wrote in 2005.[1] "It works in the long term, and is about reshaping the world rather than winning short-term tussles. And when we stop looking at the world through American eyes, we can see that each element of European 'weakness' is in fact a facet of its extraordinary transformative power."

More than anything, the sanguine forecasts from the late 1990s and the early 2000s appear today as artifacts of America's 'unipolar moment.' As long as the United States acted as the unquestioned guarantor of the continent's security, Europeans themselves faced notably few security threats or sources of regional instability. In a benign global environment, the idea of a looming European century driven by soft power, progress, and a global spread of liberal and democratic values may have seemed plausible. Yet, with Russia's invasion of Ukraine in 2014 and 2022, conflicts in the Middle East and North Africa that fueled chaotic waves of migration to Europe, emergence of China as a revisionist power, and intermittent tensions in the transatlantic partnership, the idyll is decidedly over. The election of Donald Trump as U.S. president was just one of several rude awakenings. The blustering reality TV show host had nothing but disdain for the transatlantic partnership, including for NATO, which he called "obsolete." He berated European allies for "owing vast sums of money" for U.S. protection,[2] as if the postwar bedrock of European security had been a protection racket. As a candidate, he lent his support to the cause of Brexit, unmoved by the fact that doing so was tantamount to cheering for European disintegration. Instead of pursuing deeper economic ties with the EU – as envisaged by the Transatlantic Trade and Investment Partnership, scrapped in Trump's early days in office – Trump imposed tariffs on European exports including steel and aluminium, prompting European retaliation.[3]

The new, more dangerous period that Europe faces has exposed the hollowness of the earlier, puffed up rhetoric about the EU as a qualitatively new model of conducting international politics. "The era in which we could fully rely on others is over," German Chancellor Angela Merkel told her German supporters in 2017 after a tense G7 summit, dominated by Trump's mercurial presence, recognizing that Europe's soft, slowly transformative power had worked only in conjunction with America's hard power.[4] As she introduced her

Commission to the European Parliament in 2019, the incoming EC president, Ursula von der Leyen, promised that Europeans were about to take on a much more significant role in the world: "The world needs our leadership more than ever. To keep engaging with the world as a responsible power. To be a force for peace and for positive change."[5] In 2019, French president Emmanuel Macron called NATO "brain dead" due to American indifference.[6] Of course, the refrain of European 'strategic autonomy,' or the idea of the continent as a cohesive actor independent from Washington, is an old one. France, as one of the few continental European powers with significant military capabilities and a semi-plausible claim to great power status has long harbored an ambivalent attitude toward the post-World War II settlement in Europe, which was organized around America's military might and its commitment to the continent's security. During Charles de Gaulle's presidency, France gradually withdrew its forces from NATO's joint command in the 1960s – a situation that lasted effectively until the Strasbourg summit of 2009.

Yet, the Europeans' rhetorical flourishes have been rarely matched by concrete deliverables, which are always somehow awaiting in the future. "The aftermath of Afghanistan will accelerate the agenda of *strategic autonomy* with everything that it entails," Macron opined after the U.S. withdrawal.[7] "2022 will be the year of European defence," the European Council's president Charles Michel pledged in October 2021. If that happens to be the case, it will have been a result of Russia's wholesale invasion of Ukraine, which provided a wake-up call to European governments to start taking their security seriously, rather than of earlier European initiatives. To be sure, the EU was quick to introduce an unprecedented sanctions regime against Russia, in coordination with allies, and the German Chancellor Olaf Scholz vowed to increase his country's defense spending to meet NATO's 2 percent target.[8] Yet, it remains to be seen whether the sudden display of European, and of Western, unity in the face of Russian aggression proves durable. Shocking as Russian aggression seems, it has not altered the fundamentals of the EU's decision-making and power relations. Speaking days after the beginning of Russian operations, the High Representative for Foreign Affairs and Security Policy Josep Borrell vowed that the EU would provide Ukraine with fighter jets to strengthen its air defenses.[9] However, the EU does not have any fighter jets of its own – the member states do. And while some member states were eager to provide their equipment to the Ukrainians, most notably Poland, the efforts collapsed as the Biden administration refused to back the effort. Proceeding without the support of other allies – most notably the United States but also other EU countries – would risk singling out Poland for possible retaliation by Russia without a clear understanding that either NATO or the EU would stand by its side. While a number of actors can be blamed for this failure, it remains an illustration of the disconnect between the EU's aspirations and its limited means.

The formal groundwork for the EU's putative rise as a world superpower was laid down a long time ago. Since the Lisbon Treaty, the EU has had its own 'foreign minister' and a dedicated foreign service. The EU has also hinted at building shared defense capabilities. In 2017, 25 member states (other than Denmark and Malta) founded the Permanent Structured Cooperation in the Area of Defence and Security (PESCO), followed by the creation of a European Defence Fund (EDF) endowed with a modest budget of close to €8 billion for the period 2021–27.[10] None of these changes have made much substantive difference, however. National militaries continue to be underfunded and a European one remains a pipe dream, notwithstanding the momentum provided by Russian aggression in 2022. The efforts to build up the EU's own diplomatic capacities also coincided with a sequence of internal crises: the debt crisis in the Eurozone, the refugee crisis, the U.K.'s decision to leave, as well as the Covid-19 pandemic. As a result, not only have foreign policy questions been displaced by other more pressing matters pertaining most frequently to the economy, but also the tenor of European foreign policy conversations, especially at the level of the Council, has been overwhelmingly one of constant firefighting and addressing internal emergencies – at the expense of longer-term, outward-looking, and strategic thinking.[11] On the diplomatic front, the EU's High Representatives for Foreign Affairs and Security Policy have been recruited from lower tiers of European politics, reflecting lowest-common-denominator compromises rather than imaginative efforts at European leadership. The first of its 'foreign ministers,' Catherine Ashton, worked for the Campaign for Nuclear Disarmament in the U.K. during the Cold War and served in several, relatively minor government roles under Prime Minister Tony Blair – before becoming the Labour leader in the House of Lords and later European Commissioner. Her successor, Federica Mogherini, a member of the Italian Communist Youth Federation in her early years, was a member of the European Parliament and later Italian Parliament, and then served less than a year as Italy's foreign minister before being catapulted to the position of the EU's top diplomat. The current High Representative Josep Borrell was Spain's foreign minister, leader of the opposition, and president of the European Parliament for half a term. A unitary executive with a recognized leadership and a political mandate to make foreign and security policy in real time seems like an obvious precondition for the EU to emerge as a coherent geopolitical player. However, that option remains outside the realm of possibility because of the EU's underlying diversity and disagreements on what are highly sensitive and politically salient matters. Neither the High Representative and their EEAS apparatus nor the Commission have the mandate to make such decisions on behalf of all member states. Unlike national governments, they also lack control over significant policy resources. Instead of decisive leadership at the top, European positions on matters related to foreign policy are crafted painstakingly through compromises between foreign ministers or leaders of individual countries, which carry the veto power over any EU decisions in this domain.

A FECKLESS GIANT IN TEMPESTUOUS TIMES

That has an obvious downside. Even in emergencies, the EU's joint action has been often slow and diluted to the point of irrelevance. The aftermath of Belarus' fraudulent presidential election in August 2020 provides one illustration. The initial reaction from High Representative Josep Borrell and Enlargement Commissioner Oliver Várhelyi criticized the regime's crackdown against the opposition and expressed the expectation (unrealistic by that point) that votes would be counted accurately.[12] Later, speaking on behalf of the Council, the High Representative stated that Lukashenko's new presidential mandate lacked democratic legitimacy and called for a new election.[13] However, any concrete action was blocked for weeks by Cyprus. Only on October 1, 2020 did the EU introduce the first round of sanctions – which were later escalated in the light of the regime's intensifying repression.[14] In May 2021, the Lukashenko regime used a fighter jet to hijack a Ryanair flight connecting two EU capitals, Athens and Vilnius. Short of actual war, this represented the most blatant use of hard power against the EU in years. While some praised the EU's supposedly swift reaction – simply a function of a fortuitous timing of its Council meeting the day after the hijacking – the response was minimalistic.[15] It called for an "international investigation" and promised to deploy additional sanctions, to be tailored by the Commission and adopted by the Council of the EU at a later stage, without even considering the wide range of escalatory moves that the EU could have easily deployed at very little cost to itself. Those included a comprehensive trade and investment embargo, perhaps, or working with the United States to cut Belarusian banks off SWIFT, the standardized system of transactions between banks worldwide, and seeking to exclude the regime from the UN's International Civil Aviation Organization.

The Europeans' unwillingness to respond *disproportionately* to acts of aggression and other violations of international norms meant that no effective deterrence was established. The costs of EU sanctions for Lukashenko's regime were perfectly predictable and had been surely factored in as the Belarussian dictator was making his decision. Furthermore, the EU's decision to disregard the obvious role played by the Kremlin in the brazen act also allowed Moscow to move first by banning EU flights that are avoiding Belarusian airspace,[16] placing the EU again into a position of a second mover instead of being the one to set the terms of engagement. Later in 2021, Lukashenko's regime orchestrated a migration crisis on the country's border with Lithuania and

Poland. Calibrated carefully to use immigration as a wedge issue dividing the EU, Belarus recruited thousands of prospective migrants in the Middle East, particularly in Northern Iraq, and arranged for their transport to the Polish or Lithuanian border – oftentimes coercing them into illegal border crossing attempts.[17] In December of 2021, the EU responded by imposing trivial sanctions on Belarusian political officials, high-ranking judges, and propagandists, as well as individuals and entities involved in human trafficking: altogether 17 individuals and 11 organizations.[18] The far-reaching sanctions adopted by the EU in the wake of Russia's invasion of Ukraine in February 2022[19] were hailed by many as a dramatic turning point, signaling a more forceful European posture against Russian and, by extension, Belarusian revanchism. Notwithstanding the applause that the move attracted, it was not a sign of policy success. Quite the contrary; the need to impose sanctions was a result of the EU's previous *failure* to deter Putin's regime – either because the Kremlin had been determined to attack regardless of the threat of European sanctions or because the West had not been clear in communicating just how far it had been willing to go in response to Russia's aggression. Moreover, the Russian economy and its public finances had adapted successfully to earlier waves of sanctions, largely due to a conservative fiscal policy resulting in dramatic accumulation of foreign exchange reserves. With oil and gas revenue still flowing into the regime's pockets and with workarounds inevitably developed with Chinese assistance, the overall impact of the sanctions is bound to be smaller than the self-congratulatory tone from the West suggests.

A similar pattern of sleepwalking into predictable crises and not responding in real time with effective tools characterizes the EU's engagement with other regions of the world, only occasionally punctured by successful initiatives by individual member states or their coalitions, as with the 2011 bombing campaign in Libya,[20] or the Merkel-negotiated agreement with Turkey which halted migration along the Eastern Mediterranean route in 2016. More often than not, Europeans are left on the back foot, reacting late to decisions made by others instead of advancing any coherent, strategically minded agenda of their own. The 2021 withdrawal from Afghanistan provides another example. The decision made by the Biden administration was unilateral in character and took Europeans by surprise – notwithstanding the president's insistence on America's departure as well as continuity on the matter between Biden and Trump. Europeans were understandably aggravated – yet they also followed America to exit instead of stepping up themselves, missing an opportunity for the EU to fill the void. The reconstruction of Afghanistan and keeping the country secure, after all, were as much a European project as it was an American one. For example, 150,000 German troops served in the country and 59 of them died – in addition to at least €12.5 billion of costs underwritten by the German taxpayer.[21] France had lost 88 troops before it wound down its presence in 2012,[22] while 44 Polish troops were killed. Although the plan to withdraw U.S. troops had long been known and shared by both presidents Trump and Biden, Europeans had shown little interest in trying to either fill the void created by the departure of what was then a small American contingent, or in seeking to stabilize the situation.

On the weekend of Kabul's downfall, High Representative Borrell was tweeting about a plethora of subjects unrelated to Afghanistan, including the G20 meeting and North Macedonia.[23] Only during the following week, when presented with a new fait accompli in Afghanistan, did the foreign ministers and the High Representative issue a statement which expressed a general sense of "support to the Afghan people and to democracy, good governance, human rights and social and economic development in the country, including efforts to prevent and manage the risks associated with an unstable Afghanistan in continued conflict, resulting in regional instability, drug trafficking and uncontrolled irregular migration" – without providing any details about how such goals were going to be met.[24] This was followed by another vacuous statement following the meeting of the ministers of home affairs on August 31, 2021, in which concern was expressed about the repercussions of the Taliban's takeover on "international protection, migration and security" – again, without articulating what was to be done on the EU's part, if anything.[25]

As another case of the EU's toothlessness, consider its reaction to the autocratic takeover in Tunisia. Tunisia was long the lone success story of the Arab Spring, delicately nurturing a parliamentary democracy reconciling secular constitutionalism with conservative, Islamist political impulses – until the summer of 2021. Assisted by the military, the country's president Kais Saied suspended parliament for 30 days, dismissed the prime minister, and started arresting opposition figures.[26] The EU's response was limited to a five-sentence statement about the importance of "preserving democracy and stability in the country," without any indication of the bloc's next steps unless what currently looks like a coup is reversed by constitutional means.[27] "We cannot go any further at this juncture," according to the spokesperson of the EU's High Representative for foreign policy Josep Borrell.[28]

Most new democracies of the Middle East and North Africa died before they had a chance to take their first breath. Tunisia was an exception, and its success seems firmly in the European interest, as the destabilizing counterfactual of failed states in Libya and Syria shows. Instead of a 'Marshall Plan' for the Middle East,[29] Tunisia has received over €2 billion from the EU since 2011[30] – a modest though not a trivial amount for an economy with an annual GDP of less than €35 billion. Yet, Brussels was slow to deploy other policy tools, such as trade and visa liberalization, technical assistance with economic reforms or better targeted funding for the country's civil society, journalism, and higher education. It took the EU until 2016 to start negotiations with Tunisia over a prospective deep and comprehensive free trade agreement.[31] Alas, those talks were abandoned in 2019, both due to pressures within Tunisian politics and a lack of appetite in Brussels.[32] With the EU's high tariffs on agricultural imports and Tunisia's persistent rural poverty, an opportunity was lost not only to bring Tunisia closer economically to the West but also to show that democratic governance can deliver tangible material benefits. The sad outcome of Tunisia's story and the EU's quiet acceptance that the return on its investment into promoting democracy and good governance has been lost does not bode well for the EU as an effective advocate of its own interests.

WHERE YOU SIT IS WHERE YOU STAND

The central reason for such fiascos is the same as the reason why the talk of the EU's 'sovereignty' or 'strategic autonomy' continues to ring hollow: the differences between European countries in their strategic outlooks and perceptions of their security environments. Those were already apparent during the time of the U.S.-led war in Iraq, which pitted 'old' member states against 'new Europe,' as the late Donald Rumsfeld, then U.S. Secretary of Defense, put it.[33] Unlike most Western European governments, Poland, the Czech Republic, and other post-communist countries on the eve of their accession did not hesitate to join the American coalition. This led to pushback, including from France's President Jacques Chirac, who dismissed Central and Eastern European support for the U.S. initiative as "not well brought-up behaviour," adding that the governments "missed a good opportunity to keep quiet."[34] It was Chirac's outburst, however, that missed a deeper point. Only few in the region shared the earnestness of the Czech president Václav Havel who alluded in his discussions about the U.S.-led intervention with President George W. Bush to "the Czech pre-war experience. Had the world confronted Germany early, millions of lives could have been saved."[35] For others, the decision to join the U.S. coalition reflected the understanding that the security of post-communist countries – primarily from a future Russian threat – hinged on America's, rather than France's or Germany's, willingness to defend the region and invest in credible deterrence. "Poland did not send a brigade to fight in the ill-conceived war in Iraq out of fear of weapons of mass destruction there," the country's former defense and foreign minister Radosław Sikorski wrote retrospectively.

> We did not send another brigade to Afghanistan in response to the September 11 attacks because we feared that the Taliban will come to Warsaw and enslave our girls. I did not sign the agreement for a US missile defence system site on Polish soil because I feared that Iran might attack us. We do not buy F-16s from Lockheed Martin, airliners from Boeing or missiles from Raytheon because they are necessarily better than European alternatives. *We did all of that because successive Polish leaders are invested in the US security guarantee.*[36]

Western European elites cheered on the election of Barack Obama. The cerebral figure of the first African American president was seen as a guarantee of a constructive future for the transatlantic partnership, damaged by the war in Iraq and America's supposed 'unilateralism.' Eastern European leaders, in contrast, were prescient about the dangers of the Obama administration's 'reset' of U.S.–Russia relations and its 'pivot to Asia.' A few months before the U.S. election of 2008, Russia's war against Georgia foreboded the much bigger regional wars that Putin's regime would eventually unleash. The prospect of restored Russian domination, dismissed in Western European capitals as mere post-Soviet paranoia, was integral to the strategic outlook cultivated not only by the Kremlin but also by Russian elites. If successful, the revanchism would end Europe's post-1991 settlement, based on rules and the principle of national self-determination. This early episode prompted little response from the Bush administration, dragging through its final months. By the time President Obama took office, it had been largely forgotten in most Western capitals. Yet, "the political impact of that war on the region has already been felt," senior statesmen and diplomats from Eastern Europe, including former president Havel, wrote to President Obama.

> Many countries were deeply disturbed to see the Atlantic alliance stand by as Russia violated the core principles of the Helsinki Final Act, the Charter of Paris, and the territorial integrity of a country that was a member of NATO's Partnership for Peace and the Euroatlantic Partnership Council – all in the name of defending a sphere of influence on its borders.[37]

Eastern Europeans had good reasons to expect that the looming 'pivot to Asia' would mean a lessened focus on security of the European continent. Indeed, the new U.S. administration scrapped earlier plans for a missile defense shield in Poland and the Czech Republic.[38] The 'borderlands' between Russia and Western Europe never became a priority for the Obama administration, which resulted in frequent cycles of disappointment, reversed partly only during the Trump years with the strengthening of the U.S. military presence in Poland and in the Baltic States – his own bashing of NATO and affinity toward Vladimir Putin notwithstanding.

Until Russia's invasion of Ukraine in 2022, Western Europeans and Americans alike had little patience for the sense of existential dread that undergirded, say, the Polish and Estonian perceptions of Putin's Russia and of the vital role played by the transatlantic partnership. By the time the specter of a revisionist Kremlin started to preoccupy policymakers in Western European capitals (and indeed in Washington), it was too late. While predictable and fully in line with Putin's previous anti-Ukrainian escalation,[39] both the EU and the Obama administration were caught off guard by Russia's annexation of Crimea and its attack on Eastern Ukraine in 2014. The brazen action led eventually to the imposition of a durable yet modest sanction regime against Russia. The West thus achieved a freezing of the conflict and de facto acquiescence to Russia's illegal occupation of Crimea. The unrealistic agreements from Minsk provided the Kremlin – assisted by the West – with additional leverage over successive Ukrainian governments. For eight years, Russia's war against Ukraine, always below the threshold of a full-fledged military campaign, accompanied by various forms of hybrid warfare against the West – from disinformation campaigns to state-sponsored terror attacks and poisonings – was not enough to break through the blasé and transactional attitude toward Moscow dominating in the West. Prior to the 2022 invasion, the German–Russian Nord Stream 2 project was moving ahead shepherded by successive German governments in spite of sanctions imposed by the Trump administration and the protests of post-communist countries, culminating in a U.S.–German deal struck by the Biden administration over the heads of Eastern Europeans. In a prescient opinion piece in the *Frankfurter Allgemeine Zeitung*, the Polish foreign minister Zbigniew Rau described the pipeline as yet another iteration of the imperial power politics of the past, which the EU was supposed to end. In reality, Putin's pitch to German elites is for a "German-dominated European Union to become part of a broader community together with the Russian-dominated Eurasian Union," without much regard for countries on the EU's eastern flank, which were at risk of being left vulnerable to Russian extortion.[40] In the weeks leading to Russia's invasion of Ukraine, faced with the Kremlin's military build-up, Western Europeans were more concerned about the possible fallout from additional economic sanctions, such as cutting off Russia's access to SWIFT, the international bank settlement mechanism, than about the risks of a large-scale war to their east.[41] Germany's defense minister, Christine Lambrecht, for example, warned against "dragging" the Nord Stream 2 pipeline "into this conflict."[42]

While it is hard to see how Putin could not have been encouraged and emboldened by Western hesitations and displays of weakness, the subject of Russia did not always pit the 'old' member states against the 'new' ones. The Nordic countries and the U.K. were long alarmed by the Kremlin's belligerence in early 2022 and spearheaded efforts to provide aid to Ukraine. Conversely, in a 2020 Pew poll, 60 percent of Slovaks and 73 percent of Bulgarians saw Russia favorably – the highest share in the world.[43] One country has stood out even more: Hungary. The Orbán government's deteriorating relations with Ukraine has placed it at odds with most of its NATO allies and European partners. In 2014, after Russia had cut off natural gas supplies to Ukraine, Hungary followed suit, notwithstanding the EU's concerted efforts to provide Ukraine with energy.[44] Hungary's government also opposed Ukraine's participation at the NATO summit in Brussels in July of 2018.[45] Days before Russia's invasion in February of 2022, Viktor Orbán traveled to Moscow to implore Vladimir Putin for an increase in natural gas supplies and to finalize plans to produce the Russian Sputnik V vaccine in Hungary. In 2019, furthermore, the government of Hungary concluded an agreement with the International Investment Bank (IIB), a relic of the Cold War era currently based in Moscow, to move its headquarters to Budapest and grant the largely Russian operation privileges and immunities that are extended to international organizations, including the right to bring all "advisors and experts acting in the Bank's interest" to enter Hungary – and therefore the Schengen Area – potentially circumventing the EU's travel bans against representatives of Putin's regime.[46]

The EU is coping with similar internal divisions when it comes to China. Having experienced Beijing's bullying at first hand, the Czech Republic and Lithuania may be extremely wary of China's growing influence in Europe. Following its outreach to Taiwan, Lithuania has faced a de facto trade embargo from Beijing (the country is missing as a clearance option in Chinese customs), without European institutions retaliating for what was a clearly discriminatory move in the EU–China trade relationship. In Berlin and Paris, meanwhile, policymakers have been seeking to compartmentalize different facets of the EU–China relationship – from potentially cooperative ones such as on trade questions or on climate change to more contentious issues of Chinese human rights abuses, intellectual property theft, or cyber-attacks. Accordingly, the EU's strategic documents over China refer to it, simultaneously, as a "negotiating partner," a "competitor," and a "systemic rival." The dividing line, once again, does not necessarily run neatly between 'old' and 'new' member states. Rather, it is a subject of constant contestation both across and within member states. Tellingly, Orbán's Hungary also serves as an outpost of Chinese influence in Europe, regularly blocking any EU initiatives aiming to hold Beijing accountable, most prominently for its crackdown in Hong Kong in 2020.[47] Orbán called Hungary a "pillar" of the Belt and Road Initiative (BRI).[48] The Initiative's most tangible manifestation to date has been the Chinese-funded construction of a new railway connection between Budapest and Belgrade, ostentatiously built to better connect Greek ports bringing in Chinese exports with European markets. Details of the contract, worth $1.9 billion, were classified.[49]

SLOGANS OR COOPERATION?

A divergence of interests and views does not have to prevent cooperation. For example, the Czech Republic has counted among the most active countries involved in the French-led counterterrorism operations in the Sahel and in stabilizing and rebuilding the region – in spite of the fact that concerns over the Sahel are hardly at the top of the Czech Republic's security agenda.[50] It is the insistence on common European positions that has a paralyzing effect on the bloc, and leads to belated and watered-down policies. The requirement of unanimity leads to difficult processes of bargaining and compromising while neither the EEAS nor the European Commission nor the figure of the High Representative are in a position to transcend the disagreements. The set-up also encourages larger member states to go over the heads of smaller ones and seek to present them with fait accomplis. That was the route taken by Berlin and Paris in the EU negotiations with China over a CAI, signed just weeks before President Joe Biden's arrival in office and then defeated in the European Parliament.

As a result, in contrast to the lofty rhetoric of European 'sovereignty' or 'strategic autonomy,' the reality of a common European foreign and security policy often underwhelms. From the perspective of national governments, EU-wide solutions are desirable when they amplify their influence in the pursuit of their own goals – hence the German backing of CAI with China. However, when a European solution rubs against the grain of national interests (say, scrapping the project of Nord Stream 2 for the sake of Europe's energy security and the integrity of the single energy market – yet at an economic cost to Germany) even the most vocal pro-European leaders go silent. If nation states and their oftentimes divergent interests remain the prime movers of the EU's foreign policy, the question is how those interests can be managed, coordinated, and harnessed in constructive ways, instead of becoming a cacophony of ad hoc fixes, cynical deals, and dissonant rhetoric of European unity.

The status quo presents real risks for the EU, as it invites outside actors such as Russia and China to pursue a divide-and-conquer strategy: co-opting some member governments and counting on the resulting paralysis of the Council to fail to respond to actions inimical to the EU's interests. But there is no top-down fix to the problem. Not even a shift to QMV on matters of foreign policy would act as a silver bullet. Its advocates are correct to point out that by turning every government into a veto player, unanimity sets a bar far too high for the EU to be a nimble and determined global player.[51] The extension of QMV to foreign policy questions, furthermore, is possible without a change to the Treaties by using Article 31 (3) of the *Lisbon Treaty* (one of its 'passerelle clauses').[52] Yet, abandoning unanimity would not be without its dangers. Since foreign and security policy are the core functions of any government, the prospect of being outvoted on such matters is unattractive to European governments – particularly smaller ones, aware of their own fragility. After the catastrophic fiasco of the use of QMV to adopt relocation quotas and in light of the erosion of trust between member states, such a reform – even if it were politically feasible – would risk speeding up the EU's hollowing out, with more countries defying the EU's decisions and perhaps even contemplating exit after being railroaded on issues of vital national interest. There is a possible way around the problem: to accompany the reform, which would require the agreement of all member states, with an explicit list of questions that would remain being governed by unanimity. National governments could thus enumerate specific issues on which they could not be outvoted, whether they have to do with legacies of historical border disputes, status of ethnic minorities, or other subjects – allowing, however, QMV to be used to decide other issues of foreign policy.

The problem with such a bargain is at least threefold. One, in the same 'passerelle clause,' the Lisbon Treaty states that military and defense questions cannot be subject to QMV, thus relegating questions of hard power outside of the scope of any reform conceivable within the framework of existing treaties. More fundamentally, moreover, in a world characterized by change and uncertainty, it might not be possible to enumerate, in advance, all the sensitive subjects which ought to be governed by unanimity. At the time of the Lisbon Treaty's ratification, it was difficult to imagine a crisis situation in which QMV would be applied to home and justice affairs to adopt a reset-tlement quota system vociferously opposed and de facto derailed by a subset of member states. Third and relatedly, Article 31 (2) gives governments an emergency break through which "for vital and stated reasons of national policy" any government can block a QMV decision on a question that has been derogated from unanimity to QMV voting under the 'passerelle clause.' Once again, barring a change of the Treaty – which would again require unanimous ratification across member states – a conceivable QMV regime on foreign policy questions cannot be made credible as it would always be subject to veto by any member state.

If, in contrast, disagreement is seen as a permanent feature, not as a bug of the EU's foreign policy, then efforts to eliminate it through clever reforms of the decision-making process are futile. Instead of yearning for a coherent European foreign policy, the EU should be seen as a springboard for devel-oping horizontal relationships between member states, which take initiative on matters that are salient to them instead of waiting for the emergence of shared, lowest-common-denominator solutions. Even with Cyprus stalling the EU's action on Belarus, for example, the remaining 26 member states could have responded to Lukashenko's fraudulent election at a time when doing so could have made a difference to the outcome of public protests in the country. Similarly, in the winter of 2021–22 it was vitally important that Eastern European member states worked alongside Ukraine, the United States, and other actors (most notably the United Kingdom) to increase the costs to the Kremlin's belligerence against Ukraine, instead of waiting for a grand European compromise.

PESCO, counting 25 of the EU's 27 members, is in fact an example of a horizontal, polycentric initiative that fits into a decentralized vision of the

EU, rather than a top-down effort at European sovereignty. The informal Three Seas Initiative, with its 12 members sharing concerns over Russia's influence and seeking to strengthen their ties with the United States, is another. Similarly, though more controversially, the strategic partnership concluded between France and Greece in September 2021 through which the Greek government committed to the purchase of three French frigates – following a sizeable purchase of French fighter jets earlier – is yet another example. Of course, the main purpose of the pact is to extend, in some form, French security guarantees to Greece, which finds itself in an adversarial position relative to Turkey. Of course, France, Greece, and Turkey are NATO member states, which makes the alliance of the two against the other highly ironic. However, the arrangement, like the previous ones, simply reflects the fact that the interests of some EU, or indeed NATO, members are aligned more closely than others.

In international politics, an old 'realist' adage says there are no permanent enemies and no permanent friends, only permanent interests. One does not have to embrace foreign policy realism to see that neither the EU nor NATO are permanent and immutable expressions of European, or Western, values and allegiances. The changing membership base of both organizations and the dramatic transformation of the world relative to the time of their inceptions both belie such essentialist interpretations. That renders neither of them obsolete or irrelevant, as some would argue. Yet, it does mean that both organizations will continue to feature shifting coalitions of members involved in cooperative and less-than-cooperative behaviors in the pursuit of their interests. It also means that, at times, tight cooperation is necessary with non-members of both organizations. Notwithstanding its departure from the EU, the U.K. continues to play an important role in maintaining European security, particularly on its Eastern flank, where British troops are part of NATO's rotation under the Enhanced Forward Presence. Norway is another non-member whose geopolitical interests are closely aligned with those of many EU member states, particularly in its concerns over Russia's regime.

The mismatch between the static nature of both the EU and NATO and the shifting geopolitical landscapes means that there will be disagreements, if not outright conflicts, between member states on matters of foreign policy and security. The EU's ambition cannot be to eliminate such disagreements and conflicts – a positively utopian aspiration – but to manage them in constructive ways. It is, for example, conceivable that different countries will choose different forms of relationships with the United States and the Anglosphere. For France, the desire for a degree of autonomy appears to be an overriding principle. In Germany, notwithstanding the change brought about by Russia's invasion of Ukraine, Atlanticism has been an important part of its security architecture. For the countries of Central and Eastern Europe, America's security guarantees are vital and the prospect of hypothetical European defense capabilities, controlled by the EU as a whole, remains a very inadequate substitute. The role of the EU should thus be the facilitation of effective strategic dialog between member states for which there has been very little time and space in recent years. The aim should be to define the EU's interests in very broad, consensual terms, thus identifying areas of foreign and security policy in which the EU is capable of acting as a whole, and to draw clear red lines, which coalitions of member states (and non-members) would not be allowed to cross. There already are tenets of EU law, particularly of the single market, that have implications for the EU's posture toward players such as China or Russia. A proposal is in the works to beef up the Commission's capacity to crack down on state aid, not only to EU companies operating in the single market, but also to foreign companies, receiving support from foreign governments.[53] Simultaneously, the role of the High Representative and of the EEAS needs clarification in order to prevent them from acting as substitutes for national diplomatic efforts on subjects on which they lack explicit mandates and where their initiative is not welcome. Perhaps more importantly, the EEAS and the Commission have a role to play in preventing particularly the big member states or their coalitions from pretending to act on behalf of all the EU, over the heads of smaller members, in situations when EU-wide consensus is lacking.

AFTER EUROPEAN ILLUSIONS

Until recently, the decades of life under the U.S. security umbrella appeared to Western Europeans as natural as the water that they were drinking and the air that they were breathing. Not expending scarce resources on hard power and not having to make difficult choices over deterrence, military intervention overseas, and war, were not understood as privileges of living in a world in which geopolitical heavy lifting was relegated to Washington. Rather, they were seen as a sign of European moral sophistication and a new, better way of managing global affairs.[54] For that reason, Trump's presidency with its reminders for Europe to "pay its share" did not prompt action that would be warranted by the timely if rude wake-up call but rather served as an opportunity for rhetorical grandstanding, contrasting Trump's version of crude, egotistical realpolitik against Europe's mature and principled embrace of a rules-based international order.

Several national governments, however, did get Trump's message. As of 2021, Croatia, France, Greece, Poland, Romania, and the Baltic States met the 2 percent spending target, as did Norway and the United Kingdom, both outside the EU[55] – and more are expected to do so as well after Russia's invasion of Ukraine in 2022. True, the need to build defense capacity has been often eclipsed by the quintessentially European debate about building EU-centric defense and military capabilities and thus pushing the integration project forward. In the end, however, instead of creating the basis for pan-European military structures, both PESCO and EDF serve as platforms for ad hoc defense – and military-related projects – common training, evaluation, simulation facilities, and the development of a European drone and a new generation of European attack helicopters. Perhaps the most consequential among those is the Military Mobility project, also known as 'military Schengen,' which seeks to simplify bureaucratic and other procedures surrounding the movement of allied troops and military equipment throughout EU countries in order to increase readiness. Another is the Crisis Response Operation Core, which involves a cataloging of national forces that can be put at the EU's disposal in emergency situations.

As it currently stands, PESCO provides a platform for horizontal, polycentric cooperation between EU governments. Not all PESCO members participate in all projects, while some non-EU countries take part in some of them. While potentially useful, it is also obviously self-limiting, particularly if it continues to be seen by European policymakers as a stepping stone toward a putative 'European army.' European governments are nowhere near willing to unconditionally pool their military resources and give up control over them. While successful projects can deepen trust and lead to more cooperation in the future, differences of interests, opinions, and strategic culture between member states remain real – hence PESCO's tentativeness and the scattered participation of countries in different PESCO projects. For that reason, the expectation that PESCO could be a precursor to a genuine European military force is fanciful. An overemphasis on PESCO risks exacerbating the collective action problem involved in efforts to boost the defense budgets of European countries both to make them more meaningful contributors to NATO's system of collective defense and to help Europe take on a greater role, in case the United States continues to shift its attention elsewhere. This is particularly true if the EU's officialdom leans too heavily into the initiative as a distinctly *European* project, as opposed to one that remains owned and managed by member states themselves. Given that national defense spending has steep political opportunity costs, the EU-wide initiative can serve as a cover for national politicians who are not willing to invest in their national capabilities and shift the responsibility to the EU level, where the momentum needed for big budget increases is unlikely to ever materialize.

The disconnect between the EU's ambitions as a global player and its ability to deliver is not only a result of a lack of capacity. Given the continent's formidable economic resources, Europeans are in a comfortable position to invest jointly or individually in planes, ships, tanks, drones, nuclear deterrent, or any other military hardware, if they so choose. What is harder to overcome is the EU's distinct ideological outlook, rooted in the self-understanding of the EU as a project aimed at superseding the international conflict and atavism of the past with a rules-based system of cooperation. There is, once again, an odd paradox in the Europeans' perception of U.S. foreign policy, as practiced by neoconservatives and liberal internationalists, as ideologically driven – in contrast to seeing the EU's own posture as transcending both crude power politics and ideological divides through its forward-looking pragmatism. In fact, it is the EU's foreign policy that remains heavily ideological. Since its founding, the aim of the European project was not just about addressing European problems and delivering European public goods. Rather, it was conceived as a universalist, civilizing project. Likewise, the EU's enlargements can be seen not simply as pragmatic (and largely successful) responses to new geopolitical circumstances at the end of the Cold War, but primarily as a way of exporting European norms and politics: turning the rest of the world into a version of peaceful, law-abiding, and prosperous postwar Europe, while forgetting the contingent nature of the latter. Of course, much of the success of those endeavors was driven by the fact that the truly difficult decisions over security and defense of the European continent were held firmly in the hands of the United States.

To a large extent, that model has exhausted itself. For one, it was predicated on a role that the United States may not be willing to play indefinitely. It also rested on a high degree of European self-confidence – about the functioning of the EU and its ability to accommodate new members and about the universal character of Europe's version of democratic capitalism. For a variety of reasons, that self-confidence has been shaken both in the EU and elsewhere in the world. What results is an unsteady mix of self-interest and toothless, universalist rhetoric. In many areas, the penchant for universal abstractions asserts itself in the form of an excessive weight attributed to multilateralism and a quest for carving a "European role," typically within abstract and nebulous schemes – such as fighting against climate change, or 'connectivity.' Yet, when they want to and are given space to do so by national governments, European institutions are able to show ruthlessness in protecting their interests by setting inflexible, rules-based, red lines around access to the single market in its Brexit negotiations with the U.K. – or in their dealings with Switzerland.[56] Oddly, similar ruthlessness and insistence on red lines were too often absent in its dealings with real adversaries, such as China or Russia, especially at times when following through would require bearing real costs.

The ideological mantra of multilateralism and of the EU as a vehicle for a new, qualitatively different form of international governance eclipses strategic conversations about subjects such as Iran or climate change. The EU embraced the Joint Comprehensive Plan of Action, spearheaded by the Obama administration, even when it was clear that the agreement gave Iran leeway to destabilize its neighborhood – with adverse consequences for the EU itself. It has also taken as a given that the only solution to climate change lies in collective action at the global level, hence the extraordinary significance attributed to climate summitry and to formal pledges to reduce carbon emissions. The problem, however, is that global collective action is a utopian idea that may have once seemed plausible but was conclusively discredited with the failure of the Copenhagen Climate Change Conference in 2009, which failed to produce binding commitment to reducing emissions. Furthermore, policies that can be effective in either curbing the growth in emissions (carbon taxes, public investment into nuclear energy, or R&D aimed at making renewable energy cost competitive) or in responding to the damage that climate change entails (improved water management and anti-flood infrastructure, improving agricultural practices in affected countries, etc.) are highly localized and diverse.

Even when confronted with the long-term strategic challenge of China, the EU's instinct is to frame its response in abstract, conceptual terms – rather than as a matter of geopolitics and power. "Sustainable, comprehensive and rules-based connectivity will contribute to the enhanced prosperity, safety and resilience of people and societies in Europe and Asia," the EU characterizes its 'connectivity agenda' – an effort to build an alternative to China's BRI. The problem with such a sanitized framing, of course, is that it obfuscates the true goal of the project, which is to confront China and push back against its influence in countries that might otherwise be tempted to join Beijing by using economic means. Without being explicit about the goals, the toolbox used to attain those goals, and metrics of success, it becomes impossible to assess the project's effectiveness and to sell it politically.

DO NOT THROW OUT THE BABY WITH THE BATHWATER

The idea that multilateralism, diplomacy, and rules are intrinsically valuable seems to be integral to the EU's self-understanding as a project of historical progress. A world that would adopt European norms and rely on rules and multilateral forums to sort out conflicts would certainly be a safer, freer, and more prosperous one. But such a world is also fundamentally out of reach. Understanding that there are limits to the transformative power of "Eutopia"[57] in shaping geopolitical outcomes in Europe's neighborhood, however, should not be tantamount to giving up on enlargements as a tool of the EU's foreign policy, even if it might require taking a more nuanced and more flexible approach to it. Critics of future enlargements, such as President Macron, who refused to open accession negotiations with North Macedonia and Albania in 2019, do have a point in comparing the EU to a poorly managed house in which some residents refuse to fix the lights and invest in repairs – yet are always encouraging their new friends to move in. However, as Chapter 2 sought to demonstrate, the doubling of the number of EU members over two decades – from 12 at the beginning of 1994 to 28 in the latter months of 2013 – was certainly not a failure.

However, enlargements within an unbundled, polycentric EU are not necessarily a binary choice between keeping the doors shut and following a rigid accession template, unsuited to the needs of countries that are visibly far from full membership. Instead, many highly desirable benefits of membership – access to the single market, the Schengen Area, free movement of labor, mutual recognition of university diplomas and other qualifications, or participation in common European initiatives in areas from education to defense – can be extended to non-members and even used as sources of geopolitical leverage. In fact, in the 1990s, the idea of 'variable' forms of enlargement had currency – particularly in light of the wide opposition to enlargements across the EU. In 1999, for example, only 42 percent of EU citizens were in favor of enlargement, including just 35 percent in Germany and 34 percent in France.[58] One prominent response to the trade-off posed by the EU's widening and deepening was proposed by the leader of the CDU/CSU group in the Bundestag, Wolfgang Schäuble and its foreign policy spokesman, Karl Lamers. In a joint policy paper, they argued that enlargements were in the EU's and German interests but needed to be handled carefully, relying on long periods of transition and 'variable geometry.' In fact, the proposal suggested that new members would not be required to adopt the full *acquis communautaire* upon their accession and that the EU would effectively become a two-tier structure featuring a tightly integrated core of its five or six founding members and a looser periphery.

Whether the Schäuble–Lamers proposal amounted to a workable alternative to the more ambitious template used in the following years, or whether it reflected a form of cynical 'orientalism' and 'othering' of post-communist member states, can be debated. Considering both the effects of previous enlargements on the EU's internal cohesion and the lack of enthusiasm for further enlargements in 'old' member countries, however, the likely alternative to a flexible form of enlargement is not its ambitious version undertaken in 2004 but rather no enlargement at all. Yet, what happens east and south of the EU's borders matters. The bloc cannot afford to leave the regions to become an unstable no man's land and a playground for the EU's main adversaries, notably China and Russia.

One lesson of Eastern European enlargements has become doubly relevant in the era of growing concerns over economic interdependence with China. The counterfactual to the massive flow of investment and shifts of production capacity from Western Europe to Eastern Europe around the time of enlargements was not the preservation of the status quo; rather, it was the prospect of European businesses moving even further east, sacrificing close geographic and transport links to Western Europe in favor of even lower costs and wages. With the benefit of hindsight, the EU's move to encourage, through the accession process, the emergence of a broad-based manufacturing base for the EU in Central and Eastern Europe in the 2000s appears prescient and strategically astute. If the West is seeking to reduce its reliance on Chinese manufacturing and bring production to friendlier and more reliable jurisdictions, especially in strategically sensitive sectors, economic integration with such friendlier and more reliable countries is in order, using enlargement-like tools.[59] Market access arrangements have to involve strict conditionalities – particularly to rule out dual geopolitical loyalties of countries such as Serbia, participating in the BRI. Simultaneously, they have to be flexible enough to bring into the economic fold countries which are strategically important yet which are unlikely to qualify for membership, particularly in the case of countries that are seeking with some urgency to extricate themselves from their post-Soviet legacies and be safe from Russian aggression, such as Ukraine and Georgia.

Moreover, taking a hard-line approach toward the EU's closest friends and allies is unhelpful. Whatever one's views of Brexit, maintaining a close economic and political relationship with the U.K. remains in the EU's best interest. It likewise helps nobody if the EU's economic ties to Switzerland unravel due to Brussels' unwillingness to continue in the peculiar market access regime that has characterized Switzerland's participation in the single market. Given the size of the EU's economy, the market access tool can be wielded also to foster deeper economic ties between the EU and like-minded, strategically important partners all over the world. Despite a revival of EU-led trade negotiations during the Juncker Commission, the bloc's attempts at trade agreements with other partners around the world – such as Mercosur, India, or emerging economies of sub-Saharan Africa – have stalled. To accept the current stasis would be a mistake, particularly given the steady erosion of the multilateral trading system.

The prescriptions outlined in this chapter may sound unsatisfying. Accepting the EU's diverse membership base with its diverging views of security threats and strategic priorities runs contrary to pipe dreams of the continent's 'strategic autonomy.' Yet, those dreams reflect a view of the EU as a project of state-building transcending national divisions, which has proven to be disconnected from reality. There are no top-down shortcuts to remedy challenges of diversity, which are not institutional, but rather political and substantive. Rather than insisting on unrealistic end goals of European unity, for example by requiring that foreign and defense policy questions be tackled by the EU in unison, it is time to reconceptualize the EU in more modest terms: by identifying the minimum on which the EU is able and willing to act in concert (trade and neighborhood policy, for example) and by accepting that on essentially everything the heavy lifting will have to come from individual member states acting individually or as part of ad hoc coalitions, tamed of course by the EU's overarching system of rules.

Whether that will be enough and whether it will be complemented with a boosting of capacities of European countries to project their power – a function of national politics, the health of European economies, and strategic culture in European capitals rather than of the EU, per se – is, of course, an open question. What is not an open question, in contrast, is that the EU is bound to make itself irrelevant if its officialdom continues on the alternative trajectory of pretending that there is European unity and European capacity for action when in truth there are none.

NOTES

1. Leonard (2005a).
2. Deutsche Welle (2018).
3. Harte (2018).
4. Süddeutsche Zeitung (2017).
5. Von der Leyen (2019).
6. *The Economist* (2019).
7. Le Point (2021).
8. AFP (2022).
9. Michaels (2022).
10. European Defence Agency (2021).
11. See Chryssogelos (2016).
12. European External Action Service (2020).
13. Council of the EU (2020a).
14. Council of the EU (2020b).
15. European Council (2021).
16. Ilyushina (2021).
17. Gerdžiūnas (2022).
18. Council of the EU (2021b).
19. European Council (2022).
20. Fabbrini (2014).
21. Glucroft (2021).
22. Crumley (2012).
23. Ilves (2021a).
24. Council of the EU (2021a).
25. Council of the EU (2021c).
26. Amara and Mcdowall (2021).
27. Council of the EU (2021d).
28. Burchard and Barigazzi (2021).
29. Viilup (2021).
30. European Commission (2021c).
31. European Commission (2016b).
32. Rudloff (2020).
33. Rumsfeld (2003).
34. Quoted in CNN (2003).

35. Quoted in IDNES (2002).
36. Sikorski (2018).
37. Adamkus et al. (2009).
38. Harding and Traynor (2009).
39. See, e.g., Kramer (2013).
40. Rau (2021).
41. Nardelli et al. (2022).
42. Reuters (2022).
43. Huang and Cha (2020).
44. BBC News (2014).
45. Gongadze (2018).
46. Fuller and Rohac (2019).
47. Zsíros (2021); Burchard and Barigazzi (2021).
48. Cabinet Office of the Prime Minister (2017).
49. Reuters (2020).
50. Horký-Hlucháň et al. (2021).
51. In 2018, the European Commission's president Jean-Claude Juncker called on national leaders to adopt QMV on questions of foreign policy – without much effect. See Juncker (2018).
52. *Consolidated version*, Article 31 (3).
53. European Commission (2021d).
54. See, e.g., Jarausch (2021).
55. NATO (2021).
56. Rohac (2021a).
57. Nicolaïdis and Howse (2002).
58. See Annex 2, European Parliament (1999).
59. Schimmelfennig (1999) argued that most of the economic gains from enlargements could have been realized using alternative tools. This time around, those alternative tools might be the only ones available.

References

Abnett, Kate and Simon Jessop (2022). "EU drafts plan to label gas and nuclear investments as green." *Reuters*, January 1, 2022, https://www.reuters.com/markets/commodities/eu-drafts-plan-label-gas-nuclear-investments-green-2022-01-01/.

Acharya, Viral, Itamar Drechsler and Philipp Schnabl (2014). "A Pyrrhic Victory? Bank Bailouts and Sovereign Credit Risk." *Journal of Finance*, Vol. 69, No. 6, pp. 2689–739.

Ackerman, Bruce (1994). *The Future of Liberal Revolution.* New Haven, CT: Yale University Press.

Act LXXVI of 2017 on the Transparency of Organisations Receiving Foreign Funds, https://www.helsinki.hu/wp-content/uploads/LexNGO-adopted-text-unofficial-ENG-14June2017.pdf (unofficial English translation).

Act XII of 2020 on the containment of coronavirus, http://abouthungary.hu/media/DocumentsModell-file/1585661547-act-xii-of-2020-on-the-containment-of-coronavirus.pdf (unofficial English translation).

Adami, Marina (2021). "Czech president labels transgender people as 'disgusting'." *Politico.eu*, June 28, 2021, https://www.politico.eu/article/czech-president-milos-zeman-says-he-finds-transgender-people-disgusting/.

Adamkus, Valdas, Martin Bútora, Emil Constantinescu, Pavol Demeš, Luboš Dobrovský, Mátyás Eörsi, István Gyarmati, Václav Havel, Rastislav Káčer, Sandra Kalniete, Karel Schwarzenberg, Michal Kováč, Ivan Krastev, Alexander Kwaśniewski, Mart Laar, Kadri Liik, János Martonyi, Janusz Onyszkiewicz, Adam Rotfeld, Vaira Vike-Freiberga, Alexandr Vondra and Lech Wałęsa (2009). *An Open Letter to the Obama Administration from Central and Eastern Europe*, July 16, 2009, https://www.rferl.org/a/An_Open_Letter_To_The_Obama_Administration_From_Central_And_Eastern_Europe/1778449.html.

Adams, Tim (2019). "Guy Verhofstadt: 'If you want to see what nationalists have done, come to Britain'." *The Guardian*, May 19, 2019, https://www.theguardian.com/politics/2019/may/19/guy-verhofstadt-brexit-interview-nationalists-london-european-elections.

AFP (2022). "'A new era': Germany rewrites its defence, foreign policies." *France 24*, February 27, 2022, https://www.france24.com/en/live-news/20220227-a-new-era-germany-rewrites-its-defence-foreign-policies

Aiello, Francesco and Valeria Pupo (2012). "Structural Funds and the Economic Divide in Italy." *Journal of Policy Modeling*, Vol. 34, No. 3, pp. 403–18.

Al Jazeera (2019). "Poland left out of EU's 2050 climate neutrality targets." *Al Jazeera*, December 13, 2019, https://www.aljazeera.com/economy/2019/12/13/poland-left-out-of-eus-2050-climate-neutrality-targets.

Alesina, Alberto and Nicola Fuchs-Schündeln (2007). "Good-bye Lenin (or Not?): The Effect of Communism on People's Preferences." *American Economic Review*, Vol. 97, No. 4, pp. 1507–28.

Amara, Tarek and Angus Mcdowall (2021). "Tunisian president says he will not become a dictator after MP arrest." *Reuters*, July 30, 2021, https://www.reuters

.com/world/africa/tunisian-security-forces-arrest-mp-who-criticised-president-2021 -07-30/.

Analysgruppen (2019). "Kraftigt ökat stöd för kärnkraft i Sverige [Significantly increased support for nuclear power in Sweden]." *Analysgruppen – Energiföretagen*, November 22, 2019, https://www.analys.se/wp-content/uploads/2019/11/20191122 -analysgruppen-opinion-pressmeddelande.pdf.

Anderson, Benedict (2016). *Imagined Communities: Reflections on the Origin and Spread of Nationalism*. London: Verso.

Anderson, Perry (2021). "Ever Closer Union?" *London Review of Books*, Vol. 43, No.1, https://www.lrb,co,uk/the-paper/v43/n01/perry-anderson/ever-closer-union.

Appel, Hilary and Mitchell A. Orenstein (2018). *From Triumph to Crisis: Neoliberal Economic Reform in Postcommunist Countries*. Cambridge: Cambridge University Press.

Applebaum, Anne (2020). *Twilight of Democracy: The Seductive Lure of Authoritarianism*. New York: Doubleday.

Ashworth, Lucian (2013). "A New Politics for a Global Age: David Mitrany's *A Working Peace System*." In H. Bliddal, C. Sylvest and P. Wilson (eds.), *Classics of International Relations*. London: Routledge, pp. 59–68.

Aslund, Anders and Simeon Djankov (2017). *Europe's Growth Challenge*. Oxford: Oxford University Press.

Attali, Jacques (2008). *Rapport de la Commission pour la libération de la croissance française: 300 décisions pour changer la France*, January 23, 2008, https://www .vie-publique.fr/rapport/29532-rapport-de-la-commission-pour-la-liberation-de-la -croissance-francaise.

Auer, Štefan (2014). "Limits of Transnational Solidarity and the Eurozone Crisis in Germany, Ireland, and Slovakia." *Perspectives on European Politics and Society*, Vol. 15, No. 3, pp. 322–34.

Auer, Štefan (2019). "Merkel's Germany and the European Union: Between Emergency and the Rule of Rules." *Government and Opposition*, Vol. 56, No. 1, pp. 1–19.

Avaro, Mayris and Henri Sterdyniak (2014). "Banking Union: A Solution to the Euro Zone Crisis?" *Revue de l'OFCE/Debates and Policies*, Vol. 132, pp. 195–241.

Bánkuti, Miklós, Gábor Halmai and Kim Lane Scheppele (2012). "Hungary's Illiberal Turn: Disabling the Constitution." *Journal of Democracy*, Vol. 23, No. 3, pp. 138–46.

Barroso, José Manuel Durão (2013). *A new narrative for Europe*. Speech by President Barroso, April 23, 2013, https://ec.europa.eu/commission/presscorner/detail/en/ SPEECH_13_357/.

Barysch, Katinka (2006). "Is Enlargement Doomed?" *Public Policy Research*, Vol. 13, No. 2, pp. 78–85.

Bauer, Matthias (2016). "The Political Power of Evoking Fear: The Shining Example of Germany's Anti-TTIP Campaign Movement." *European View*, Vol. 15, pp. 193–212.

Baume, Maïa de la (2021). "Orbán's Fidesz quits EPP group in European Parliament." *Politico.eu*, March 3, 2021, https://www.politico.eu/article/epp-suspension-rules -fidesz-european-parliament-viktor-orban-hungary/.

BBC News (2014). "Hungary suspends gas supplies to Ukraine." *BBC News*, September 26, 2014, https://www.bbc.com/news/business-29374151.

BBC News (2018). "Poland reinstates Supreme Court judges following EU ruling." *BBC News*, December 17, 2018, https://www.bbc.com/news/world-europe-46600425.

BBC News (2019). "Berlin Wall anniversary: Merkel warns democracy is not 'self-evident'." *BBC News*, November 9, 2019, https://www.bbc.com/news/world -europe-50361173.

BBC News (2020). "Poland abortion: Top court bans almost all terminations." *BBC News*, October 23, 2020, https://www.bbc.com/news/world-europe-54642108.

BBC News (2021). "Nord Stream 2: Biden waives US sanctions on Russian pipeline." *BBC News*, May 20, 2021, https://www.bbc.com/news/world-us-canada-57180674.

Becker, Markus, Veronika Hackenbroch, Martin Knobble, Christoph Schult and Thomas Schulz (2020). "Germany and Europe could fall short on vaccine supplies." *Der Spiegel*, December 18, 2020, https://www.spiegel.de/international/europe/the -planning-disaster-germany-and-europe-could-fall-short-on-vaccine-supplies-a -3db4702d-ae23-4e85-85b7-20145a898abd.

Bell, Chloe and Nika Bačić Selanec (2016). "Who Is a 'Spouse' Under the Citizens' Rights Directive? The Prospect of Mutual Recognition of Same-Sex Marriages in the EU." *European Law Review*, Vol. 41, No. 5, pp. 655–86.

Bell, Daniel (1977). "The Future World Disorder: The Structural Context of Crises." *Foreign Policy*, No. 27, pp. 109–35.

Bénassy-Quéré, Agnès, Markus K. Brunnermeier, Henrik Enderlein, Emmanuel Farhi, Marcel Fratzscher, Clemens Fuest, Pierre-Olivier Gourinchas, Philippe Martin, Florence Pisani, Hélène Rey, Nicolas Véron, Beatrice Weder di Mauro and Jeromin Zettelmeyer (2018). "Reconciling risk sharing with market discipline: A constructive approach to euro area reform." *CEPR Policy Insight*, No. 91, https://cepr.org/ active/publications/policy_insights/viewpi.php?pino=91.

Berchin, Issa Ibrahim, Isabela Blasi Valduga, Jéssica Garcia and José Baltazar Salgueirinho Osório de Andrade Guerra (2017). "Climate Change and Forced Migrations: An Effort Towards Recognizing Climate Refugees." *Geoforum*, Vol. 84, pp. 147–50.

Best, Edward, Thomas Christiansen and Pierpaolo Settembri (2010). "Effects of Enlargement on the EU's Institutions and Decision-making after Enlargement: Not quite Business as Usual." Brussels: *Trans European Policy Studies Association*, https://www.researchgate.net/publication/261287312_Effects_of_Enlargement _on_the_EU's_Institutions_and_Decision-making_after_Enlargement_Not_quite _Business_as_Usual.

Beunderman, Mark (2006). "Giscard demands second chance for EU constitution in France." *EU Observer*, May 23, 2006, https://euobserver.com/institutional/21674.

Bilbiie, Florin, Tommaso Monacelli and Roberto Perotti (2021). "Fiscal Policy in Europe: Controversies over Rules, Mutual Insurance, and Centralization." *Journal of Economic Perspectives*, Vol. 35, No. 2, pp. 77–100.

Blenkinsop, Philip, Sabine Siebold and Gabriela Baczynska (2021). "'Too much': EU leaders confront Hungary's Orban over new anti-LGBT law." *Reuters*, June 24, 2021, https://www.reuters.com/world/europe/leaders-16-eu-states-call-block-fight -lgbti-discrimination-2021-06-24/.

Blocker, Joel (1998). "Europe: German economists advocate postponement of monetary union." *Radio Free Europe – Radio Liberty*, February 9, 1998, https://www.rferl .org/a/1087924.html.

Blokker, Paul (2019). "Populism as a Constitutional Project." *International Journal of Constitutional Law*, Vol. 17, No. 2, pp. 536–53.

Bobić, Ana (2017). "Constitutional Pluralism Is Not Dead: An Analysis of Interactions Between Constitutional Courts of Member States and the European Court of Justice." *German Law Journal*, Vol. 18, No. 6, pp. 1395–428.

Bogaards, Matthijs (2018). "De-democratization in Hungary: Diffusely Defective Democracy." *Democratization*, Vol. 25, Vol. 8, pp. 1481–99.

Bolt, Jutta and Jan Luiten van Zanden (2020). *Maddison style estimates of the evolution of the world economy. A new 2020 update*, https://www.rug.nl/ggdc/historicalde velopment/maddison/releases/maddison-project-database-2020 (accessed December 15, 2021).

Borrell, Josep (2021). *Speech by High Representative/Vice-President Josep Borrell at the Annual Conference of European Defence Agency.* Brussels, December 7, 2021, https://eeas.europa.eu/headquarters/headquarters-homepage/108482/european -defence-agency-speech-high-representativevice-president-josep-borrell-annual_en.

Börzel, Tanja A. and Frank Schimmelfennig (2017). "Coming Together or Drifting Apart? The EU's Political Integration Capacity in Eastern Europe." *Journal of European Public Policy*, Vol. 24, No. 2, pp. 278–96.

Bouin, Jérôme (2008). "Sarkozy rejette deux propositions du rapport Attali." *Le Figaro*, January 23, 2008, https://www.lefigaro.fr/economie/2008/01/23/04001 -20080123ARTFIG00421-sarkozy-rejette-deux-propositions-du-rapport-attali.php.

Brauers, Anna and Pao-Yu Oei (2020). "The Political Economy of Coal in Poland: Drivers and Barriers for a Shift Away from Fossil Fuels." *Energy Policy*, Vol. 144, article 111621.

Britské listy (2015). "Czech President Miloš Zeman: Refugees will stone unfaithful women to death." *Britské listy*, October 17, 2015, https://blisty.cz/art/79464-czech -president-milos-zeman-refugees-will-stone-unfaithful-women-to-death.html.

Buchanan, James M. (1965). "An Economic Theory of Clubs." *Economica*, Vol. 32, No. 125, pp. 1–14.

Burchard, Hans von der and Jacopo Barigazzi (2021). "Germany slams Hungary for blocking EU criticism of China on Hong Kong." *Politico.eu*, May 10, 2021, https:// www.politico.eu/article/german-foreign-minister-slams-hungary-for-blocking-hong -kong-conclusions/.

Burgess, Michael (1996). "Introduction: Federalism and Building the European Union." *Publius*, Vol. 26, No. 4, pp. 1–15.

Burgess, Michael (2000). *Federalism and European Union: The Building of Europe, 1950–2000*. London: Routledge.

Buti, Marco, István Székely and Filip Keereman (2009). "Five years after the enlarge-ment of the EU." *VoxEU*, June 20, 2009, https://voxeu.org/article/eu-15-eu-27 -impact-enlargement.

Cabinet Office of the Prime Minister (2017). *Hungary is an ideal pillar of the One Belt, One Road initiative.* June 1, 2017, https://miniszterelnok.hu/hungary-is-an-ideal -pillar-of-the-one-belt-one-road-initiative/.

CBInsights (2021). *Global Unicorn Club: Private Companies Valued at 1B+*. https:// www.cbinsights.com/research-unicorn-companies (accessed October 1, 2021).

Cheikh Ali, Hana, Christel Querton and Elodie Soulard (2012). *Gender related asylum claims in Europe. A comparative analysis of law, policies and practice focusing on women in nine EU Member States France, Belgium, Hungary, Italy, Malta, Romania, Spain, Sweden and the United Kingdom*. Brussels: European Parliament, https://www.europarl.europa.eu/meetdocs/2009_2014/documents/femm/dv/asylum _claims_/asylum_claims_en.pdf.

Cheneval, Francis (2011). *The Government of the Peoples: On the Idea and Principles of Multilateral Democracy*. London: Palgrave.

Cheneval, Francis (2019). "Demoicratic Self-Government in the European Union's Polycentric System: Theoretical Remarks." In Josephine van Zeben and Ana Bobić (eds.), *Polycentricity in the European Union*, pp. 51–77. Cambridge: Cambridge University Press.

Christ, Carl F. (1994). "The Cowles Commission Contributions to Econometrics at Chicago: 1939–1955." *Journal of Economic Literature*, Vol. 32, No. 1, pp. 30–59.

Chryssogelos, Angelos (2016). *The EU's Crisis of Governance and European Foreign Policy*. London: Chatham House, November 2016, https://www.chathamhouse.org/sites/default/files/publications/research/2016-11-18-eu-crisis-governance-foreign-policy-chryssogelos_0.pdf.

Chyong, Chi Kong (2019). "European Natural Gas Markets: Taking Stock and Looking Forward." *Review of Industrial Organization*, Vol. 55, No. 1, pp. 89–109.

Clinton, Hillary (2016). *Hard Choices: A Memoir*. New York: Simon and Schuster.

CNN (2003). "Chirac lashes out at 'new Europe'." *CNN*, February 18, 2003, https://edition.cnn.com/2003/WORLD/europe/02/18/sprj.irq.chirac/.

Collins, Sarah (2008). "Demonstrators claim EU is trying to railroad Irish voters." *Irish Times*, December 12, 2008, https://www.irishtimes.com/news/world/europe/demonstrators-claim-eu-is-trying-to-railroad-irish-voters-1.922609.

Congleton, Roger D. (2010). *Perfecting Parliament: Constitutional Reform, Liberalism, and the Rise of Western Democracy*. Cambridge: Cambridge University Press.

Consolidated version of the Treaty on European Union. Official Journal of the European Union C 326/13, https://eur-lex.europa.eu/resource.html?uri=cellar:2bf140bf-a3f8-4ab2-b506-fd71826e6da6.0023.02/DOC_1&format=PDF.

Constitutional Tribunal of the Republic of Poland (2021). *Judgment of 7 October 2021 – Assessment of the conformity to the Polish Constitution of selected provisions of the Treaty on European Union*. K 3/21, https://trybunal.gov.pl/en/hearings/judgments/art/11662-ocena-zgodnosci-z-konstytucja-rp-wybranych-przepisow-traktatu-o-unii-europejskiej.

Convention Determining the State Responsible for Examining Applications for Asylum Lodged in One of the Member States of the European Communities—Dublin Convention. August 19, 1997. Official Journal C254, https://eur-lex.europa.eu/legal-content/EN/ALL/?uri=celex%3A41997A0819%2801%29.

Coudenhove-Kalergi, Richard Nicolaus (1923). *Pan-Europa*. Vienna: Pan-Europa-Verlag, https://paneuropeanmovement.wordpress.com/2019/11/04/the-pan-european-manifesto-1923/.

Council of the EU (2020a). *Belarus: Declaration by the High Representative on behalf of the European Union on the so-called "inauguration" of Aleksandr Lukashenko*. Press Release, September 24, 2020, https://www.consilium.europa.eu/en/press/press-releases/2020/09/24/belarus-declaration-by-the-high-representative-on-behalf-of-the-european-union-on-the-so-called-inauguration-of-aleksandr-lukashenko/.

Council of the EU (2020b). *Belarus: EU imposes third round of sanctions over ongoing repression*. Press Release, December 17, 2020, https://www.consilium.europa.eu/en/press/press-releases/2020/12/17/belarus-eu-imposes-third-round-of-sanctions-over-ongoing-repression/.

Council of the EU (2021a). *Afghanistan: Declaration by the High Representative on behalf of the European Union*. August 17, 2021, https://www.consilium.europa.eu/en/press/press-releases/2021/08/17/afghanistan-declaration-by-the-high-representative-on-behalf-of-the-european-union/.

Council of the EU (2021b). *Belarus: EU adopts 5th package of sanctions over continued human rights abuses and the instrumentalisation of migrants*. Press Release, December 2, 2021, https://www.consilium.europa.eu/en/press/press-releases/2021/12/02/belarus-eu-adopts-5th-package-of-sanctions-over-continued-human-rights-abuses-and-the-instrumentalisation-of-migrants/.

Council of the EU (2021c). *Statement on the situation in Afghanistan.* August 31, 2021, https://www.consilium.europa.eu/en/press/press-releases/2021/08/31/statement-on-the-situation-in-afghanistan/.

Council of the EU (2021d). *Tunisia: declaration by the High Representative on behalf of the European Union.* July 27, 2021, https://www.consilium.europa.eu/en/press/press-releases/2021/07/27/tunisia-declaration-by-the-high-representative-on-behalf-of-the-eu/.

Council Regulation (EC) No 343/2003 of 18 February 2003 establishing the criteria and mechanisms for determining the Member State responsible for examining an asylum application lodged in one of the Member States by a third-country national. Official Journal of the European Union L50, https://eur-lex.europa.eu/legal-content/EN/TXT/?uri=celex%3A32003R0343.

Crozet, Matthieu, Marius Brülhart and Pamina Koenig (2004). "Enlargement and the EU Periphery: The Impact of Changing Market Potential." *HWWA Discussion Paper*, No. 270, https://www.econstor.eu/bitstream/10419/19241/1/270.pdf.

Crumley, Bruce (2012). "Ceremony for returning troops closes French combat mission in Afghanistan." *Time*, December 8, 2012, https://world.time.com/2012/12/08/ceremony-for-returning-troops-closes-french-combat-mission-in-afghanistan/.

ČTK (2011). "Klaus a Schwarzenberg odmítli dopis velvyslanců k pochodu gayů." *Týden.cz*, August 8, 2011, https://www.tyden.cz/rubriky/domaci/klaus-a-schwarzenberg-odmitli-dopis-velvyslancu-k-pochodu-gayu_208981.html.

Dahrendorf, Ralf (1996). *Why Europe Matters: A Personal View.* London: Centre for European Reform, https://www.cer.eu/publications/archive/report/1996/why-europe-matters-personal-view.

Dall'Erba, Sandy and Fang Fang (2017). "Meta-analysis of the Impact of European Union Structural Funds on Regional Growth." *Regional Studies*, Vol. 51, No. 6, pp. 822–32.

Davis, Christian (2018). "Poland's Supreme Court constitutional crisis approaches a standoff." *The Guardian*, July 2, 2018, https://www.theguardian.com/world/2018/jul/02/polands-supreme-court-constitutional-crisis-comes-to-a-head.

Day, Matthew (2013). "Angela Merkel compared to Nazis by Hungary." *The Daily Telegraph*, May 20, 2013, https://www.telegraph.co.uk/news/worldnews/europe/germany/10068917/Angela-Merkel-compared-to-Nazis-by-Hungary.html.

Deutsche Welle (2014). "Slovakia opens reverse-flow pipeline to carry gas to Ukraine." *Deutsche Welle*, September 2, 2014, https://www.dw.com/en/slovakia-opens-reverse-flow-pipeline-to-carry-gas-to-ukraine/a-17895333.

Deutsche Welle (2015). "Germany's Schäuble likens migrant wave to 'avalanche'." *Deutsche Welle*, November 12, 2015, https://www.dw.com/en/germanys-sch%C3%A4uble-likens-migrant-wave-to-avalanche/a-18844624.

Deutsche Welle (2018). "Germany owes 'vast' sums of money for NATO, claims US President Donald Trump." *Deutsche Welle*, March 18, 2018, https://www.dw.com/en/germany-owes-vast-sums-of-money-for-nato-claims-us-president-donald-trump/a-38008374.

Directive 2003/33/EC of the European Parliament and of the Council of 26 May 2003 on the approximation of the laws, regulations and administrative provisions of the Member States relating to the advertising and sponsorship of tobacco products, https://eur-lex.europa.eu/legal-content/EN/TXT/?uri=celex%3A32003L0033.

Directive 2006/123/EC of the European Parliament and of the Council of 12 December 2006 on services in the internal market. Official Journal of the European

Union   L   376/36,   https://eur-lex.europa.eu/legal-content/EN/TXT/?uri=celex
%3A32006L0123.

*Directive 2009/72/EC of the European Parliament and of the Council of 13 July
2009 concerning common rules for the internal market in electricity and repealing
Directive 2003/54/EC*. Official Journal of the European Union L 211, https://eur-lex
.europa.eu/legal-content/EN/ALL/?uri=celex%3A32009L0072.

*Directive 2009/73/EC of the European Parliament and of the Council of 13 July
2009 concerning common rules for the internal market in natural gas and repealing Directive 2003/55/EC*. Official Journal L 211, https://eur-lex.europa.eu/legal
-content/EN/ALL/?uri=celex:32009L0073.

*Directive 2018/957 of the European Parliament and of the Council of 28 June 2018
amending Directive 96/71/EC concerning the posting of workers in the framework
of the provision of services*. Official Journal of the European Union L 173/16,
https://eur-lex.europa.eu/legal-content/EN/TXT/PDF/?uri=CELEX:32018L0957&
from=EN.

Djankov, Simeon (2015). "Hungary under Orbán: Can Central Planning Revive Its
Economy?" *Peterson Institute Policy Brief* PB 15-11, https://piie.com/sites/default/
files/publications/pb/pb15-11.pdf.

Djankov, Simeon, Elena Nikolova and Jan Žilinský
(2016). "The Happiness Gap in Eastern Europe." *Journal of Comparative Economics*,
Vol. 44, No. 1, pp. 108–24.

Draghi, Mario (2012). Speech at the Global Investment Conference in London, July
26, 2012, https://www.ecb.europa.eu/press/key/date/2012/html/sp120726.en.html.

Dustmann, Christian and Tommaso Frattini (2014). "The Fiscal Effects of Immigration
to the UK." *Economic Journal*, Vol. 124, No. 580, pp. F593–F643.

Dustmann, Christian, Tommaso Frattini and Anna Rosso (2015). "The Effect of
Emigration from Poland on Polish Wages." *Scandinavian Journal of Economics*,
Vol. 117, No. 2, pp. 522–64.

Dyson, Kenneth (2017). "Hans Tietmeyer, Ethical Ordo-Liberalism, and the
Architecture of the EMU: Getting the Fundamentals Right." In Kenneth Dyson and
Ivo Maes (eds.), *Architects of the Euro: Intellectuals in the Making of European
Monetary Union*, pp. 138–69. Oxford: Oxford University Press.

Dyson, Kenneth and Ivo Maes (2017). "Intellectuals as Policy-Makers: The Value of
Biography in the History of European Monetary Union." In Kenneth Dyson and
Ivo Maes (eds.), *Architects of the Euro: Intellectuals in the Making of European
Monetary Union*, pp. 1–30. Oxford: Oxford University Press.

Dzurinda, Mikuláš (2021). Interview with author, July 21, 2021.

Easterly, William and Tobias Pfutze (2008). "Where Does the Money Go? Best and
Worst Practices in Foreign Aid." *Journal of Economic Perspectives*, Vol. 22, No.
2, pp. 29–52.

Ederveen, Sjef, Henri L. de Groot and Richard Nahuis (2006). "Fertile Soil for
Structural Funds? A Panel Data Analysis of the Conditional Effectiveness of
European Cohesion Policy." *Kyklos*, Vol. 59, No. 1, pp. 17–42.

Eikeland, Per Ove (2011). "The Third Internal Energy Market Package: New Power
Relations among Member States, EU Institutions and Non-state Actors?" *Journal of
Common Market Studies*, Vol. 49, No. 2, pp. 243–63.

Einaudi, Luigi (1945). *I problemi economici della federazione europea*, http://www
.luigieinaudi.it/doc/i-problemi-economici-della-federazione-europea-2/?id=282.

Eisen, Norman (2021). Interview with author, August 9, 2021.

Epstein, Rachel A. and Wade Jacoby (2014). "Eastern Enlargement Ten Years On: Transcending the East–West Divide?" *Journal of Common Market Studies*, Vol. 52, No. 1, pp. 1–16.

Erdélyi, Katalin (2019). "The Mészáros empire won public tenders worth €826 million last year, 93 percent of which came from European Union funds." *Atlatszo*, January 17, 2019, https://english.atlatszo.hu/2019/01/17/the-meszaros-empire-won-public -tenders-worth-e826-million-last-year-93-percent-of-which-came-from-european -union-funds/.

EuroNews (2020). "Hungarian MEP facing expulsion from EPP group over Gestapo comments." *EuroNews*, December 2, 2020, https://www.euronews.com/2020/12/02/ hungarian-mep-facing-expulsion-from-epp-group-over-gestapo-comments.

European Automobile Manufacturers Association (2021). *Vehicles per capita, by country*, https://www.acea.be/statistics/tag/category/vehicles-per-capita-by-country (accessed December 15, 2021).

European Central Bank (2018). *Financial Integration in Europe*. Frankfurt: European Central Bank, https://www.ecb.europa.eu/pub/pdf/fie/ecb.financialintegrationineu rope201805.en.pdf.

European Commission (2015). *Antitrust: Commission sends Statement of Objections to Gazprom for alleged abuse of dominance on Central and Eastern European gas supply markets*. Press release, April 22, 2015, https://ec.europa.eu/commission/ presscorner/detail/en/IP_15_4828.

European Commission (2016a). "Hungary Country Profile." In *Public Procurement—A Study on Administrative Capacity in the EU*. Brussels: European Commission, http://ec.europa.eu/regional_policy/sources/policy/how/improving -investment/public-procurement/study/country_profile/hu.pdf.

European Commission (2016b). *The texts proposed by the EU for a Deep and Comprehensive Free Trade Area (DCFTA) with Tunisia*, April 29, 2016, https:// trade.ec.europa.eu/doclib/press/index.cfm?id=1490.

European Commission (2017a). *White Paper on the Future of Europe. Reflections and scenarios for the EU27 by 2025*, https://www.politico.eu/wp-content/uploads/2017/ 03/WhitePaper_POLITICO.pdf.

European Commission (2017b). *Report from the Commission to the European Parliament and the Council on the Single Supervisory Mechanism established pursuant to Regulation (EU) No 1024/2013*. Brussels: European Commission, https://ec .europa.eu/info/sites/default/files/171011-ssm-review-report_en.pdf.

European Commission (2017c). *Commission calls for the completion of all parts of the Banking Union by 2018*. Press Release, October 11, 2017, https://ec.europa.eu/ commission/presscorner/detail/en/IP_17_3721.

European Commission (2019a). *Clean energy for all Europeans*, https://op.europa .eu/en/publication-detail/-/publication/b4e46873-7528-11e9-9f05-01aa75ed71a1/ language-en?WT.mc_id=Searchresult&WT.ria_c=null&WT.ria_f=3608&WT.ria _ev=search.

European Commission (2019b). *EU–China – A strategic outlook*. Joint Communication to the European Parliament, the European Council and the Council, March 12, 2019, https://ec.europa.eu/info/sites/info/files/communication-eu-china-a-strategic -outlook.pdf.

European Commission (2019c). *European Fiscal Board 2018 Annual Report*, https://ec .europa.eu/info/sites/default/files/2018-efb-annual-report_en.pdf.

European Commission (2019d). *Mergers: Commission prohibits Siemens' proposed acquisition of Alstom*. Press Release, February 6, 2019, https://ec.europa.eu/ commission/presscorner/detail/sv/IP_19_881.

European Commission (2019e). *The European Green Deal*. Brussels: European Commission, https://eur-lex.europa.eu/legal-content/EN/TXT/?qid= 1596443911913&uri=CELEX:52019DC0640#document1.

European Commission (2020a). *State of the Union Address 2020*. Brussels: European Commission, https://ec.europa.eu/info/sites/info/files/soteu_2020_en.pdf.

European Commission (2020b). *The Commission's proposal for Horizon Europe*, https://ec.europa.eu/info/horizon-europe-next-research-and-innovation-framework -programme/commissions-proposal-horizon-europe_en.

European Commission (2021a). *Climate Change. Special Eurobarometer 513*. Brussels: European Commission, https://ec.europa.eu/clima/sites/default/files/support/docs/ report_2021_en.pdf.

European Commission (2021b). Communication from the Commission to the European Parliament and the Council: *A more inclusive and protective Europe: extending the list of EU crimes to hate speech and hate crime*. COM (2021) 777, https://ec.europa .eu/info/sites/default/files/1_1_178542_comm_eu_crimes_en.pdf.

European Commission (2021c). *European Neighbourhood Policy and Enlargement Negotiations: Tunisia*, https://ec.europa.eu/neighbourhood-enlargement/european -neighbourhood-policy/countries-region/tunisia_en.

European Commission (2021d). *Proposal for a Regulation of the European Parliament and of the Council on foreign subsidies distorting the internal market*. May 5, 2021, https://ec.europa.eu/competition/international/overview/proposal_for_regulation .pdf.

European Commission (2021e). *Questions and Answers: COVID-19 vaccination in the EU*. January 8, 2021, https://ec.europa.eu/commission/presscorner/detail/en/qanda _20_2467.

European Commission (2021f). *Subsidiarity control mechanism*. European Commission website, https://ec.europa.eu/info/law/law-making-process/adopting-eu-law/ relations-national-parliaments/subsidiarity-control-mechanism_en#procedures -triggered-so-far (accessed December 14, 2021).

European Council (1992). *Overall Approach to the Application by the Council of the Subsidiarity Principle and Article 3b of the Treaty on the European Union*. Conclusions of the Presidency, Edinburgh, UK, December 12, 1992, http://www .europarl.europa.eu/summits/edinburgh/a1_en.pdf.

European Council (2020a). *European Council meeting (10 and 11 December 2020) – Conclusions*. December 11, 2020, https://www.consilium.europa.eu/media/47296/ 1011-12-20-euco-conclusions-en.pdf.

European Council (2020b). *Special meeting of the European Council (17, 18, 19, 20 and 21 July 2020) – Conclusions*. July 21, 2020, https://www.consilium.europa.eu/ media/45109/210720-euco-final-conclusions-en.pdf.

European Council (2021). *European Council conclusions on Belarus*. May 24, 2021, https://www.consilium.europa.eu/en/press/press-releases/2021/05/24/european -council-conclusions-on-belarus-24-may-2021/.

European Council (2022). *EU restrictive measures in response to the crisis in Ukraine*. Updated March 4, 2022, https://www.consilium.europa.eu/en/policies/sanctions/ restrictive-measures-ukraine-crisis/.

European Court of Human Rights (2013). *Case OF N.K.M. v. Hungary.* Application No. 66529/11, JUDGMENT, May 14, 2013, https://fra.europa.eu/en/caselaw-reference/ecthr-application-no-6652911-judgment.

European Court of Human Rights (2016). *Case of András Baka v. Hungary.* Application no. 20261/12, Judgment, June 23, 2016, https://hudoc.echr.coe.int/eng?i=001-115532.

European Court of Justice (1963). *Judgment of the Court of 5 February 1963, NV Algemene Transport- en Expeditie Onderneming van Gend & Loos v Netherlands Inland Revenue Administration.* Case 26-62, https://eur-lex.europa.eu/legal-content/EN/ALL/?uri=CELEX:61962CJ0026.

European Court of Justice (1964). *Judgment of the Court of 15 July 1964, Flaminio Costa v ENEL.* Case 6-64, https://eur-lex.europa.eu/legal-content/EN/TXT/?uri=CELEX%3A61964CJ0006.

European Court of Justice (1974). *Judgment of the Court of 11 July 1974, Procureur du Roi v Benoît and Gustave Dassonville.* Case 8/74, http://eur-lex.europa.eu/legal-content/EN/TXT/?uri=CELEX:61974CJ0008.

European Court of Justice (1993). *Judgment of the Court of 24 November 1993, Criminal proceedings against Bernard Keck and Daniel Mithouard.* Joined Cases C-267/91 and C-268/91, https://eur-lex.europa.eu/legal-content/EN/TXT/?uri=CELEX%3A61991CJ0267/.

European Court of Justice (2000). *Judgment of the Court of 5 October 2000, Federal Republic of Germany v. European Parliament and Council of the European Union.* Case C-376/98, https://eur-lex.europa.eu/legal-content/EN/TXT/?uri=CELEX%3A61998CJ0376.

European Court of Justice (2006). *Judgment of the Court (Second Chamber) of 7 September 2006. Kingdom of Spain v Council of the European Union.* Case C-310/04, http://curia.eu.europa.eu/juris/liste.jsf?language=en&num=C-310/04/.

European Court of Justice (2012). *Decision of the Court of November 6 2012, European Commission Against Hungary.* Case C-286/12, http://curia.europa.eu/juris/liste.jsf?num=C-286/12.

European Court of Justice (2014). *Judgment of the Court (Grand Chamber) of 8 April 2014, Digital Rights Ireland Ltd v Minister for Communications, Marine and Natural Resources and Others and Kärntner Landesregierung and Others.* Joined Cases C-293/12 and C-594/12, https://eur-lex.europa.eu/legal-content/EN/TXT/?uri=CELEX%3A62012CJ0293.

European Court of Justice (2018). *Judgment of the Court (Grand Chamber) of 5 June 2018 – Coman, Hamilton and Asociatia Accept v Inspectoratul General pentru Imigrări and Ministerul Afacerilor Interne,* Case C-673/16, https://curia.europa.eu/juris/document/document.jsf?text=&docid=202542&doclang=EN.

European Court of Justice (2019). *Judgment of the Court (Grand Chamber) of 19 November 2019, Joined cases C-585/18, C-624/18 and C-625/18. A. K. and Others v Sąd Najwyższy, CP v Sąd Najwyższy and DO v Sąd Najwyższy,* https://curia.europa.eu/juris/liste.jsf?num=C-585/18.

European Court of Justice (2020a). *Judgment of the Court (Grand Chamber) of 18 June 2020 – C-78/18 European Commission v Hungary,* https://curia.europa.eu/juris/liste.jsf?num=C-78/18.

European Court of Justice (2020b). *Judgment of the Court (Sixth Chamber) of 2 April 2020 – Caisse pour l'avenir des enfants,* Case C-802/18, https://curia.europa.eu/juris/liste.jsf?num=C-802/18.

European Court of Justice (2021a). *Judgment of the Court (Grand Chamber) of 14 December 2021 – V.M.A. v Stolichna obshtina, rayon "Pancharevo".* Case C-490/20, https://curia.europa.eu/juris/liste.jsf?lgrec=fr&td=%3BALL&language= en&num=C-490/20&jur=C.

European Court of Justice (2021b). *Judgment of the General Court of 12 May 2021, Grand Duchy of Luxembourg, Amazon EU Sàrl and Amazon.com, Inc. v European Commission.* Case T-816/17, https://curia.europa.eu/juris/liste.jsf?num=T-816/17.

European Defence Agency (2021). *What We Do: European Defence Fund,* https:// eda.europa.eu/what-we-do/EU-defence-initiatives/european-defence-fund-(edf) (accessed October 8, 2021).

European Environment Agency (2021). *EEA greenhouse gases.* European Environment Agency, https://www.eea.europa.eu/data-and-maps/data/data-viewers/greenhouse -gases-viewer (accessed December 15, 2021).

European External Action Service (2020). *Belarus: Joint Statement by High Representative/Vice-President Josep Borrell and Neighbourhood and Enlargement Commissioner Olivér Várhelyi on the Presidential elections.* August 10, 2020, https://eeas.europa.eu/headquarters/headquarters-homepage/83935/belarus-joint -statement-high-representativevice-president-josep-borrell-and-neighbourhood -and_en.

European Parliament (1999). "Public opinion on enlargement in the EU Member States and applicant countries." *Briefing* No. 41, April 22, 1999, https://www.europarl .europa.eu/enlargement/briefings/41a3_en.htm.

European Parliament (2018). *European Parliament resolution of 12 September 2018 on a proposal calling on the Council to determine, pursuant to Article 7(1) of the Treaty on European Union, the existence of a clear risk of a serious breach by Hungary of the values on which the Union is founded.* 2017/2131(INL), https://www.europarl .europa.eu/doceo/document/TA-8-2018-0340_EN.html.

European Parliament (2021). *FAQ: Political parties and political foundations at European level,* https://www.europarl.europa.eu/news/en/faq/3/political-parties-and -political-foundations-at-the-european-level.

European Union Agency for the Cooperation of Energy Regulators (2020). *Annual Report on the Results of Monitoring the Internal Electricity and Natural Gas Markets in 2019,* https://extranet.acer.europa.eu/en/Electricity/Market%20monitoring/ Documents/MMR%202019%20-%20SNAPSHOT.pdf.

European Union Agency for the Cooperation of Energy Regulators (2021). *Mission,* https://acer.europa.eu/en/The_agency/Mission_and_Objectives/Pages/default.aspx.

Eurostat (2019). "Regional GDP per capita ranged from 31% to 626% of the EU average in 2017." Eurostat News Release 34/2019, February 26, 2019, https://ec.europa .eu/eurostat/documents/2995521/9618249/1-26022019-AP-EN.pdf/f765d183-c3d2 -4e2f-9256-cc6665909c80.

Eurostat (2021a). *First instance decisions on applications by citizen- ship, age and sex – annual aggregated data (rounded) [migr_asy- dcfsta],* https://appsso.eurostat.ec.europa.eu/nui/show.do?query= BOOKMARK_DS-057070_QID_-4D8EC040_UID_-3F171EB0&layout=TIME,C ,X,0;GEO,L,Y,0;CITIZEN,L,Z,0;SEX,L,Z,1;AGE,L,Z,2;DECISION,L,Z,3;UNIT ,L,Z,4;INDICATORS,C,Z,5;&zSelection=DS-057070CITIZEN,EXT_EU27 _2020;DS-057070AGE,TOTAL;DS-057070UNIT,PER;DS-057070DECISION ,TOTAL_POS;DS-057070SEX,T;DS-057070INDICATORS,OBS_FLAG;& rankName1=DECISION_1_2_-1_2&rankName2=UNIT_1_2_-1_2&rankName3 =INDICATORS_1_2_-1_2&rankName4=SEX_1_2_-1_2&rankName5=

CITIZEN_1_2_-1_2&rankName6=AGE_1_2_-1_2&rankName7=TIME_1_0_0
_0&rankName8=GEO_1_2_0_1&sortC=ASC_-1_FIRST&rStp=&cStp=&rDCh=
&cDCh=&rDM=true&cDM=true&footnes=false&empty=false&wai=false&time
_mode=ROLLING&time_most_recent=false&lang=EN&cfo=%23%23%23%2C
%23%23%23.%23%23%23 (accessed December 15, 2021).

Eurostat (2021b). *First permits by reason, length of validity and citizenship [migr_res-first]*, https://appsso.eurostat.ec.europa.eu/nui/show.do?dataset=migr_resfirst&lang=en (accessed December 15, 2021).

Eurostat (2021c). *Gross nuclear electricity production from 1990 to 2019*, https://ec.europa.eu/eurostat/statistics-explained/index.php?title=File:Gross_nuclear_electricity_production_from_1990_to_2019_(in_gigawatt-hour).png (accessed June 21, 2021).

Eurostat (2021d). *Employment and activity by sex and age – annual data*, https://ec.europa.eu/eurostat/databrowser/bookmark/c3998de9-4dcf-4aec-a012-a6c94e43c54c?lang=en (accessed 13 December 2021).

Eurostat (2021e). *Educational attainment statistics*, https://ec.europa.eu/eurostat/statistics-explained/index.php?title=Educational_attainment_statistics (accessed December 13, 2021).

Fabbrini, Sergio (2014). "The European Union and the Libyan Crisis." *International Politics*, Vol. 51, No. 2, pp. 177–95.

Fazekas, Mihály, Jana Chvalkovská, Jiří Skuhrovec, János István, János Tóth and Lawrence P. King (2013). "Are EU Funds a Corruption Risk? The Impact of EU Funds on Grand Corruption in Central and Eastern Europe." In Alina Mungiu-Pippidi (ed.), *The Anticorruption Frontline*, pp. 68–89. *The ANTICORRP Project*, vol. 2, Berlin: Barbara Budrich Publishers.

Federal Constitutional Court of Germany (2020). *Judgment of 5 May 2020. 2 BvR 859/15, 2 BvR 980/16, 2 BvR 2006/15, 2 BvR 1651/15*, https://www.bundesverfassungsgericht.de/SharedDocs/Pressemitteilungen/EN/2020/bvg20-032.html.

Federal Law of 20 July 2012 N 121-FZ "On Amending Certain Legislative Acts of the Russian Federation Regarding the Regulation of the Activities of Non-Profit Organizations Performing the Functions of a Foreign Agent" ("О внесении изменений в отдельные законодательные акты Российской Федерации в части регулирования деятельности некоммерческих организаций, выполняющих функции иностранного агента"), http://base.garant.ru/70204242/#ixzz6LsYKfYEE.

Federal Reserve Bank of St. Louis (2021). Constant GDP per capita for Italy, https://fred.stlouisfed.org/series/NYGDPPCAPKDITA (accessed December 15, 2021).

Feitz, Anna (2020). "Hydrogène: la France détaille son plan à 7 milliards d'euros" ["Hydrogen: France details its plan to 7 billion euros"], *LesEchos*, September 8, 2020, https://www.lesechos.fr/industrie-services/energie-environnement/hydrogene-la-france-detaille-a-son-plan-a-7-milliards-deuros-1240547.

Feldstein, Martin (1997). "The Political Economy of the European Economic and Monetary Union: Political Sources of an Economic Liability." *Journal of Economic Perspectives*, Vol. 11, No. 4, pp. 23–42.

Flynn, Tom (2021). "Constitutional Pluralism and Loyal Opposition." *International Journal of Constitutional Law*, Vol. 19, No. 1, pp. 241–68.

Freedom House (2021). *Freedom in the World 2021*, https://freedomhouse.org/report/freedom-world/2021/democracy-under-siege.

Frontex (2019). Risk Analysis for 2019, Warsaw: *Frontex*, p. 41, https://frontex.europa.eu/assets/Publications/Risk_Analysis/Risk_Analysis/Risk_Analysis_for_2019.pdf.

Frontex (2020). *Budget 2021*, https://frontex.europa.eu/about-frontex/key-documents/?category=budget.

Fukuyama, Francis (1992). *The End of History and the Last Man*. New York: Free Press.

Fuller, Clay R. and Dalibor Rohac (2019). "It is time for America's Eastern European allies to withdraw from Putin's fake multilateral bank." *AEI Ideas*, March 9, 2019, https://www.aei.org/publication/it-is-time-for-americas-eastern-european-allies-to-withdraw-from-putins-fake-multilateral-bank/.

Fundamental Law of Hungary. April 25, 2011, http://2010-2014.kormany.hu/download/e/2a/d0000/THE%20FUNDAMENTAL%20LAW%20OF%20HUNGARY.pdf.

Garrett, Amanda (2019). "The refugee crisis, Brexit, and the reframing of immigration in Britain." *Europe Now*, September 9, 2019, https://www.europenowjournal.org/2019/09/09/the-refugee-crisis-brexit-and-the-reframing-of-immigration-in-britain/.

Gateva, Eli (2013). "Post-Accession Conditionality – Translating Benchmarks into Political Pressure?" *East European Politics*, Vol. 29, No. 4, pp. 420–42.

Gay-Padoan, Luna (2020). "'Nous avons une chance historique, c'est le nucléaire', selon Emmanuel Macron" ["'We have a historic chance, namely nuclear power,' according to Emmanuel Macron"]. *TV5Monde*, February 12, 2020, https://information.tv5monde.com/info/nous-avons-une-chance-historique-c-est-le-nucleaire-selon-emmanuel-macron-346444.

Gellner, Ernest (1983). *Nations and Nationalism*. Ithaca, NY: Cornell University Press.

Gerdžiūnas, Benas (2022). "Almost all migrants on Lithuania's border are Kurds. Why?" *LRT English*, January 3, 2022, https://www.lrt.lt/en/news-in-english/19/1571999/almost-all-migrants-on-lithuania-s-border-are-kurds-why.

Gillingham, John (2003). *European Integration 1950–2003: Superstate or New Market Economy?* Cambridge: Cambridge University Press.

Glucroft, William (2021). "After Afghanistan: Germany rethinks its military missions." *Deutsche Welle*, August 19, 2021, https://www.dw.com/en/after-afghanistan-germany-rethinks-its-military-missions/a-58912418.

Gongadze, Myroslava (2018). "Ukraine to take part in NATO summit despite Hungarian objection." *Voice of America*, July 5, 2018, https://www.voanews.com/a/nato-summit-ukraine/4466125.html.

Grässler, Bernd (2014). "The labor reforms that set off a boom." *Deutsche Welle*, December 31, 2014, https://www.dw.com/en/the-labor-reforms-that-set-off-a-boom/a-18164351.

Gray, John (2000). *Two Faces of Liberalism*. Cambridge: Polity Press.

Grossman, Emiliano and Cornelia Woll (2011). "The French Debate over the Bolkestein Directive." *Comparative European Politics*, Vol. 9, No. 3, pp. 344–66.

Guarascio, Freseco (2020). "EU criticises 'hasty' UK approval of COVID-19 vaccine." *Reuters*, December 2, 2020, https://www.reuters.com/article/us-health-coronavirus-britain-eu/eu-criticises-hasty-uk-approval-of-covid-19-vaccine-idUSKBN28C1B9.

Gutiérrez, Germán and Thomas Philippon (2019). "How EU markets became more competitive than US markets: A study of institutional drift." *NBER Working Paper* No. 24700, https://www.nber.org/papers/w24700.

Hall, Richard (2016). "Trump's new ad plays on Europe's refugee crisis—and the videographer is fuming." *Global Post*, November 7, 2016, https://www.pri.org/stories/2016-11-07/trumps-new-ad-plays-europes-refugee-crisis-and-videographer-fuming.

Halmai, Gábor (2018). "Silence of Transitional Constitutions: The 'Invisible Constitution' Concept of the Hungarian Constitutional Court." *International Journal of Constitutional Law*, Vol. 16, No. 3, pp. 969–84.

Hanreich, Günther (2004). "Eurostat takes issue with former Greek PM on reasons for the revision of economic data." *Financial Times*, December 28, 2004, http://www.ft.com/cms/s/0/745b2b44-5874-11d9-9940-00000e2511c8.html#ixzz3hs1pRwyY.

Harding, Luke and Ian Traynor (2009). "Obama abandons missile defence shield in Europe." *The Guardian*, September 17, 2009, https://www.theguardian.com/world/2009/sep/17/missile-defence-shield-barack-obama.

Harte, Roderick (2018). *US tariffs: EU response and fears of a trade war*. Brussels: European Parliamentary Research Service, July 21, 2018, https://www.europarl.europa.eu/RegData/etudes/ATAG/2018/623554/EPRS_ATA(2018)623554_EN.pdf.

Hayek, Friedrich August von (1945). "Introduction." In Wilhelm Röpke. *The German Question*, pp. 11–15 (translated by E. W. Dickes). London: George Allen & Unwin.

Hayek, Friedrich August von (1948). "The Economic Conditions of Interstate Federalism." In *Individualism and Economic Order*, pp. 255–71. Chicago, IL: University of Chicago Press.

Hayek, Friedrich August von (1978). *Law, Legislation, and Liberty*, Vol. 2. Chicago, IL: University of Chicago Press.

Hayek, Friedrich August von (1988). *The Fatal Conceit: The Errors of Socialism*. Edited by W. W. Bartley III. Chicago, IL: University of Chicago Press.

Heath, Anthony and Lindsay Richards (2019). "How do Europeans differ in their attitudes to immigration? Findings from the European Social Survey 2002/03–2016/1." *OECD Social, Employment and Migration Working Paper* No. 222, https://doi.org/10.1787/0adf9e55-en.

Hobbing, Peter (2005). "Integrated Border Management at the EU Level." *CEPS Working Document* No. 227, August 1, 2005, http://aei.pitt.edu/6672/1/1254_227.pdf.

Hoekstra, Ruth, Cécile Horstmann, Juliane Knabl, Derek Kruse and Sarah Wiedemann (2007). "Germanizing Europe? The evolution of the European Stability and Growth Pact." *Arbeitspapiere für Staatswissenschaft*, No. 24, https://www.econstor.eu/bitstream/10419/41344/1/637002695.pdf.

Hoffmann, Mathias, Egor Maslov, Bent Sørensen and Iryna Stewen (2019). "Banking integration in the EMU: Let's get real!" *VoxEU*, January 10, 2019, https://voxeu.org/article/banking-integration-emu-let-s-get-real.

Hooghe, Liesbet and Gary Marks (2001). *Multi-Level Governance and European Integration*. Lanham, MD: Rowman and Littlefield.

Horký-Hlucháň, Ondřej, Jan Daniel and Ondřej Ditrych (2021). *Stability, Sustainability, and Success in the Sahel: The Next Steps for the Czech Engagement*. Prague: Institute of International Relations, June 24, 2021, https://www.iir.cz/en/stability-sustainability-and-success-in-the-sahel-the-next-steps-for-the-czech-engagement-1.

Horsey, David (2014). "Putin's Crimea grab shows he misunderstands 21st century." *Los Angeles Times*, March 4, 2014, https://www.latimes.com/opinion/topoftheticket/la-xpm-2014-mar-04-la-na-tt-putins-crimea-grab-20140303-story.html.

Huang, Christine and Jeremiah Cha (2020). "Russia and Putin receive low ratings globally." *Pew Research Center*, February 7, 2020, https://www.pewresearch.org/fact-tank/2020/02/07/russia-and-putin-receive-low-ratings-globally/.

Human Progress (2021). *Asthma deaths per 100,000 people, 1990–2017*. HumanProgress.org, https://www.humanprogress.org/dataset/asthma-deaths/?countries=338 (accessed December 15, 2021).

Hungarian Constitutional Court (2010). *184/2010. (X. 28.) AB határozat* ("Decision 184/2010. (X. 28) AB"), https://europaialkotmanyjog.eu/?p=108.

Hungarian Constitutional Court (2012). *Decision 33/2012. (VII. 17) AB.* Official English translation, https://hunconcourt.hu/uploads/sites/3/2017/11/en_0033_2012.pdf.

Hungary Helsinki Committee (2020). *Never Ending Story? Rapid analysis of the Bill on Terminating the State of Danger (T/10747) & the Bill on Transitional Provisions related to the Termination of the State of Danger (T/10748)*, https://www.helsinki.hu/en/never-ending-story/.

Hungary Today (2018). "EU anti-fraud office accuses Orbán's son-in-law of corruption in lighting contracts." *Hungary Today*, February 14, 2018, https://hungarytoday.hu/eu-anti-fraud-office-accuses-orbans-son-law-corruption-lighting-contracts-57635/.

IDNES (2002). "Havel a Bush: Zlu v Iráku je třeba čelit." *IDNES*, September 18, 2002, https://www.idnes.cz/zpravy/zahranicni/havel-a-bush-zlu-v-iraku-je-treba-celit.A020717_104025_zpr_nato_inc.

Ilves, Toomas Hendrik (2021a). Post on Twitter, August 15, 2021, https://twitter.com/IlvesToomas/status/1427103624447111174.

Ilves, Toomas Hendrik (2021b). Interview with author, July 19, 2021.

Ilyushina, Mary (2021). "Russia blocks flights as West's standoff with Belarus over diverted plane hits international air travel." *CBS News*, May 27, 2021, https://www.cbsnews.com/news/russia-belarus-blocks-flights-putin-backs-lukashenko-standoff-with-west/.

Imlauf, Antonín (2016). "Socialistický trh s auty: Mototechna, Tuzex, čekání a drahota" ["Socialist-era market with cars: Mototechna, Tuzex, wait times, and priciness"]. *Idnes.cz*, November 10, 2016, https://www.idnes.cz/auto/historie/auta-socialismus-trh-nakup-znacky-cena.A161107_234234_auto_ojetiny_fdv.

International Monetary Fund (2021a). *Gender and the IMF.* IMF website, https://www.imf.org/external/themes/gender/ (accessed June 1, 2021).

International Monetary Fund (2021b). *World Economic Outlook Database.* April 2021, https://www.imf.org/en/Publications/WEO/weo-database/2021/April.

Jaillard, Marion et al. (2010). *Setting up a Common European Asylum System: Report on the application of existing instruments and proposals for the new system.* Brussels: European Parliament, https://www.europarl.europa.eu/meetdocs/2009_2014/documents/libe/dv/pe425622_/pe425622_en.pdf.

Jakubcová, Hana (2020). "Kdo dostaví blok v Dukovanech? Odpověď bude v roce 2022" ["Who will build the block in Dukovany? The answer will be in 2022"]. *Třebíčský deník*, April 29, 2020, https://trebicsky.denik.cz/zpravy_region/kdo-dostavi-blok-v-dukovanech-odpoved-bude-v-roce-2022-20200429.html.

Jarausch, Konrad H. (2021). *Embattled Europe: A Progressive Alternative.* Princeton, NJ: Princeton University Press.

Jay, John (1787). "Federalist 2: Concerning Dangers from Foreign Force and Influence." *The Independent Journal*, https://avalon.law.yale.edu/18th_century/fed02.asp.

Johnson, Simon, David T. Kotchen and Gary W. Loveman (1995). "How One Polish Shipyard Became a Market Competitor." *Harvard Business Review*, November/December 1995, https://hbr.org/1995/11/how-one-polish-shipyard-became-a-market-competitor.

Jones, Will and Alexander Teytelboym (2017). "Matching Systems for Refugees." *Journal of Migration and Human Security*, Vol. 5, No. 3, pp. 667–81.

Jordan, Andrew, Dave Huitema, Harro van Asselt and Johanna Forster (eds.) (2018). *Governing Climate Change: Polycentricity in Action?* Cambridge: Cambridge University Press.

Juncker, Jean-Claude (2016). *Pour une Europe ambitieuse.* Speech delivered October 7, 2016, at Institut Delors, https://institutdelors.eu/wp-content/uploads/2020/08/europeambitieuse-juncker-ijd-oct16-1.pdf/.

Juncker, Jean-Claude (2018). *State of the Union 2018.* September 12, 2018, https://ec.europa.eu/info/priorities/state-union-speeches/state-union-2018_en.

Kaiser, Wolfram (2007). *Christian Democracy and the Origins of European Union.* Cambridge: Cambridge University Press.

Kant, Immanuel (1983). *Perpetual Peace and Other Essays* (translated by Ted Humphrey). Indianapolis, IN: Hackett Publishing Company.

Kauranen, Anne (2019). "Finland's long-delayed Olkiluoto three nuclear reactor granted operating licence." *Reuters*, March 7, 2019, https://www.reuters.com/article/us-finland-nuclear/finlands-long-delayed-olkiluoto-three-nuclear-reactor-granted-operating-licence-idUSKCN1QO1IC.

Keefer, Philip (2007). "Clientelism, Credibility, and the Policy Choices of Young Democracies." *American Journal of Political Science*, Vol. 51, No. 4, pp. 804–21.

Kelemen, R. Daniel (2018). "The Dangers of Constitutional Pluralism." In: Gareth Davies and Matej Avbelj (eds.), *Research Handbook on Legal Pluralism and EU Law*. Cheltenham, UK and Northampton, MA: Edward Elgar Publishing, pp. 392–406.Kelemen, R. Daniel (2020). "The European Union's Authoritarian Equilibrium." Journal of European Public Policy, Vol. 27, No. 3, pp. 481–99.

Kelemen, R. Daniel, Anand Menon and Jonathan Slapin (2014). "Wider and Deeper? Enlargement and Integration in the European Union." *Journal of European Public Policy*, Vol. 21, No. 5, pp. 647–63.

Kelemen, R. Daniel and Kathleen R. McNamara (2022). "State-building and the European Union: Markets, War, and Europe's Uneven Political Development." *Comparative Political Studies*, Vol. 55, No. 6, pp. 963–91.

Keynes, John M. (1936). *The General Theory of Employment, Interest and Money.* London: Palgrave Macmillan.

Kinsky, Ferdinand (1979). "Personalism and Federalism." *Publius*, Vol. 9, No. 4, pp. 131–56.

Klaus, Václav (2009). *Speech of the President of the Czech Republic Václav Klaus in the European Parliament.* February 19, 2009, https://www.klaus.cz/clanky/310.

Kletzer, Christoph (2006). "Alexandre Kojeve's Hegelianism and the Formation of Europe." *Cambridge Yearbook of European Legal Studies*, Vol. 8, pp. 133–51.

Kochenov, Dimitry (2014). "Overestimating Conditionality." *University of Groningen Faculty of Law Research Paper Series*, No. 03/2014, https://www.researchgate.net/publication/310463453_Overestimating_Conditionality.

Kornai, János (1979). *Economics of Shortage.* Amsterdam: North-Holland.

Kornai, János (2015). *Hungary's U-Turn.* April 3, 2015, http://www.kornai-janos.hu/Kornai_Hungary's%20U-Turn%20-%20full.pdf.

Kovács, Zoltán and György Vida (2015). "Geography of the New Electoral System and Changing Voting Patterns in Hungary." *Acta Geobalcanica*, Vol. 1, No. 2, pp. 55–64.

Kramer, Andrew (2013). "Chocolate factory, trade war victim." *New York Times*, October 29, 2013, https://www.nytimes.com/2013/10/30/business/international/ukrainian-chocolates-caught-in-trade-war-between-europe-and-russia.html?pagewanted=all&_r=0.

Krastev, Ivan (2017). "The Refugee Crisis and the Return of the East–West Divide in Europe." *Slavic Review*, Vol. 76, No. 2, pp. 291–6.

Krastev, Ivan and Stephen Holmes (2020). *The Light that Failed: Why the West is Losing the Fight for Democracy*. New York: Pegasus Books.

Kreuzbergová, Eva (2006). "Banking Socialism in Transition: The Experience of the Czech Republic." *Global Business and Economics Review*, Vol. 8, Nos. 1–2, pp. 161–77.

Krugman, Paul (1990). "A Europe-wide currency makes no economic sense." *Los Angeles Times*, August 5, 1990, https://www.latimes.com/archives/la-xpm-1990-08 -05-fi-453-story.html.

Krzyżanowski, Michał (2018). "Discursive Shifts in Ethno-Nationalist Politics: On Politicization and Mediatization of the 'Refugee Crisis' in Poland." *Journal of Immigrant & Refugee Studies*, Vol. 16, Nos. 1–2, pp. 76–96.

Kukathas, Chandran (2007). *The Liberal Archipelago: A Theory of Diversity and Freedom*. Oxford: Oxford University Press.

Kukavica, Jaka (2020). "(Rule of) law in the time of Covid-19: warnings from Slovenia." *Verfassungsblog*, March 25, 2020, https://verfassungsblog.de/rule-of-law -in-the-time-of-covid-19-warnings-from-slovenia/.

Kundnani, Hans (2020). "Europe's sovereignty conundrum." *Berlin Policy Journal*, May 13, 2020, https://berlinpolicyjournal.com/europes-sovereignty-conundrum/.

Kundnani, Hans (2021). "What does it mean to be 'pro-European' today?" *The New Statesman*, February 4, 2021, https://www.newstatesman.com/ideas/2021/02/what -does-it-mean-be-pro-european-today.

Landes, David (1998). *The Wealth and Poverty of Nations: Why Some Are So Rich and Some So Poor*. New York: W. W. Norton.

Le Point (2021). "Macron insiste sur 'l'autonomie stratégique' de l'UE face à des eurodéputés" ["Faced with MEPs, Macron insists on the EU's 'strategic autonomy'"]. *Le Point*, September 6, 2021, https://www.lepoint.fr/politique/macron -insiste-sur-l-autonomie-strategique-de-l-ue-face-a-des-eurodeputes-06-09-2021 -2441868_20.php.

Leo XIII (1891). *Rerum Novarum*. Encyclical of Pope Leo XIII on Capital and Labor, https://www.vatican.va/content/leo-xiii/en/encyclicals/documents/hf_l -xiii_enc_15051891_rerum-novarum.html.

Leonard, Mark (2005a). "Europe: The new superpower." *The Irish Times*, February 18, 2005, https://www.cer.org.uk/in-the-press/europe-new-superpower.

Leonard, Mark (2005b). *Why Europe Will Run the 21st Century*. New York: Public Affairs.

Levy, David (1992). *Interview with Milton Friedman*. Federal Reserve Bank of Minneapolis, June 1, 1992, https://www.minneapolisfed.org/article/1992/interview -with-milton-friedman.

Limerick, Patricia Nelson (1987). *The Legacy of Conquest: The Unbroken Past of the American West*. New York: W. W. Norton.

Lipka, Michael and David Masci (2019). "Where Europe stands on gay marriage and civil unions." Pew Research Center, October 2019, https://www.pewresearch.org/ fact-tank/2019/10/28/where-europe-stands-on-gay-marriage-and-civil-unions/.

Lührmann, Anna and Staffan I. Lindberg (2019). "A Third Wave of Autocratization Is Here: What Is New About It?" *Democratization*, Vol. 26, No. 7, pp. 1095–113.

Maçães, Bruno (2020). *History Has Begun*. New York: Oxford University Press.

Macours, Karen and Johan F. M. Swinnen (2006). "Rural Poverty in Transition Countries." *LICOS Discussion* Paper No. 169/2006, https://dx.doi.org/10.2139/ssrn.947433.

Madison, James (1785). *Memorial and Remonstrance against Religious Assessments*. June 20, 1785, Founders Online, National Archives, https://founders.archives.gov/documents/Madison/01-08-02-0163.

Maes, Ivo (2002). *Economic Thought and the Making of the European Monetary Union*. Cheltenham, UK and Northampton, MA, USA: Edward Elgar Publishing.

Majone, Giandomenico (2014). *Rethinking the Union of Europe Post-Crisis: Has Integration Gone Too Far?* Cambridge: Cambridge University Press.

Masini, Fabio (2017). "Tommaso Padoa-Schioppa: EMU as the Anchor Stone for Building a Federal EUrope." In Kenneth Dyson and Ivo Maes (eds.), *Architects of the Euro: Intellectuals in the Making of European Monetary Union*, pp. 193–211. Oxford: Oxford University Press.

Matić, Predrag Fred (2021). *Report on the situation of sexual and reproductive health and rights in the EU, in the frame of women's health*. 2020/2215(INI), https://www.europarl.europa.eu/doceo/document/A-9-2021-0169_EN.html.

Matrix Insight et al. (2010). *What system of burden-sharing between Member States for the reception of asylum seekers?* Brussels: European Parliament, https://www.europarl.europa.eu/RegData/etudes/etudes/join/2010/419620/IPOL-LIBE_ET(2010)419620_EN.pdf.

McCabe, David (2021). *Liberalism, Modus Vivendi, and Polycentricity: Mapping the Terrain*. Working paper.

McGinnis, Michael and Elinor Ostrom (1992). *Design Principles for Local and Global Commons*. Paper prepared for a conference on "Linking Local and Global Commons," Cambridge, MA, April 23–25, 1992.

Mesík, Juraj (2020). "'Enfant terrible' of the Eurozone – Why did Slovakia refuse to bail out Greece?" *Heinrich Böll Stiftung*, August 31, 2010, https://cz.boell.org/en/2014/03/24/enfant-terrible-eurozone-why-did-slovakia-refuse-bail-out-greece.

Michaels, Daniel (2022). "EU member countries in talks to supply Ukraine with jet fighters." *Wall Street Journal*, February 27, 2022, https://www.wsj.com/livecoverage/russia-ukraine-latest-news-2022-02-26/card/eu-member-countries-will-supply-ukraine-with-jet-fighters-borrell-says-zjCJ5iME2keSkxfiaIpr.

Middelaar, Luuk Van (2019). *Alarums and Excursions: Improvising Politics on the European Stage.* Newcastle upon Tyne: Agenda Publishing.

Mikloš, Ivan (2021). Interview with author, July 12, 2021.

Milanovic, Branko (1998). *Income, Inequality, and Poverty During the Transition From Planned to Market Economy*. Washington, DC: World Bank.

Milanovic, Branko and Lire Ersado (2010). "Reform and Inequality during the Transition: An Analysis Using Panel Household Survey Data, 1990–2005." *UNU–WIDER Working Paper* No. 2010/62, https://www.wider.unu.edu/sites/default/files/wp2010-62.pdf.

Ministry of Immigration and Integration (2021). "Now anti-democratic donations to recipients in Denmark are banned" ["Nu bliver antidemokratiske donationer til modtagere i Danmark forbudt"]. Press Release, March 9, 2021, https://uim.dk/nyhedsarkiv/2021/marts/nu-bliver-antidemokratiske-donationer-til-modtagere-i-danmark-forbudt/.

Mises, Ludwig von (1985). *Liberalism*. Irvington-on-Hudson, NY: Foundation for Economic Education.

Mitrany, David (1943). *A Working Peace System*. Oxford: Oxford University Press.

Moens, Gabriél A. and John Trone (2015). "The Principle of Subsidiarity in EU Judicial and Legislative Practice: Panacea or Placebo?" *Journal of Legislation*, Vol. 41, No. 1, pp. 65–102.

Mohl, Philipp and Tobias Hagen (2010). "Do EU Structural Funds Promote Regional Growth? New Evidence from Various Panel Data Approaches." *Regional Science and Urban Economics*, Vol. 40, No. 5, pp. 353–65.

Monnet, Jean (1985). *Mémoires*. Paris: Fayard.

Moraga, Jesús Fernández-Huertas and Hillel Rapoport (2015). "Tradable Refugee-Admission Quotas (TRAQs), the Syrian Crisis and the New European Agenda on Migration." *IZA Discussion Paper* No. 9418, October 2015, pp. 6–7, http://ftp.iza.org/dp9418.pdf.

Moravcsik, Andrew (2002). "Reassessing Legitimacy in the European Union." *Journal of Common Market Studies*, Vol. 40, No. 4, pp. 603–24.

Mortkowitz, Siegfried (2019). "Czech prosecutor reopens Babiš subsidy fraud case." *Politico.eu*, December 5, 2019, https://www.politico.eu/article/czech-prosecutor-reopens-andrej-babis-subsidy-fraud-case/.

Mos, Martijn (2020). "The Anticipatory Politics of Homophobia: Explaining Constitutional Bans on Same-Sex Marriage in Post-Communist Europe." *East European Politics*, Vol. 36, No. 3, pp. 395–416.

Mounk, Yascha (2019). *The People vs. Democracy: Why Our Freedom Is in Danger and How to Save It*. Cambridge, MA: Harvard University Press.

Müller, Julian F. (2019). *Political Pluralism, Disagreement and Justice: The Case for Polycentric Democracy*. London: Routledge.

Mundell, Robert A. (1961). "A Theory of Optimum Currency Areas." *American Economic Review*, Vol. 51, No. 4, pp. 657–65.

Nardelli, Alberto, Nick Wadhams and Jennifer Jacobs (2022). "Europe fears economic hit if Russia is sanctioned heavily." *Bloomberg*, January 9, 2022, https://www.bloomberg.com/news/articles/2022-01-09/europe-frets-about-economic-hit-if-russia-is-sanctioned-heavily.

NATO (2021). *Defence Expenditure of NATO Countries (2014–2021)*. Press Release, June 11, 2021, https://www.nato.int/nato_static_fl2014/assets/pdf/2021/6/pdf/210611-pr-2021-094-en.pdf.

Nauert, Heather (2017). *Poland: Independence of the Judiciary*. Press statement, U.S. Department of State, July 21, 2017, https://www.state.gov/r/pa/prs/ps/2017/07/272791.htm.

Nehammer, Karl, Boyko Rashkov, Nicos Nouris, Jan Hamáček, Mattias Tesfaye, Kristian Jaani, Panagiotis Mitarachi, Sándor Pintér, Agnė Bilotaitė, Maria Golubeva, Mariusz Kamiński and Roman Mikulec (2021). *Letter to Margaritis Schinas, Vice-President, European Commission, and Ylva Johansson, Commissioner for Home Affairs, European Commission, on "Adaptation of the EU legal framework to new realities"*. October 7, 2021, https://www.politico.eu/wp-content/uploads/2021/10/07/Joint-letter_Adaptation-of-EU-legal-framework-20211007.pdf.

Nelsen, Brent F. and James L. Guth (2015). *Religion and the Struggle for the European Union: Confessional Culture and the Limits of Integration*. Washington, DC: Georgetown University Press.

Nicolaïdis, Kalypso (2013). "European Demoicracy and Its Crisis." *Journal of Common Market Studies*, Vol. 51, No. 2, pp. 351–69.

Nicolaïdis, Kalypso and Robert Howse (2002). "'This is my EUtopia …': Narrative as Power." *Journal of Common Market Studies*, Vol. 40, No. 4, pp. 767–92.

Notzon, Francis C., Yuri M. Komarov, Sergei P. Ermakov, Christopher T. Sempos, James S. Marks and Elena V. Sempos (1998). "Causes of Declining Life Expectancy in Russia." *JAMA*, Vol. 279, No. 10, pp. 793–800.

Novotný, Vít (2021). *A Dictatorship from Brussels or a Paradise of Subsidiarity? National Prerogatives and EU Immigration Policy*. Brussels: Wilfried Martens Centre for European Studies, https://www.martenscentre.eu/publication/a-brussels -based-dictatorship-or-a-paradise-of-subsidiarity-national-prerogatives-and-eu -migration-policy/.

Öberg, Jacob (2017a). "Subsidiarity as a Limit to the Exercise of EU Competences." *Yearbook of European Law*, Vol. 36, No. 1, pp. 393–4.

Öberg, Jacob (2017b). "The Rise of the Procedural Paradigm: Judicial Review of EU Legislation in Vertical Competence Disputes." *European Constitutional Law Review*, Vol. 13, No. 2, pp. 248–80.

Oliver, Christian (2020). "How Bulgaria became the EU's mafia state." *Politico.eu*, September 9, 2020, https://www.politico.eu/article/bulgaria-how-it-became-mafia -state-of-eu/.

Orren, Karen and Stephen Skowronek (2017). *The Policy State: An American Predicament*. Cambridge, MA: Harvard University Press.

Ostrom, Vincent (1991). *The Meaning of American Federalism: Constituting a Self-Governing Society*. San Francisco, CA: Center for Contemporary Studies.

Ostrom, Vincent, Charles M. Tiebout and Robert Warren (1961). "The Organization of Government in Metropolitan Areas: A Theoretical Inquiry." *American Political Science Review*, Vol. 55, No. 4, pp. 831–42.

Palmer, James (2020). "Slovenia PM frantically tries to justify congratulatory Trump call." *Foreign Policy*, November 7, 2020, https://foreignpolicy.com/2020/11/07/ slovenia-prime-minister-trump-call-election/.

Pansardi, Pamela and Pier Domenico Tortola (2021). "A 'More Political' Commission? Reassessing EC Politicization through Language." *Journal of Common Market Studies*, https://doi.org/10.1111/jcms.13298.

Pápajová, Hedviga and Viera Hermanová (1989). "Sledovanie dynamiky výskytu kadmia, olova a zinku pri technologickom spracovaní mlieka" ["Observing the dynamics of presence of cadmium, lead, and zinc in the technological treatment of milk"], *Bulletin PV*, Vol. 28, No. 3, pp. 303–8, https://www.vup.sk/index.php ?mainID=2&navID=36&version=1&volume=28&article=167.

Paravicini, Giulia and Joshua Posaner (2016). "Budapest metro scheme tainted by fraud." *Politico.eu*, December 21, 2016, https://www.politico.eu/article/budapest -metro-scheme-tainted-by-fraud/.

Pellegrini, Guido Flavia Terribile, Ornella Tarola, Teo Muccigrosso and Federica Busillo (2013). "Does EU Regional Policy Enhance Growth?" *Papers in Regional Science*, Vol. 92, pp. 217–33.

Pew Research Center (2018). *Eastern and Western Europeans Differ on Importance of Religion, Views of Minorities, and Key Social Issues*. Pew Research Center, October 29, 2018, https://www.pewforum.org/2018/10/29/eastern-and-western-europeans -differ-on-importance-of-religion-views-of-minorities-and-key-social-issues/.

Pew Research Center (2019). *Attitudes on Same-Sex Marriage*. Pew Research Center, May 14, 2019, https://www.pewforum.org/fact-sheet/changing-attitudes-on-gay -marriage/.

Piketty, Thomas (2018). "2018, the year of Europe." *Le blog de Thomas Piketty*, January 16, 2018, https://www.lemonde.fr/blog/piketty/2018/01/16/2018-the-year -of-europe/.

Pisani-Ferry, Jean and Jeromin Zettelmeyer (2018). "Could the 7+7 report's proposals destabilise the euro? A response to Guido Tabellini." *VoxEU*, August 20, 2018, https://voxeu.org/article/could-77-report-s-proposals-destabilise-euro-response -guido-tabellini.

Pop-Eleches, Grigore and Joshua A. Tucker (2017). *Communism's Shadow: Historical Legacies and Contemporary Political Attitudes*. Princeton, NJ: Princeton University Press.

Potočár, Radovan (2020). "Kvalitné potraviny za socializmu sú mýtus. Režim problémy ututlával" ["Quality food under socialism is a myth. The regime covered up problems"], *Denník N*, March 3, 2020, https://dennikn.sk/blog/1782915/kvalitne -potraviny-za-socializmu-su-mytus-rezim-problemy-ututlaval/.

Proposal for an amendment to Bill T/16365 on stricter measures against pedophile offenders and amending certain laws to protect children ["Javaslat módosítási szándék megfogalmazásához a Törvényalkotási bizottság számára a pedofil bűnelkövetőkkel szembeni szigorúbb fellépésről, valamint a gyermekek védelme érdekében egyes törvények módosításáról szóló T/16365, számú törvényjava-slathoz"], https://www.parlament.hu/documents/129291/40734520/T16365_1.pdf/ a244e10a-33a1-df89-24c2-70edbe9f7622?t=1623263262629.

Protocol (No. 2) on the application of the principles of subsidiarity and proportionality. Consolidated version of the Treaty on Functioning of the European Union, OJ 115, 09/05/2008, pp. 206–9, https://eur-lex.europa.eu/legal-content/EN/TXT/HTML/?uri =CELEX:12008E/PRO/02&from=EN.

Przeworski, Adam, Michael Alvarez, José Antonio Cheibub and Fernando Limongi (2000). *Democracy and Development: Political Institutions and Well-Being in the World, 1950–1990*. New York: Cambridge University Press.

Przybylski, Wojciech (2018). "Explaining Eastern Europe: Can Poland's Backsliding Be Stopped?" *Journal of Democracy*, Vol. 29, No. 3, pp. 52–64.

Pucher, John (1999). "The Transformation of Urban Transport in the Czech Republic, 1988–1998." *Transport Policy*, Vol. 6, No. 4, pp. 225–36.

Ranking, Jennifer (2018). "How Hungarian PM's supporters profit from EU-backed projects." *The Guardian*, February 12, 2018, https://www.theguardian.com/world/ 2018/feb/12/how-hungarian-pms-supporters-profit-from-eu-backed-projects.

Rau, Zbigniew (2021). Article by Minister Zbigniew Rau in the *Frankfurter Allgemeine Zeitung*, June 30, 2021, https://www.gov.pl/web/diplomacy/article-by-minister -zbigniew-rau-in-the-frankfurter-allgemeine-zeitung.

Rech, Walter and Janis Grzybowski (2016). "Between Regional Community and Global Society: Europe in the Shadow of Schmitt and Kojève." *Journal of International Political Theory*, Vol. 13, No. 2, pp. 143–61.

Regulation (EC) No 713/2009 of the European Parliament and of the Council of 13 July 2009 establishing an Agency for the Cooperation of Energy Regulators. Official Journal of the European Union L 211, https://eur-lex.europa.eu/legal-content/EN/ ALL/?uri=celex%3A32009R0713.

Regulation (EC) No 714/2009 of the European Parliament and of the Council of 13 July 2009 on conditions for access to the network for cross-border exchanges in electricity and repealing Regulation (EC) No 1228/2003. Official Journal of the European Union L 211, https://eur-lex.europa.eu/legal-content/EN/ALL/?uri=celex %3A32009R0714.

Regulation (EC) No 715/2009 of the European Parliament and of the Council of 13 July 2009 on conditions for access to the natural gas transmission networks and repealing Regulation (EC) No 1775/2005. Official Journal of the European Union L 211, https://eur-lex.europa.eu/legal-content/EN/ALL/?uri=celex%3A32009R0715.

Regulation 2020/2092 of the European Parliament and of the Council of 16 December 2020 on a general regime of conditionality for the protection of the Union budget. Official Journal of the European Union L 433I, https://eur-lex.europa.eu/legal-content/EN/ALL/?uri=uriserv:OJ.LI.2020.433.01.0001.01.ENG.

Reho, Federico Ottavio (2018). *The Four "Classical Federalisms"*. Brussels: Wilfried Martens Centre for European Studies.

Reho, Federico Ottavio (2019). "Subsidiarity in the EU: Reflections on a Centre-right Agenda." *European View*, Vol. 18, No. 1, pp. 6–15.

Reid, Thomas Roy (2004). *The United States of Europe*. London: Penguin Books.

Reuters (2017). "Ruling Fidesz party wants Soros-funded NGOs 'swept out' of Hungary." *Reuters*, January 11, 2017, https://www.reuters.com/article/us-hungary-fidesz-soros/ruling-fidesz-party-wants-soros-funded-ngos-swept-out-of-hungary-idUSKBN14V0P2.

Reuters (2019a). "EU audit finds Czech Prime Minister Babis in conflict of interest: report." *Reuters*, December 1, 2019, https://www.reuters.com/article/us-czech-eu-babis/eu-audit-finds-czech-prime-minister-babis-in-conflict-of-interest-report-idUSKBN1Y51CO.

Reuters (2019b). "EU executive open to making new proposal to push deposit guarantee idea forward." *Reuters*, June 12, 2019, https://www.reuters.com/article/us-eurozone-integration-edis/eu-executive-open-to-making-new-proposal-to-push-deposit-guarantee-idea-forward-idUSKCN1TD18F.

Reuters (2020). "Hungary classifies Budapest–Belgrade Chinese rail project." *Reuters*, May 19, 2020, https://www.reuters.com/article/hungary-china-railway-law/hungary-classifies-budapest-belgrade-chinese-rail-project-idUSL8N2D14V2.

Reuters (2022). "Don't drag Nord Stream 2 into conflict over Ukraine, German defmin says." *Reuters*, January 13, 2022, https://www.reuters.com/business/energy/dont-drag-nord-stream-2-into-conflict-over-ukraine-german-defmin-says-2022-01-13/.

Reynolds, Emma (2020). "'Living in fear': Hungary's new ban throws its transgender community into limbo." *CNN*, June 2020, https://www.cnn.com/interactive/2020/06/world/hungary-transgender-portraits-cnnphotos/.

Ritterband, Charles E. (2013). "The Constitutional Court forces Orbán's government to change the law" ["Das Verfassungsgericht zwingt die Regierung Orbán zu Gesetzesänderung"], *Neue Zürcher Zeitung*, January 4, 2013, http://www.nzz.ch/aktuell/international/das-verfassungsgericht-zwingt-dieregierung-Orbán-zu-gesetzesaenderung-1.17921786.

Rodrik, Dani (2000). "How Far Will International Economic Integration Go?" *Journal of Economic Perspectives*, Vol. 14, No. 1, pp. 177–86.

Rohac, Dalibor (2020). *How green will Europe's recovery be?* Testimony to the House Committee on Foreign Affairs Subcommittee on Europe, Eurasia, Energy, and the Environment, September 23, 2020, https://www.aei.org/research-products/testimony/how-green-will-europes-recovery-be/.

Rohac, Dalibor (2021a). "How the EU treats friends worse than foes." *The Dispatch*, June 3, 2021, https://thedispatch.com/p/how-the-eu-treats-friends-worse-than.

Rohac, Dalibor (2021b). "Poland's right-wing ruling party is baiting the European Union." *UnPopulist*, October 19, 2021, https://theunpopulist.substack.com/p/polands-right-wing-ruling-party-is.

Rohac, Dalibor (2021c). "How Viktor Orbán became China's most reliable European ally." *The Dispatch*, June 30, 2021, https://thedispatch.com/p/how-viktor-orban -became-chinas-most.

Rohac, Dalibor (2021d). "Sputnik V's biggest legacy may be political turmoil." *Foreign Policy*, April 14, 2021, https://foreignpolicy.com/2021/04/14/sputnik-vs -biggest-legacy-may-be-political-turmoil/.

Romania Insider (2019). "European Socialists freeze relations with Romanian ruling party." *Romania Insider*, April 12, 2019, https://www.romania-insider.com/european -socialists-freeze-relations-psd.

Rossetto, Niccolo (2020). *Unbundling in the European electricity and gas sectors.* Florence School of Regulation, European University Institute, May 20, 2020, https:// fsr.eui.eu/unbundling-in-the-european-electricity-and-gas-sectors.

Rqiq, Yassine, Jesus Beyza, Jose M. Yusta and Ricardo Bolado-Lavin (2020). "Assessing the Impact of Investments in Cross-Border Pipelines on the Security of Gas Supply in the EU." *Energies*, Vol. 13, No. 11, pp. 1–23.

Rudloff, Bettina (2020). *A Stable Countryside for a Stable Country? The Effects of a DCFTA with the EU on Tunisian Agriculture."* SWP Research Paper 2, German Institute for International and Security Affairs, https://www.swp-berlin.org/ publications/products/research_papers/2020RP02_rff.pdf.

Ruhs, Martin and Carlos Vargas-Silva (2012). *The Labour Market Effects of Immigration.* Briefing, January 17, 2012, Migration Observatory at the University of Oxford, https://www.bl.uk/britishlibrary/~/media/bl/global/social-welfare/pdfs/non -secure/l/a/b/labour-market-effects-of-immigration.pdf.

Rumsfeld, Donald H. (2003). Secretary Rumsfeld briefs at the Foreign Press Center, January 22, 2003, https://web.archive.org/web/20140228200949/http://www .defense.gov/transcripts/transcript.aspx?transcriptid=1330.

Sabev, Dimitar, Ondřej Kopečný, Marek Trošok, Vojtěch Kotecký, Leonárd Máriás, Peter Učeň, Andrei Rizea and Alina Calistru (2021). *Where Does the EU Money Go? An Analysis of the Implementation of CAP Funds in Bulgaria, the Czech Republic, Hungary, Slovakia and Romania.* A report commissioned by the Greens/EFA group in the European Parliament, February 2021, https://extranet.greens-efa.eu/public/ media/file/1/6769.

Sargent, Thomas J. (2012). "Nobel Lecture: United States Then, Europe Now." *Journal of Political Economy*, Vol. 120, No. 1, pp. 1–40.

Scheppele, Kim Lane (2013). *Understanding Hungary's Constitutional Revolution.* Testimony before the U.S. Commission on Security and Cooperation in Europe (Helsinki Commission). March 19, 2013, https://law.yale.edu/system/files/ understanding_hungarys_constitutional_revolution.pdf.

Schimmelfennig, Frank (1999). *The Double Puzzle of Enlargement: Liberal Norms, Rhetorical Action, and the Decision to Expand to the East.* Paper Presented at the ECSA Sixth Biennial International Conference, Pittsburgh, June 3–5, 1999, https://www.researchgate.net/publication/5014670_The_Double_Puzzle_of_EU _Enlargement_-_Liberal_Norms_Rhetorical_Action_and_Expansion_to_the_East.

Schimmelfennig, Frank (2007). "European Regional Organizations, Political Conditionality, and Democratic Transformation in Eastern Europe." *East European Politics and Societies*, Vol. 21, No. 1, pp. 126–41.

Schuck, Peter H. (1997). "Refugee Burden-Sharing: A Modest Proposal." *Yale Journal of International Law*, Vol. 22, No. 2, pp. 243–97.

Schuman, Robert (1950). *The Schuman Declaration.* May 9, 1950, https://europa.eu/ european-union/about-eu/symbols/europe-day/schuman-declaration_en/.

Schwab, Klaus (ed.) (2019). *The Global Competitiveness Report 2019*. Cologne: World Economic Forum, http://www3.weforum.org/docs/WEF_TheGlobalCompe titivenessReport2019.pdf.

Sénécat, Adrien (2017). "La baisse du nucléaire à 50% en 2025, une promesse jamais suivie de moyens" ["The reduction of nuclear power to 50% in 2025, a promise never followed up on"], *Le Monde*, November 8, 2017, https://www.lemonde.fr/les -decodeurs/article/2017/11/08/la-baisse-du-nucleaire-a-50-en-2025-une-promesse -jamais-suivie-de-moyens_5212107_4355770.html.

Shehadi, Sebastian (2021). "How Hungary's elite made a fortune from the EU." *New Statesman*, March 23, 2021, https://www.newstatesman.com/business/finance/2021/ 03/how-hungarys-elite-made-fortune-eu.

Sierhej, Robert and Christoph B. Rosenberg (2007). "Interpreting EU Funds Data for Macroeconomic Analysis in the New Member States." *IMF Working Paper* No. 07/77, April 2007, https://www.imf.org/en/Publications/WP/Issues/2016/12/ 31/Interpreting-EU-Funds-Data-for-Macroeconomic-Analysis-in-the-New-Member -States-20620.

Sikorski, Radosław (2018). "Anticipating Putin's next war." *Washington Post*, July 17, 2018, https://www.washingtonpost.com/news/theworldpost/wp/2018/07/17/putin/.

Simms, Brendan (2012). "Towards a Mighty Union: How to Create a Democratic European Superpower." *International Affairs*, Vol. 88, No. 1, pp. 49–62.

Smith, Adam (1904) [1776]. *An Inquiry into the Nature and Causes of the Wealth of Nations*. London: Methuen & Co.

Smyth, Jamie (2008). "MEPs transparent in their suspicions about Libertas." *Irish Times*, September 30, 2008, https://www.irishtimes.com/news/meps-transparent-in -their-suspicions-about-libertas-1.941575.

Sobolewski, Matthias and Paul Carrel (2008). "Germany adopts 500 billion euro bank rescue package." *Reuters*, October 13, 2008, https://www.reuters.com/article/ us-financial-germany/germany-adopts-500-billion-euro-bank-rescue-package -idUSTRE49C5PX20081013.

Spinelli, Altiero (1985). *Il progetto europeo* [*The European Project*]. Bologna: Il Mulino.

Spinelli, Altiero and Ernesto Rossi (1941). *The Manifesto of Ventotene*. The Altiero Spinelli Institute for Federalist Studies, https://www.cvce.eu/en/obj/the_manifesto _of_ventotene_1941-en-316aa96c-e7ff-4b9e-b43a-958e96afbecc.html.

Štambergová, Monika, Jitka Svobodová and Eva Kozubíková (2009). *Raci v České republice*. Prague: Agentura ochrany přírody a krajiny ČR, http://www .forumochranyprirody.cz/sites/default/files/raci_v_cr.pdf.

Steinmetz, Katy (2015). "See Obama's 20-year evolution on LGBT rights." *Time*, April 10, 2015, https://time.com/3816952/obama-gay-lesbian-transgender-lgbt-rights/.

Šťovíček, Vladimír and Miroslav Šuta (2017). "Byla šunka 'za totáče' zdravější?" *Český rozhlas*, February 21, 2017, https://plzen.rozhlas.cz/byla-sunka-za-totace -zdravejsi-6718043.

Strban, Grega (2020). "Case C-802/18 Caisse pour l'avenir des enfants v FV, GW: Equal treatment of workers or of children?: Note on Case C-802/18 Caisse pour l'avenir des enfants, 2 April 2020 and Pending Cases against Austria." *Maastricht Journal of European and Comparative Law*, Vol. 27, No. 4, pp. 522–8.

Submission of a Bill on the Amendment of Certain Electoral Laws ["Egyes választási tárgyú törvények módosításáról"]. Parliament of Hungary, Filing no. T/13679, https://www.parlament.hu/irom41/13679/13679.pdf.

Süddeutsche Zeitung (2017). "Wir Europäer müssen unser Schicksal in unsere eigene Hand nehmen" ["We, Europeans, must take our destiny into our own hands"], *Süddeutsche Zeitung*, May 28, 2017, https://www.sueddeutsche.de/politik/g-krise-wir-europaeer-muessen-unser-schicksal-in-unsere-eigene-hand-nehmen-1.3524718.

Supreme Court of the United States (1856). *Dred Scott v. Sandford*. 60 U.S. 393, https://www.law.cornell.edu/supremecourt/text/60/393.

Surubaru, Neculai-Cristian (2021). "European Funds in Central and Eastern Europe: Drivers of Change or Mere Funding Transfers? Evaluating the Impact of European Aid on National and Local Development in Bulgaria and Romania." *European Politics and Society*, Vol. 22, No. 2, pp. 203–21.

Swedberg, Richard (1994). "Saint-Simon's Vision of a United Europe." *European Journal of Sociology*, Vol. 35, No. 1, pp. 145–69.

Szuleka, Małgorzata, Marcin Wolny and Marcin Szwed (2016). *The Constitutional Crisis in Poland, 2015–2016*. Warsaw: Helsinki Foundation for Human Rights, http://www.hfhr.pl/wp-content/uploads/2016/09/HFHR_The-constitutional-crisis-in-Poland-2015-2016.pdf.

Tabellini, Guido (2018). "Risk sharing and market discipline: Finding the right mix." *VoxEU*, July 16, 2018, https://voxeu.org/article/risk-sharing-and-market-discipline-finding-right-mix.

The Economist (2019). "Emmanuel Macron in his own words (English)." *The Economist*, November 7, 2019, https://www.economist.com/europe/2019/11/07/emmanuel-macron-in-his-own-words-english.

The Guardian (2006). "Hungary PM: we lied to win election." *The Guardian*, September 18, 2006, https://www.theguardian.com/world/2006/sep/18/1.

Timmermans, Frans (2019). *Letter of 10 May 2019*, https://cdn.g4media.ro/wp-content/uploads/2019/05/Scrisoare-Timmermans-Rule-of-law-Framework.pdf.

Toshkov, Dimiter D. (2017). "The Impact of the Eastern Enlargement on the Decision-making Capacity of the European Union." *Journal of European Public Policy*, Vol. 24, No. 2, pp. 177–96.

Transparency International (2020). Corruption Perceptions Index 2020, https://www.transparency.org/en/cpi/2020/index/hun.

Trantidis, Aris (2018). *Clientelism and Economic Policy: Greece and the Crisis*. London: Routledge.

Treaty Establishing a Constitution for Europe, October 29, 2004, http://europa.eu/eu-law/decision-making/treaties/pdf/treaty_establishing_a_constitution_for_europe/treaty_establishing_a_constitution_for_europe_en.pdf.

Tryfonidou, Alina (2019). "The ECJ Recognises the Right of Same-Sex Spouses to Move Freely between EU Member States: The Coman Ruling." *European Law Review*, Vol. 44, No. 5, pp. 663–79.

Trzeciakowski, Rafal (2017). "Restrictions on the posting of workers: protectionism against the poorer member states." *4Liberty.eu*, September 21, 2017, http://4liberty.eu/restrictions-on-the-posting-of-workers-protectionism-against-the-poorer-member-states/.

Tusk, Donald (2020). Post on Twitter, December 2, 2020, https://twitter.com/donaldtuskEPP/status/1334119966820491266.

UNHCR (2012). "Claims to Refugee Status based on Sexual Orientation and/or Gender Identity within the context of Article 1A(2) of the 1951 Convention and/or its 1967 Protocol relating to the Status of Refugees." *Guidelines on International Protection* No. 9, https://www.unhcr.org/509136ca9.pdf.

U.S. Embassy Slovakia (2019). Joint Statement on LGBTI+ Rights, July 17, 2019, https://sk.usembassy.gov/joint-statement-on-lgbti-rights/.

Valero, Jorge (2020). "Commission eyes new proposal to unblock deposit insurance scheme." *Euractiv*, December 7, 2020, https://www.euractiv.com/section/banking-union/news/commission-eyes-new-proposal-to-unblock-deposit-insurance-scheme/.

van Zeben, Josephine and Ana Bobić (eds.) (2019). *Polycentricity in the European Union*. Cambridge: Cambridge University Press.

Venice Commission (2017). *Opinion on the Draft Law on the Transparency of Organisations Receiving Support from Abroad*. June 16–17, 2017, http://www.venice.coe.int/webforms/documents/default.aspx?pdffile=CDL-AD(2017)015-e.

Venice Commission and OSCE/ODIHR (2012). "Joint Opinion on The Act on The Elections of Members of Parliament Of Hungary." *Opinion* No. 662/2012, https://www.osce.org/odihr/elections/91534?download=true.

Verseck, Keno (2012). "Amendment alarms opposition: Orbán cements his power with new voting law." *Spiegel Online*, October 30, 2012, http://www.spiegel.de/international/europe/hungarian-parliament-amendselection-law-a-864349.html.

Vestager, Margrethe (2020). *Speech by Executive Vice-President Margrethe Vestager: Building trust in technology*. EPC Webinar, Digital Clearinghouse, October 29, 2020, https://ec.europa.eu/commission/commissioners/2019-2024/vestager/announcements/speech-executive-vice-president-margrethe-vestager-building-trust-technology_en.

Viilup, Elina (2021). "EU's weak and slow reaction to Arab spring has no excuses." Opinión CIDOB, no. 108, *Barcelona Center for International Affairs*, https://www.cidob.org/en/publications/publication_series/opinion/europa/eu_s_weak_and_slow_reaction_to_arab_spring_has_no_excuses.

Vladisavljevic, Anja (2020). "Slovenia seen emulating Hungary, Poland with media reforms." *Balkan Insight*, July 22, 2020, https://balkaninsight.com/2020/07/22/slovenia-seen-emulating-hungary-poland-with-media-reforms/.

Von der Leyen, Ursula (2019). Speech by President-elect von der Leyen in the European Parliament Plenary on the occasion of the presentation of her College of Commissioners and their programme. November 27, 2019, https://ec.europa.eu/commission/presscorner/detail/en/speech_19_6408.

Walker, Shaun (2021). "Viktor Orbán using NSO spyware in assault on media, data suggests." *The Guardian*, July 18, 2021, https://www.theguardian.com/news/2021/jul/18/viktor-orban-using-nso-spyware-in-assault-on-media-data-suggests.

Walshe, David and Orlando Crowcroft (2020). "Jan Kuciak murder: The crime and trial that sparked a 'renaissance of civil society'." *EuroNews*, September 3, 2020, https://www.euronews.com/2020/09/03/jan-kuciak-murder-the-crime-and-trial-that-sparked-a-renaissance-of-civil-society-.

Waterfields, Bruno (2009). "EU intervention in Irish referendum 'unlawful.'" *Daily Telegraph*, September 29, 2009, http://www.telegraph.co.uk/news/worldnews/europe/eu/6239933/EU-intervention-in-Irish-referendum-unlawful.html.

Weiler, Joseph H. H. (2011). "The political and legal culture of European integration: An exploratory essay." *International Journal of Constitutional Law*, Vol. 9, Nos. 3–4, pp. 678–94.

Wike, Richard, Jacob Poushter, Laura Silver, Kat Devlin, Janell Fetterolf, Alexandra Castillo and Christine Huang (2019a). "European public opinion three decades after the fall of communism." *Pew Research*, October 15, 2019, https://www.pewresearch

.org/global/2019/10/15/european-public-opinion-three-decades-after-the-fall-of -communism/.

Wike, Richard, Jacob Poushter, Laura Silver, Kat Devlin, Janell Fetterolf, Alexandra Castillo and Christine Huang (2019b). "Minority groups: European public opinion three decades after the fall of communism." *Pew Research*, October 14, 2019, https://www.pewresearch.org/global/2019/10/14/minority-groups/.

Wiśniewski, Jakub and Marta Zahorska (2020). "Reforming Education in Poland." In F. Reimers (ed.), *Audacious Education Purposes*. Cham: Springer, https://link .springer.com/chapter/10.1007/978-3-030-41882-3_7.

World Bank (2021). *World Development Indicators*, https://databank.worldbank.org/ source/world-development-indicators (accessed December 13, 2021).

Wyplosz, Charles (2010). "The failure of the Lisbon strategy." *VoxEU*, January 12, 2010, https://voxeu.org/article/failure-lisbon-strategy.

Wyplosz, Charles (2018). *Creating a Decentralized Eurozone*. Brussels: Wilfried Martens Centre for European Studies, https://www.martenscentre.eu/publication/ creating-a-decentralised-eurozone/.

Zachová, Aneta (2020). "Ako premiér Babiš nepresadil jadro ako zelený zdroj energie" ["As prime minister, Babiš did not convince the EU to label nuclear power as a green source of energy"]. *Euractiv*, April 29, 2020, https://euractiv.sk/section/energetika/ opinion/ako-premier-babis-nepresadil-jadro-ako-zeleny-zdroj-energie/.

Zalan, Eszter (2021). "EU leaders confront Orbán on anti-LGBTQ law." *EU Observer*, June 25, 2021, https://euobserver.com/democracy/152253.

Zampano, Giada (2017). "Italy decrees liquidation of Veneto Banca and Banca Popolare di Vicenza." *Politico.eu*, June 25, 2017, https://www.politico.eu/article/ italy-decrees-liquidation-of-veneto-banca-and-banca-popolare-di-vicenza/.

Zsíros, Sándor (2021). Post on Twitter, March 22, 2021, https://twitter.com/EuroSandor/ status/1373942948904239107?s=20.

Index